John Paul Jones
Maverick Hero

JOHN PAUL JONES

JONES

MAVERICK HERO

by

Frank Walker

SPELLMOUNT

British Library Cataloguing in Publication Data:
A catalogue record for this book is available
from the British Library

Copyright © Frank Walker 2007

10 ISBN 1-86227-375-8
13 ISBN 978-1-86227-375-7

Published in the UK in 2007 by
Spellmount Limited
The Mill, Brimscombe Port
Stroud, Gloucestershire, GL5 2QG

Tel: 01453 883300
Fax: 01453 883233
E-mail: enquiries@spellmount.com
Website: www.spellmount.com

1 3 5 7 9 8 6 4 2

Printed in Great Britain by
Oaklands Book Services
Stonehouse, Gloucestershire GL10 3RQ

Contents

Introduction

I first became aware of John Paul Jones more than fifteen years ago, when I retired from my work as a lecturer and came to live in Cumbria. During a visit to Whitehaven, an old seaport on the Cumbrian coast, I discovered that Paul Jones is remembered there with good cause and with understandably mixed feelings. I soon became very interested in the chequered career and swashbuckling adventures of this controversial eighteenth-century Scottish seafarer, who eventually became a hero of the American War of Independence, and started to look into his life and times. Born to an ordinary, respectable family opposite Whitehaven on the Scottish side of the Solway Firth, he grew into a complex and often difficult man.

Whatever his origins, John Paul Jones was certainly not a conventional hero, and there was always the air of the maverick about him. Historically a controversial figure, his reputation was transformed almost miraculously in the twentieth century. I leave the reader to judge whether and in what way he was a renegade, and whether the epithets thrown at him by his enemies – privateer, pirate and corsair – could be fairly applied to him. Of course, like the distinction between fame and notoriety, judgment depends on the viewpoint of the observer; in the case of Paul Jones, whether the perspective is British or American might possibly have some bearing! John Paul Jones himself was always extremely sensitive on the subject of his own status: he did not consider himself in any way a felon. Although he took many merchant ships as prizes, he was always very conscious of being a properly commissioned American naval officer, in due course attaining a ranking as 'Commodore' in France. Small in stature, he was jealous of honour and hungered for glory. The entry on him in the 1875 edition of the *Encyclopaedia Britannica* includes the comment: 'though he certainly ranked as an officer of the United States, the independent manner in which he cruised might well suggest letters of marque rather than a government commission' – in other words, there was a whiff of the privateer about him. Attitudes change as facts emerge or are highlighted. The reputation of John Paul Jones has certainly undergone a sea-change over the years, not least in America.

Towards the end of the eighteenth century, Britain's American colonies violently severed their political ties with the mother country by revolution: the American War of Independence, bitterly fought between 1775 and 1781. This strife was the context in which the reputation of John Paul Jones was forged, in the unexpected service of the fledgling Continental Navy of the American colonists; a force that with his assistance would be transformed into the United States Navy.

Writing this book has led to many visits to places around the British Isles connected with John Paul Jones and his exploits, enabling me to carry out rewarding site observation and local manuscript research – all of which was unexpectedly revealing.

The Public Record Office in London provided me with the opportunity to read with great interest the original court martial documents relating to the loss of the Royal Navy warships *Drake* and *Serapis*, as well as other documents related to John Paul Jones. The library at Lancaster University has also been of great assistance. I would have greatly appreciated the same helpful access to the historic records covering the operations of the secret police in eighteenth-century St. Petersburg, but this proved an insoluble problem.

Quite a number of books have been written about John Paul Jones in the US, but relatively few in Britain, in whose territorial waters his developing reputation blazed to a spectacular climax. Apart from contributing to the fund of knowledge about his life and exploits and opening up some fascinating and seemingly unexplored lines of inquiry (for example in relation to his traumatic experience of Russia), I hope that by looking at events from a different viewpoint I have been able to furnish some fresh and valid insights into the man.

Acknowledgements

I would like to gratefully acknowledge my debt to previous writers as set out in the bibliography. I wish to thank the numerous interested and helpful library and archive staff with whom I have made very pleasant and fruitful acquaintance over the years; especially in Kendal, Whitehaven, Carlisle, Kirkcudbright, Dumfries, North Shields (Whitby), Morpeth and Edinburgh. The British Library loan service through the library in Kendal has been a wonderful help, with both book and microfiche/microfilm research. I have also had unstinting assistance from the Royal Armouries in Leeds and Fareham (Fort Nelson), the Royal Naval Museum in Portsmouth, and the National Maritime Museum in Greenwich, as well as from the UK Hydrographic Office in Taunton, the BL's Newspaper Library (Colindale), and last but by no means least the Beacon Heritage Centre in Whitehaven. With thanks to many very helpful and friendly contacts in America, especially those at the U.S. Naval Academy Museum in Annapolis, as well as Masonic librarians in both Britain and the United States.

On a personal note, I would like to thank David Bradbury, whom I met by chance one day in the Cumbria Record Office at Whitehaven. He was of critical assistance to me that day in finding a set of documents for which I had been fruitlessly searching on a poor reference. One of David's publications, which, amongst other interesting matters, includes the course of the *Ranger* plotted from the ship's log for the first time, is listed in the bibliography.

In conclusion, I would like to thank my wife, Lucy, and family for either their assistance or forbearance and very often both, especially my daughter Pam, my daughter-in-law Gaynor and my nephew Guy.

Errors are hopefully few, and on that score I can only say that I have been assiduous in my efforts. I hope the reader finds this book an engaging read, worthy of its enthralling subject.

The portrait of John Paul Jones on the front of the jacket is reproduced by kind permission of the Independence National Historical Park, Philadelphia. Unless otherwise indicated, photographs are by the author. Maps on pages 9, 106 and 119 are by Martin Brown © Spellmount Publishing Ltd.

1

Enshrined In Glory

At the centre of a magnificent circular shrine beneath the chapel of the American Naval Academy at Annapolis in Maryland, there is a sumptuous black marble sarcophagus enlivened with white, modelled on the tomb of Napoleon in Paris. Garlanded with oak leaves in wreaths and swags of dark bronze foliage, its sombre bulk is elegantly supported upon four leaping bronze dolphins. It rests under a dome, enshrined within a graceful circle of pillars. In front of the sarcophagus, boldly set into the polished marble floor in letters of bronze, are the words:

HE GAVE OUR NAVY ITS EARLIEST TRADITIONS OF HEROISM AND VICTORY

Within the sarcophagus lie the mortal remains of John Paul Jones, brought to the shores of America in 1905 from an obscure grave, hurriedly dug over a hundred years earlier in the tumultuous Paris of Revolutionary France. The body was accompanied on its crossing of the Atlantic by an honorific escort of five American warships. This squadron was augmented as the flotilla approached Chesapeake Bay by seven great battleships. In turn, each of these fired off a fifteen-gun salute, which heralded the approach of the frigate *Brooklyn*, recently distinguished in action and awarded the honour of bearing the body into the roadstead of Annapolis. Impressive patriotic ceremony accompanied the interment of the body within its hallowed sarcophagus. A perpetual guard of honour keeps vigil within the shrine.

After its lost resting place had been researched and located, the body in question had been tunnelled out from amongst a mass of graves lying under the buildings that by then covered an old protestant cemetery in the outskirts of Paris. Enclosed in an unmarked lead coffin that proved difficult to find, the body itself was formally identified only after an autopsy. Luckily, it was in a very good state of preservation, but only survived at all because it had been pickled in alcohol and sealed in its lead casket by a compassionate and far-sighted Frenchman. The American Minister Plenipotentiary in Paris at the time would have been quite happy to see the 'poor fellow' consigned to a pauper's grave, for cheapness. It was left to the French to arrange for something better, and for a modest volley to be fired over the sad grave. The Minister was not present at the funeral; he had a dinner engagement.

How did it come about that a man of no apparent consequence was transformed into one of the foremost heroes in the American pantheon? How did he become the occupant of a hallowed shrine in the crypt of the American Naval Academy chapel over a hundred years after his untimely and rather lonely death at the age of forty-five?

The key lies not in his enterprising and colourful early life, nor in his enigmatic and rather sad later years, but in two warring cruises into British home waters – both gallant and much vaunted attempts to beard the lion in his den – which took place between the 10th of April 1778 and the 4th of October 1779.

2

Rousing The British Lion –
The Renegade Makes His Mark

On the tenth of April 1778 a warship, not long constructed, quietly slipped out from the French port of Brest. She was not a French ship, however. She had recently arrived at the French naval base proudly flying a flag new across the oceans of the world: the flag of the United States of America. This newly adopted flag – though not yet in its final form – had for the first time been acknowledged ceremonially by a carefully arranged exchange of salutes with a French flagship in Quiberon Bay, in 'official' recognition of America's independent status as a nation-state. Two more salutes were arranged for good measure, the first on the following day with the same flagship, and the second in Brest two weeks later with the flagship of Admiral d'Orvilliers, commander of the French fleet there. Tantalisingly, John Paul Jones, the captain of the ship, the *Ranger*, and the person who initiated the ceremonial exchange of gun-fire, did not specify which of several early variants of the U.S. flag was saluted; he merely refers to 'American Colours'.

The fast, rakishly built vessel was large for a twenty-gun sloop-of-war (though she only mounted eighteen guns at that time) and was square rigged rather than fore and aft rigged in the normal manner of a trading sloop. As the well-built and powerful sloop rounded the island of Ushant after leaving her temporary haven at Brest, it could be seen that she was no longer flying aloft the Stars and Stripes – she now flew a British flag. This was a disguise, for this handsome vessel was an American warship with a secret and spectacular mission in British waters, one which Britain's rebellious colonies hoped would assist in bringing the American War of Independence to a successful conclusion. The British flag seems to have stayed aloft for nearly the whole cruise, giving place to the

Stars and Stripes only at the start of a sea battle, and probably at Whitehaven. *Ranger* was escorted towards St George's Channel, the southern approach to the Irish Sea, by a powerful French frigate. When this became known at a later stage in the expedition, much was made of the fact in an official communication to the British government, which was naturally very concerned about French involvement in Britain's war with her American colonists. *Ranger* entered the Irish Sea alone.

British spies were active in France, and included in their remit were the three American Commissioners in Paris. One spy, a double agent born in America but well placed on the British scene, was approached by Silas Deane, the first of the soon-to-be-three Commissioners. Deane had been his tutor in America; but Dr. Edward Bancroft was a man more inclined to the British side than the American. Although impressive intellectually, he was unscrupulous; and though paid by both the British and the Americans, he got much more financial reward from the British. As soon as Silas Deane made his approach, Bancroft got in touch with his British connections. A personable fellow, Bancroft was, through his friendly connection with Deane, soon on equally friendly terms with the other two Commissioners, Benjamin Franklin and Arthur Lee. He also became a nodding acquaintance of John Paul Jones after the *Ranger's* arrival in France. One of Bancroft's functions was to report to the British on American ship movements, including American privateers and naval vessels such as the *Ranger*. Luckily for the Americans – and for himself – Paul Jones, despite amicable relations with Bancroft, who was Franklin's confidential secretary / agent, told him nothing about his plans. Jones was extremely security conscious, complained about the lack of it in France, and was very close with everyone – including his employers – as to what his real intentions were. The British were clearly unaware what Paul Jones was really up to during 1778 and 1779 when his reputation was made, for good or ill, in British home waters.

The first fighting in the American War of Independence had been an indecisive skirmish at Lexington, not far from Boston, in April 1775, and it was not until more than a year later, on 4 July 1776, that the colonists declared their independence in resounding terms. Fighting on land developed to the advantage of the Americans and the war at sea became increasingly vicious, with commerce raiding by American warships and punishing attacks on American civilian coastal targets by the Royal Navy. It was in this ever more savage climate of war that on 14 June 1777, the American Congress adopted the Stars and Stripes as the flag of the United States. Congress resolved 'that the Flag of the Thirteen United States be thirteen stripes, alternated red and white; that the Union be thirteen stars, white on a blue field, representing a new constellation.' Congress did not specify how the stars were to be arranged on their blue field, which led to several different early versions of the new national flag. One had the thirteen stars in a diamond pattern, one had them in a circle, and another had twelve stars in a circle with one in the centre. Yet another version had the stars in staggered rows, and it was this form of the Stars and Stripes that was later developed into the flag as we know it today.

On the same day that they adopted the new national flag, the American Congress saw fit to appoint John Paul Jones – a Scotsman by birth, an American by adoption, and a 'citizen of the world' by his own stated inclination – to be captain of their fine new warship *Ranger*, then under construction on the Piscataqua river in New England. This coincidence proved an auspicious one, and its significance would not have been lost on John Paul Jones as he prepared to undertake his secret mission – the first of its type – in British territorial waters.

Operating as part of their then very small fleet, Captain Jones had already given good service to the Americans, mainly by commerce raiding. He had also successfully carried out some minor coastal attacks, including the destruction of warehouses and oil tanks on the Canadian coast. During the course of his depredations he had been creditably involved in several encounters in the Americas with British ships of war more powerful than his own. The British naturally considered him nothing better than a pirate, and a traitor to boot. It may be that the tragic events following upon the unsuccessful Jacobite Rebellion of 1745 had instilled in Paul Jones, who was friendly with Jacobite refugees in New England and whose mother had a Highland background, a somewhat jaundiced view of patriotism as understood in London. At this crucial point in his professional life he had little hand in choosing his officers, some of whom fortunately had maritime experience, although only one had ever served in the navy (any navy).

Paul Jones already had a reputation for being difficult to get along with; he was known as a perfectionist and disciplinarian. He was not much more than five feet four inches in height, but wiry and strong in the shoulders. It is difficult to say how the wholly volunteer crew of the *Ranger* first viewed the diminutive and rather dandified Scotsman, but whatever they thought, he had been commissioned as an officer of the United States Navy and was in charge of the brand new warship in which they were departing for action in British waters. Captain Jones's handbill, put about in New England to attract recruits, referred to 'an agreeable voyage in this pleasant season of the year' for those 'who have a mind to distinguish themselves in the glorious cause of their country, and to make money'. Not unnaturally perhaps, profit from captured prizes would prove to exert more power over the minds of the crew than any thirst for glory, such as animated their dynamic captain, who placed it before money in the handbill! It was an order of priority that probably made little impression on interested readers, though they would have been very wise to note it. Amongst the recruits there were seamen of course, but also townsmen and country boys who were more attuned to a free and easy life and the enterntaining drama of New England public meetings than to the hard life aboard a warship with a distinctly authoritarian captain who ate alone in his cabin.

However, John Paul Jones was not without social graces; on the contrary he was very sociable ashore, and, after the style of his fellow countryman Robbie Burns, he was very fond of female company. He never married, but there is some pleasantly revealing correspondence extant relating to girls and older women with whom he was intimately acquainted, and – not in the least like Burns – some excruciating verse. It was rumoured that the young ladies of New England had rallied to the aid of Paul Jones with their own clothing when the rigging of the *Ranger* was frustratingly delayed, and that the Stars and Stripes at the masthead on the journey across the Atlantic was fashioned from their petticoats! It is also said that the white stars on the flag were cut from the wedding dress of the wife of John Wendell, Paul Jones's great friend in Portsmouth, New England. Having been the first to fly the Grand Union flag – the Flag of Freedom as he called it – aboard his ship *Alfred*, on 1 December, 1775, Jones would have been anxious to be the first to fly the new national flag in British waters; which he almost certainly was. The Grand Union flag still displayed the then-current British flag in a canton.

John Paul Jones was delayed in his voyage to Europe until 1 November. By the time he set sail, the Stars and Stripes (which indicated no British connection) was becoming an established national symbol, but nevertheless was probably still difficult to come by. Perhaps the rumoured contribution of the ladies of Portsmouth, New England, resulted from this. Others, less enterprising than Jones, continued to fly the Grand Union flag for a while, or were, perhaps, already at sea.

One might reasonably expect that Paul Jones, without doubt well aware of the matter, would have flown a flag in conformity with the new Congressional specification, but there is strong evidence that in European waters he included a blue stripe in his flag. Admiral Morison, in his classic biography of Paul Jones explores this and other aspects of the early flag. 'There is no reason to doubt that Jones flew the Stars and Stripes in *Ranger*, but were the stripes red and white, or red, white and blue?' He answers the question by adding 'Probably the latter,' concluding later, 'It seems clear that this was the "flag of freedom" that he preferred, and that his preference led to its unofficial recognition as the proper American naval ensign, at least in European waters.' Was this naval ensign merely the whim of a maverick? Official national symbol or eccentric personal fancy, in view of his imminent exploits, the importance of the flag at his masthead would undoubtedly have impressed itself on John Paul Jones's mind.

Paul Jones spent a deal of his own money in order to expedite and complete the fitting out of his ship at Portsmouth in New England. He expressed particular disgust at the niggardly amount of rum supplied for the crew: 'This alone', he wrote in stinging complaint, 'was enough to cause a mutiny'.

Despite the extra rum, the crewmen were not in fact happy when they arrived in France. Weather-wise, the voyage across the Atlantic had been reasonable enough, but in terms of prizes they had no luck until approaching Europe, where eventually, says Paul Jones, *Ranger* began to fall in with vessels 'every day and sometimes every hour'. A 'prize' was a captured enemy vessel eventually sold legitimately on the open market, the proceeds being divided up between the various grades of officers and crew, with the Captain getting most, of course. It was far from being done on an equal shares basis, and the Establishment had its share too. Though continued practice in stopping ships by day and by night was good training for the crew, only two of these numerous possibilities turned out to be legitimate prizes: the British-owned brigs *Mary* and *George,* under Captains Goldsmith and Richards, carrying cargoes including fruit and wine from Malaga to England. They were manned by prize crews and dispatched to the French port of Nantes (or Nantez, as the British often called it). Taking prizes imposed constraints on the vessels taking them. Obviously, prize ships had to be effectively manned in order to keep possession of them. Each one taken drained the capturing vessel of part of her crew. With luck, they might have to make choices on a value basis. *Ranger* was a naval warship, but private vessels too could take prizes, provided they were granted an official 'letter of marque': This was a written commission granted by a belligerent state to a private ship-owner allowing him to use his vessel as a warship. Such ships were permitted to take enemy vessels only. If a captain was indiscriminate and took friendly or neutral vessels he was a pirate, and subject to hanging. Because of the warring state of relations between the new United States of America and Britain, which considered the Americans to be colonists in rebellion, and certainly not nationals of a new sovereign state, the status of John Paul Jones was ambiguous. He could be, and was, considered a pirate, or at best, a privateer.

Before the *Ranger* herself reached France, the 'pleasant season of the year' featured in the recruiting handbill turned to snow and despite a bold attempt to break into a strong convoy of ten British ships sailing into the Channel, the crew could see no real prospect yet of any lucrative returns. They had in any case become increasingly sullen owing to the lack of prizes and their judgement that the captain worked them unreasonably hard, generally treating them like scum. He certainly did not have the familiar touch that the New Englanders liked, and rum was no substitute for that. Still, things brightened up somewhat when the prize money from the sale of one of the brigs was eventually shared out. The captain acknowledged the fact that his crew were homesick, and was keenly aware that they also wanted more prizes to make the fortune referred to in the handbill, copies of which were still floating around amongst the crew as a poignant reminder of why most of them were on board the *Ranger*. It was definitely not for the glory towards which the

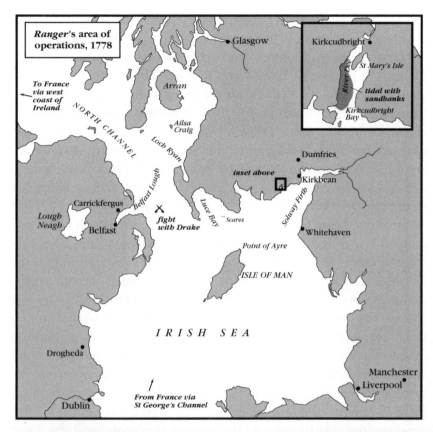

Tom Hurd's Rock fully exposed at low tide. See page 59.

Captain was hell-bent on leading them. They were not yet aware of his alarming intentions in this respect, but they soon would be.

The passage from the island of Ushant off the French coast towards St George's Channel and the Irish Sea started quite promisingly. Between the Scillies, off the Cornish peninsula, and Cape Clare, the southernmost land feature of Ireland, *Ranger* spotted and captured the brigantine *Dolphin* without a fight. But Captain Jones scuttled her with her cargo of flax seed, apparently because his crew had been so diminished by desertions that he felt unable to provide a prize crew for a vessel of such relatively trifling value. No doubt the crew watched her go down with keen regret. However, a better proposition soon loomed over the horizon: the *Lord Chatham*, a much larger and more valuable ship of 250 tons, carrying a substantial cargo of porter (dark beer made from charred malt – the Guinness of its day) in 50-gallon casks or hogsheads, as well as general merchandise and, according to a newspaper report , 'General Irwin's baggage'. Like the *Dolphin*, this ship was taken without a fight. Manned with the necessary prize crew she was dispatched quietly back to Brest – minus some of the porter one would presume – and with the crew no doubt amused by the capture of the belongings of a British General. The porter proved a contentious prize item when they finally got back to Brest.

So far, the real identity of the *Ranger*, soon roving in the heart of the Irish Sea, had been successfully concealed from the British. This situation changed when *Ranger* was off the north cape of the Isle of Man. She was spotted and challenged as suspicious by the *Hussar*, a fast government revenue vessel whose captain thought he had lighted upon a smuggler. Flying the customs house colours, the *Hussar* followed a diffident *Ranger* into the entrance to Luce Bay in Scotland – only a short sail from John Paul's birthplace. Gurley, the *Hussar*'s competent captain, managed to get his ship almost alongside the *Ranger*, as Paul Jones expected him to attempt, and which he encouraged him to do, intending to take her. *Ranger* was flying a British flag, but Gurley noted 'strange uniforms', with the captain of this ostensible merchant ship inexplicably in white – no wonder he thought they were smugglers. Unless they were disguised (as was quite often the case aboard Paul Jones's vessels) American naval officers' uniforms at that time were basically blue coats and britches with a waistcoat. This was initially red but was soon changed to white, thus resembling from a distance the regulation British uniform. The uniform of the marine officers was mainly green, but with white britches. The crew of the *Ranger* probably wore brown shirts at that time, and the marines almost certainly wore green ones. With the British flag flying aloft, what was Gurley to make of it all? He was certainly very suspicious, and must have studied any emerging finer details of the uniforms, or more varied clothes adopted as cover, with deepening puzzlement.

According to the *Cumberland Chronicle*'s report, *Ranger* brazenly asked Gurley 'whence he came' and requested that the *Hussar* provide her with a pilot – just a ruse to get closer of course. Gurley made no reply to the question, and cannily refused the request for a pilot as he 'could not spare one'. The Customs man formally demanded to know 'from whence *they* came and where bound'. The *Chronicle* says 'no answer was made to his first question', but Gurley was informed that she was the *Molly* of Glasgow, and that they were 'strangers on the coast'. Again, *Ranger* asked for a pilot, and again received the same negative answer from Gurley. Realising that Gurley was too wary to go along with him, John Paul Jones abandoned pretence and intervened decisively himself: 'Bring to, or I'll sink you directly'.

Gurley announced that he would comply, but the officer who had been exchanging words with the revenue man became suddenly suspicious of his real intent. He dropped his hailer, picked up a musket and fired at the *Hussar*, which was hovering off the knuckle of the Americans' bow – awkwardly placed by design for sinking by gunfire. Captain Jones knew he had to eliminate the *Hussar* one way or another, though he realised that she was shrewdly riding in an ideal position to make off. There was no time for niceties. Discarding his disguise as a merchantman, only convincing at a distance anyway, Paul Jones ordered the gun ports knocked open. The crew swiftly ran out a tier of guns, but they could not be brought to bear on the experienced and wily captain of the customs vessel, who kept his station very well. Instead, *Hussar* was subjected to a hail of small arms fire as she sheared off and made away in a strong wind. *Ranger* tacked and fired what Paul Jones calls 'a severe cannonade', though Gurley says that only one shot smashed into his stern and two shots passed through the mainsail. Gurley must have handled the *Hussar* well to avoid further damage from bar shot or chain shot sufficient to slow him down. The *Chronicle* reported, however, that apart from the shot in her hull the *Hussar* 'suffered much in [her] sails and rigging, having many shots through them', including 'several volleys of small arms'. The *Ranger* was square rigged and could easily outsail *Hussar*, but as the revenue cutter was fore and aft rigged she was able to constantly tack, spoiling the aim of the American sloop-of-war and gaining distance each time she did so. Paul Jones had successfully employed the very same tactic against British men o' war off the American coast when he was in command of a similar small vessel.

The Americans did not give up the pursuit until the *Hussar* entered Luce Bay near the Scarres rocks and shoals. With a fast tide running, Jones felt he dare not risk his ship in the shallow waters of the bay and reluctantly gave up the chase. The cover of the *Ranger* was well and truly blown, or so thought Jones. Remaining calm and calculating, he judiciously sank a number of small craft to prevent any further reports of an American ship of war stalking the Irish Sea for prize victims, and to make a salutary impression once the tale of the sinkings got about. Thwarted by adverse wind from looking for British warships in Belfast Lough, the *Hussar* hurried back to her home-port of Whitehaven to report the encounter. Gurley still thought the *Ranger* was a smuggler. According to the *Cumberland Chronicle* of 25 April, two days after the attack on Whitehaven:

> ...the smuggling business has, for some time past, been known to have been carried on by large vessels, with tenders to land their goods, and Captain Gurley's report, generally carrying that idea along with it, threw the inhabitants, in some degree, off their guard.

Unfortunately for Whitehaven, Gurley's view prevailed until Jones's surprise attack on the port. Early in the encounter Gurley had been convinced that the strange vessel 'was not on any fair trade', an accurate enough assessment, but one which missed the bigger picture. He had been misled by the fact that the *Ranger* appeared to have a cutter in attendance. This was a smuggling set-up Gurley thought he recognized. (It is curious that this tender, presumably brought from Brest, is not mentioned again.) Interestingly, Gurley described the *Ranger* as 'about 250 tons burthen, hake sterned [having an undercut stern] with badges on her quarters; a figurehead inclining to the left and painted yellow; her sides brown, with a yellow stroke round.' Gilkerson identifies the figurehead in his book *The Ships of John Paul Jones* as a 'rifleman', stating that the ship bore the name *Ranger* 'to honour the role of American riflemen'. Such an association most probably explains the 'badges' on her quarters. She carried plenty of red cloth to stretch as a cover along her yellow gunstroke, so that she could masquerade as a merchant vessel. Her whole battery was covered by decking and thus sheltered from small arms fire. She had twenty gun ports but actually mounted eighteen six-pounder guns, together with six swivel guns.

Out in the Irish Sea the crew of the *Ranger* was becoming increasingly disgruntled as they registered the mounting loss of prize money when each small ship they encountered sank forlornly below the waves for the sake of security and because of prize-manning constraints. They must have thought it very fortunate that whilst casting about for more worthwhile prey around the northern entrance into the Irish Sea, their captain was told by the crewmen of an easily captured and sunk small vessel that ten, or a dozen, valuable merchant ships lay at anchor nearby in Loch Ryan, Scotland. On the instant Paul Jones determined to get in amongst them and see what came of it. Fortunately for the merchantmen, but unluckily for his own prize-seeking crew, he was prevented from attacking by adverse winds. He then attempted to head off a cutter, but unable to do so pursued her doggedly as far as Ailsa Craig, a rocky island prominence in the wide mouth of the Firth of Clyde, where he abandoned the chase. He then encountered a sloop out of Dublin which he said he sank 'to prevent intelligence'.

Thwarted at Loch Ryan in what would have been an easy and profitable exercise, he crossed over the North Channel to Ireland in order to prowl about for prizes inside Belfast Lough. From the entrance to the Lough the *Ranger* could venture as far in as Carrickfergus, where the small harbour is still dominated by the daunting fortress that is Ulster's most impressive medieval structure. Hovering about the entrance to the Lough, *Ranger* took over a small fishing smack, learning from her crew that a ship that they had sighted riding at anchor in the Lough off Carrickfergus was in fact a British warship, the twenty-gun sloop *Drake*.

Paul Jones's reaction was instantaneous and positive: *Ranger* would sail down into the Lough straightaway and 'cut her out'. The crew refused absolutely to go along with this alarming proposal. They did, however, agree to make an attempt to take the totally unsuspecting *Drake* by surprise during the night. Paul Jones planned for the *Ranger* to quietly overlay the *Drake's* cable and 'fall upon her bow, so as to have all her decks open, and exposed'. From an ideal position *Ranger* would then rake her from stem to stern with musketry and shot, whilst at the same time grappling fast to her and boarding her. This plan was put into action but miscarried at the last moment when *Ranger*'s anchor caught fast on the cathead (the projecting timber through which the ropes for raising the anchor pass). The party sent forward to free the anchor, under the supervision of a quartermaster with too much drink inside him, was unable to do so before their ship had overshot the *Drake*, coming to on the British warship's port quarter only some thirty yards away. 'Unfortunately', says Paul Jones, somewhat economical with the truth in his report to the Commissioners (the drink allegation came later), 'the anchor was not let go so soon as the order was given'. There is a report that the *Drake* fired off an alerting shot; but according to Paul Jones she suspected nothing untoward as she slumbered peacefully at anchor in the timelessly secure waters of the British Isles.

It seems that *Ranger* was still successfully carrying off her disguise as a merchantman, perhaps deploying the red cloth that she specifically carried on board for camouflaging her sides. Paul Jones intended to push his luck by returning for another attempt the next night. Proceeding stealthily, he cut his anchor cable and made off into the darkness, hoping the cable would be seen as broken rather than cut. In the event, his revised plan was thwarted by a sudden onset of heavy gales accompanied by very high seas, which ruled out any return visit. The *Ranger* and the *Drake* were in fact destined to encounter each other later, in quite different circumstances; the ships of the Royal Navy having by then been alerted to the presence of the American intruder and ordered to hunt her down.

For the present, *Ranger* made off and rode out the gale overnight in the shelter of the Scottish coast. By the time the storm finally blew itself out the crew were exhausted and glad of some rest. Fortunately, the day dawned cold, clear and calm. From the deck of the *Ranger* extensive snowfalls could be seen powdering the distant hills across the waters. It was indeed a fine day, with the fresh snow sharpening the flanks of the broad fells and moorlands gleaming in the bright sunlight; such weather was unseasonal for the latter part of April. Taking in the tranquil scene on that crystal-clear morning, Paul Jones resolved to carry out the main purpose of his incursion into British waters. This was to be a spectacular attack on the port of Whitehaven, with the goal of burning out the crowded mass of ships lying helplessly aground in the harbour there at low tide. Remarkable as it may seem from walking around Whitehaven's sleepy quaysides today, at that time it was one of the most important ports in the British Isles, with over two hundred vessels lying huddled together at the time Paul Jones paid his visit. According to Jones's official account of events to the American Commissioners, a first attempt to attack Whitehaven at around 10.00pm on 18 April, the day after they took the *Lord Chatham*, was nipped in the bud when an onshore gale accompanied by high seas suddenly developed. He was about to make a second attempt when he was so unluckily spotted by the *Hussar*, and forced to postpone matters again in order to pursue her. Now that all the widespread havoc amongst the small craft plying their trade in the Irish Sea, which the chase of the revenue vessel had led to, was over, Paul Jones had his eye set once more on glory rather than on the prize money that so preoccupied his crew. But as the average mystified Englishman living in Cumbria at the time might well have asked: what on earth could possibly have motivated plans for such a devastating surprise attack on Whitehaven? The place had given Paul Jones a livelihood from the age of around twelve and he had become increasingly familiar with many of the inhabitants. Some explanation of the events that brought about this situation is required.

We have to look first at the matter from the point of view of Britain's rebellious colonists. The American Declaration of Independence, not long proclaimed in New England, included a list of grievances against King George III: 'He has plundered our seas, ravaged our coasts, burned our towns, and destroyed the lives of our people.' In truth, British actions at sea and against the sea-coast in America were rapidly becoming more brutal, and the war had not touched the British Isles in this way; they were at a safe distance and secure behind a shield of impressive sea power. No enemy since long before the living memory of the inhabitants of the British Isles had dared to attack a British port; but the British were about to get a very rude awakening. By carrying the war literally and force-fully home to the British and their government he resolved, said Paul Jones, 'to bring to an end the barbarous ravages to which the English turned in America'. In retaliation for these depredations, he had already plundered and destroyed a number of small craft in the Irish Sea, inevitably ruining livelihoods. However, as he wrote after the event in justification of his descent on Whitehaven, these deeds were purely incidental to a much more important objective which he had in mind: '... to put an end to burnings in America by making one good fire in England of shipping'. He specifically said that with regard to British conduct in America he 'had received no order at all to avenge these injuries' and 'had not at all commu-nicated my plans for this object to the American Commissioners at Paris'. However, the blanket orders that he was given by those Commissioners regarding the cruise of the *Ranger* amounted to carte blanche and included the possibility of 'an attempt on the coast of Great Britain'. The Commissioners had directed in a letter from Paris dated 16 January 1778, that after equipping the *Ranger* as he saw fit, Jones was to '... proceed with her in the manner you shall judge best for distressing the Enemies of the United States, by sea or otherwise, consistent with the laws of war and the terms of your commission'. The Commissioners expressly stated that they relied on his 'ability' and 'zeal [to] serve the cause of the United States, and therefore, do not give particular instructions as to your operations'.

Paul Jones was therefore acting within the scope of his orders, and being tight-lipped about them, not least to his crew. Significantly, he had already approached Congress for special payments to compen-sate them for the loss of possible prize money that his secret plans would involve. As the Commissioners, led by Benjamin Franklin, to whom Jones was immediately answerable, were no doubt aware, something other than commerce raiding was clearly brewing from the very outset. But based as they were in France, not at that time at war with Great Britain, they were in an awkward position.

So much for the immediate political background to the planned surprise attack on Whitehaven – what about Paul Jones himself? He had known Whitehaven intimately since early boyhood, and had become well acquainted with many of the people who lived there. What were his personal feelings about launching a diabolical incendiary attack on this familiar seaport? He never expressed any personal sentiments on the matter, and it is notable that where he does express emotions about his actions and their consequences, his words often seem to be wrapped up in euphuisitic and artificial language that does nothing for the projection of any sincerely held feeling. At a later stage in his excursions in British waters some of his contemporaries actually accused him of being callous and indifferent to casualties. To understand what made John Paul Jones tick, one must consider his background.

A Scotsman by a whisker, he was born at Kirkbean on the Scottish side of the tidal expanse of the Solway Firth. While still only a boy of twelve, or thirteen possibly, he came over the Solway to be apprenticed to the sea at Whitehaven. Fortunately, he took a liking to his English apprentice master, a Mr. Younger, who noted with satisfaction his good progress in seamanship and in due course promised him a secure future. His first major voyage as a youngster was aboard the *Friendship* of Whitehaven; a round trip to America, where his older brother was already living, and with whom he stayed in Fredericksburg, Virginia, whilst the ship was in the Rappahannock River there. He was at an impressionable age and took an immediate liking to New England, with which he soon became familiar through round trips on the *Friendship* that included prolonged stays in the Rappahannock.

Before very long, unfortunately, Younger's business began to falter, and on returning from another routine voyage to America aboard the *Friendship* in 1763, John Paul found Younger bankrupt and was released from his indentures as an apprentice, whilst still only a youngster of seventeen. Naturally anxious for work, he managed with Younger's valuable assistance to get himself taken on as third mate of the *King George*, a ship purpose-built for the slave trade and just completed in Whitehaven.

Whitehaven merchants only resorted to slaving when a switch in Government policy resulted in a catastrophic and permanent collapse of their tobacco trade with Virginia, a consequence which would have blighted the young John Paul's job prospects in the port. The *King George* sailed on her maiden voyage in 1764 with John Paul aboard, probably bound for the Windward Coast, which was favoured by Whitehaven merchants.

An actual destination in Africa – if indeed there was a recognizable one along the undeveloped and poorly mapped coastline – is unrecorded. Modern-day Liberia is in the centre of this stretch of the African coast, flanked on either side now by Sierra Leone (then the Gold Coast) and Ivory Coast. John Paul completed one round trip to Africa in the *King George*, and signed on for a second voyage. However, he left the ship after she had completed another 'middle passage' (the harrowing part of the voyage, across the Atlantic, laden with slaves) from West Africa to Jamaica.

In 1766, at the age of nineteen, he was taken on as first mate aboard the *Two Friends*, another 'blackbirder' (slaver), operating out of Kingston, Jamaica. On this ship, not put off by his experience so far, he participated in the slave trade for another two round trips until suitably recompensed with savings of around a thousand pounds – quite a sum – he left the repugnant business and eventually returned to ordinary trading.

A playbill bearing John Paul's name as one of the actors in a play written by Richard Steele has given rise to the story that around 1768 he became a member of a company of travelling players operating in the West Indies. At this particular moment in his life, with plenty of money and still only twenty-one, he could certainly afford to indulge himself and take up acting for a while. The playbill was designed to be used anywhere and cannot now be sourced to any particular island. In later life John Paul could quote Shakespeare, who was amongst his favourite poets, but there is no actual evidence that he performed in any of his plays, including the playbill. This thespian episode tenuously fills what would otherwise be an awkward gap of about a year in John Paul's biography. He then secured a passage home in the *John*, a brigantine belonging to a firm in Kirkcudbright, not far from his birthplace.

Whilst off the island of Tobago both the captain and the mate of this ship developed yellow fever and died. Since no-one else on board knew how to navigate, John Paul assumed command by common consent of the crew. To the immense pleasure and relief of the *John*'s owners, who appointed him Master in gratitude, he brought the small vessel, along with her cargo and remaining crew of seven, safely home to Kirkcudbright.

John Paul then made an uneventful round trip to the West Indies, to the satisfaction of the owners. However, on his next round trip in command of the *John* there was a dramatic example of John Paul's apparent disciplinary harshness. Furious with the new ship's carpenter, Mungo Maxwell of Kirkcudbright, John Paul had him lashed to the rigging and flogged for incompetence and disobedience. He was somewhat remorseful afterwards, but at the same time satisfied at having maintained necessary discipline. Maxwell quit the *John* in the West Indies, but soon afterwards died whilst in passage on another ship, the *Barcelona Packet*. His father, of some local standing back home in Kirkcudbright, assumed it was caused by the flogging and not by the fever, which was later certified as the cause of Mungo's death by the captain of the *Barcelona Packet*, who said that Maxwell had been 'in perfect health' when he came aboard his ship. Immediately upon his arrival in Tobago, the aggrieved Mungo had lodged a complaint about the flogging with the Admiralty Court. After personally examining Mungo's scars, the judge dismissed the complaint as frivolous, saying that the stripes were 'neither mortal nor dangerous'.

When John Paul got back from the West Indies, he was, to his complete surprise, arrested and clapped in gaol in the Tollbooth at Kirkcudbright. Mungo's father had acted as soon he learned of the alleged circumstances surrounding the distant event of his son's death.

Luckily for John Paul, he was soon permitted to return to the Caribbean and gather evidence to exonerate himself. However, despite having done this, he was dogged forever by the tale that he had once flogged a sailor to death; a version that Mungo's father continued to believe and promulgate, even though he had been a world away from the scene of events and had no real knowledge or appreciation of the facts. There were no more voyages in command of the *John*, because the ship's owners dissolved their partnership and sold the vessel, expressing in writing their satisfaction with John Paul's performance and professionalism.

A later incident in the course of his seafaring life, again in the West Indies, might well have had far more serious consequences for the future admiral, except that he hastily left for America, looking very much like a fugitive from justice. He abandoned his original name – John Paul – and adopted the new name Paul Jones.

At the age of twenty-six he had arrived in Tobago once again, on his second voyage as captain of the *Betsy* of London. In his correspondence, London seems to have evoked happy reminiscences of prostitutes in Soho's Poland Street. (He mentions one by name, a 'Miss Drew'.) Memories of these, some of the cast of *Harris's List of Covent Garden Ladies* (Harris was a pimp who collaborated with one Sam Derrick on the later successful and notorious book) must have been driven far from his mind when there occurred in Tobago what Jones would describe, in the only contemporary account of the matter, as 'the greatest misfortune of my life'.

These words appear in a letter to Benjamin Franklin, written under a misapprehension some five years after the event. John Paul Jones mistakenly thought that Franklin, the most illustrious of the American Commissioners in France, was onto a potentially very damaging story about him, and Jones wished to scotch any further speculation that might arise.

Jones carefully explained that the crew of the *Betsy* had wanted to go ashore in Tobago and were mutinous over arrears of pay, which the Captain had in his possession but wanted to invest in more cargo, to pay out later in London to their profit as well as his. The crew, living more for the present and the delights of Tobago than their Captain, thought this was outrageous. Their ringleader, whom John Paul described as a 'prodigious brute' and a man 'three times' his strength – remember that though strong and wiry he was a small man – insisted on going ashore against orders. Jones says, as background information, that this man frequently got drunk and was the main culprit involved in stealing the Captain's liquor! The man became openly aggressive when the Captain tried to prevent him leaving the ship, and forced the undoubtedly incensed Captain back into his cabin, yelling at him 'not to show his nose on deck again'. John Paul's sword happened to be lying on his cabin table, he wrote. Not to be so humiliatingly browbeaten, he grimly emerged, sword in hand and presented defensively before him. The infuriated ringleader was not put off by the blade, and leaping from a boat which was about to cast off he again came for the captain in a rage, with a bludgeon raised to connect lethally with the Captain's head. John Paul – whose account to Franklin is the only direct evidence of course – says he stepped back and encountered the edge of the open hatch as the blow was descending. He stopped suddenly; 'the fatal and unavoidable consequence of which,' he wrote, was the ringleader 'rushing upon the sword's point.' In other words: the man ran himself through on the captain's sword. The unlucky 'ringleader' then fell dead to the deck.

John Paul consulted his friends in Tobago, who, in view of the dead man's connections there (he was a native of Tobago), advised him to skedaddle until the heat was off. He jumped ship therefore, arriving not long afterwards in America, where he assumed the name of Paul Jones. The episode is difficult to interpret because at that time a captain who took extreme action to quell anything like a mutiny would normally have been backed up by the authorities and exonerated. Paul Jones says in his letter to Franklin that he offered to surrender himself, but was persuaded not to do so by the Justice of the Peace 'who called himself the Master's friend', as surrender was not necessary before the day of the trial. He further says: '… the rest of the master's friends who were present forced me to mount my horse [and] constrained me for a time to leave the Country.' He did so and never returned; and could well not have done so anyway because of developing hostilities between Great Britain and her colonies; a factor over and above the death of the 'ringleader'. His 'friends' included his partner Archibald Stewart and his agent Stuart Murray, as well as the Governor, William Young.

Eventually he ended up, through his excellent connections in New England, as a lieutenant in the newly forming American revolutionary navy. This was nearly two years after he had abandoned his ship in Tobago. Feeling more secure he modified his assumed name Paul Jones, to something closer to his original one: John Paul Jones. Jones was a surname that he could not now easily discard, and 'John Paul Jones' he remained for the rest of his life.

What happened in Tobago was without doubt known to an embarrassing number of people there, and presumably became known to people back in London. It is therefore surprising that the affair which precipitated his change of name never did seem to see the full light of day in his lifetime, even when he stepped later into the pitiless glare of the limelight, and the name subterfuge became known and was noised around. However, when the old Mungo Maxwell flogging affair had blown up unexpectedly on his return to Kirkcudbright from Tobago all those eventful years before, John Paul had fortuitously – prudently perhaps – joined the Freemasons.

They clearly found him acceptable, and he established a strong life-long connection with the society, being eventually admitted to the third degree. Maybe his Masonic involvement was in some way his salvation in Tobago after the unfortunate death of the 'ringleader'. The circumstances of his leaving Tobago were mysterious to say the least.

He certainly maintained his Masonic connections in America, being on record as having visited Lodges in Portsmouth and Boston whilst the *Ranger* was being fitted out on the Piscataqua River in New England. He may indeed have obtained his Commission in the navy through friends with Masonic connections. The brother of John Paul Jones's Masonic sponsor in Kirkcudbright was the business partner in America of Joseph Hewes, a congressman, a signatory of the Declaration of Independence, and chairman of the Marine Committee that actually created the navy, and appointed officers.

His well-documented service record clearly demonstrates that John Paul Jones was enterprising, bold, resolute and resourceful; all enviable qualities, and he made constructive contributions towards the effective development of the fledgling American navy. However, on the evidence of numerous contemporary written comments, he had an unstable and irascible temper. The evidence ranges from a complaint by a subordinate officer that he was 'unpardonably rude', to recorded displays of ungovernable temper. In a fury, he once kicked an officer several times in the backside as he was proceeding down a ladder after an altercation on deck. He had a combative nature, and perhaps his temper had come into play when he fatally ran through his crewman in Tobago and was forced to jump ship – a turn of events not at all usual amongst ships' captains.

He made and consolidated his early reputation in the American navy as a lieutenant – the very first one of such officers actually commissioned by Congress as it scraped together some kind of a navy in the early days of the American War of Independence. To his satisfaction he had been promoted to the rank of captain, and was enjoying active participation in the New England social scene by the time the *Ranger* sailed for British waters, where his qualities came into play and where he was soon to write his name in the annals of American history.

At what was clearly a critical juncture in his career, a curious glimpse into the less-than-straightforward persona of John Paul Jones – as he now boldly dubbed himself – is provided. In 1777, whilst living in Boston during the build-up to the cruise of the *Ranger*, he decided to provide himself with an Achievement of Arms of his own idiosyncratic design. Just why he assumed this heraldic invention, which he took seriously enough to keep and modify in later years, is difficult to divine, especially considering that the name Jones was a masquerade. Why he chose this surname above others to disguise his identity has never been satisfactorily explained in terms of any real connections. However, like 'Johnson', it means 'son of John'; a true statement, since John was his father's name as well as his own. So maybe this is the logic behind his choice of an urgently required alias when he fled from Tobago. However, there seems to be no logic at all in the design of heraldic quartering on his escutcheon or shield. The ermine-tailed arms characteristic of several Paul families of Gloucestershire (who are not provably connected with his own Paul family) are quartered with the stag adopted by a number of real Jones families in Wales. Admiral S.E. Morison, discussed these arms in an article which appeared in *American Neptune,* October 1958. He considered that whoever designed the Achievement of Arms 'must have had access to an armorial' – a book with depictions of coats of arms pertaining to the Paul and Jones families. He consulted one such book himself, though it was one published much later than the time of the heraldic invention, in 1884.

There are some interesting hints in the Edinburgh area about possible Paul family connections. Paul Jones's grandfather came from Fife, on the north side of the Firth of Forth, where he had been a yeoman farmer. He crossed over the Firth to take on a wayside Inn near Leith, which presumably he bought, and to run an associated market garden. Leith was very close to Edinburgh, and functioned as its port. So, in all the circumstances, we may reasonably assume that John Paul's grandfather was not without money, and had some social standing as both a yeoman farmer and an innkeeper – an occupation occasionally favoured by younger sons of the aristocracy or the 'middle classes' (misusing the term slightly) who did not wish to enter 'trade'. The surname Paul was very uncommon in the Leith/Edinburgh area around 1700. The Edinburgh Burgess Roll in

1716 lists a Col. Joshua Paul as an honorary Burgess. Tantalizingly perhaps in view of the Achievement's Gloucestershire connection, the Burgess Roll in 1723 includes a Robert Paul, Assistant Controller of Customs in South Britain. The Leith Directory for 1773 lists an actual John Paul, Bookbinder, in High School Wynd, Leith. Therefore, a connection with the Gloucestershire Pauls is perhaps not such an outrageous improbability.

Even though the combined arms might have meant something covertly logical to John Paul, his name was not 'Jones', making the whole shield display essentially bogus; and in any case hardly appropriate in a brand new republic! On the other hand, it may well have bolstered him socially, and the bold imposture no doubt tickled his fancy. The stag is used again in the crest above the shield, atop a very odd-looking helmet, which by its basic design represents, heraldically, 'esquire' ranking. There are two heraldically correct, but somewhat grotesque dolphin supporters at either side of the shield who are 'guarding' it. These same dolphins, four of them this time, in bronze and very attractively depicted, appear again after his death, literally supporting John Paul's sarcophagus in the crypt at Annapolis. Mantled around the shield are other details illustrating his seagoing life up to the point at which he set sail in the *Ranger*. The motto below the escutcheon is all-American: *Pro Republica*, 'For the Republic'. This motto is woven around cannons with ornamental roses below, and the Masonic symbols, the compass and square, are placed in the middle. Projecting from around the outer edge of the escutcheon to form the mantling are numerous artefacts, mostly connected to the grim business of war at sea. In reference to the boarding of enemy ships there is a prominent cutlass blade, together with a boarding axe. There are depictions of tools used for servicing a ship's guns: a ram, used to ram bags of black powder, the iron cannon ball and the wadding down the gun barrel; a sponge, a wetted mop stuffed down the barrel after firing to extinguish any burning remnants; and a 'worm', like a brass corkscrew, used to extract smouldering residues as well as unused or misfired powder bags from the barrel. To the top left of the Achievement is an ill-defined object, which seems to be the hilt of a sword. A grenade, a weapon much employed in close sea fights, might have been more appropriate. But perhaps Paul Jones was demonstrating that, being a gentleman, his sword was only unsheathed in justifiable circumstances, in time of war. Between the cutlass blade and the helmet there is another mysterious object that Admiral Morison thinks is either a lance or an arrow, but it could also be a harpoon-like incendiary device, as a wide variety of such devices were used in close engagements, usually fired from guns, with a flaming binding or attachment.

Also present in the Achievement are four flags, two of which were flown by the Americans prior to the introduction of the more familiar Stars and Stripes, as flown by Paul Jones in the *Ranger*. Morison in his biography also tentatively identifies a blue command pendant, as well as positively identifying a British red ensign (in merchant navy parlance 'the red duster'), the flag displayed then, as now, by the British merchant fleet. In John Paul's days, however, the red ensign was also flown by warships of the Royal Navy. Then, the fleet was divided into three squadrons, the red ensign distinguishing the red squadron from the white and the blue. As fleets got bigger the system was modified in practice, and abolished formally in 1864. Since that date the white ensign has been the flag of the Royal Navy, the blue ensign the flag of the Royal Naval Reserve, and the red the flag of the Merchant Service.

It has been claimed in the past (by Jones's biographer Lincoln Lorenz for example, see bibliography) that Paul Jones saw some short service in the British Navy quite early in his career, but there is no material evidence for this. At first sight it is tempting to think that the red ensign embellishing John Paul's coat of arms indicates such service. Unfortunately, with both merchant ships and warships flying the red ensign in the eighteenth century, the inclusion of this particular flag in the Achievement of Arms proves nothing. Of course, Paul Jones would have sailed on numerous British merchant ships displaying the red ensign, and he might well have flown it deceptively in the lead-up to an actual engagement – the element of surprise in warfare being something by which he set great store – and he frequently used British flags to assist him in achieving this. But the red ensign does not indicate that he served in the Royal Navy. He certainly studied navigation late into the night whilst staying with his brother in New England, and says in an item existing amongst Benjamin Franklin's vast collection of papers that he had made 'the art of war at sea in some degree my study'. Many merchant ships were of necessity well armed in those perilous seafaring days, and a source of valuable experience. However it was that he came to absorb the business of handling a fighting ship in battle, by general consent he practised the art of naval warfare extremely well and – very much to the point – never lost a vessel.

Whatever faults he had, and his difficult, idiosyncratic temperament was one of them, by the time he designed his rather odd and deceptive Achievement of Arms, he was sufficiently well thought of by those with power and authority in the fledgling Republic across the Atlantic to be recommended for advancement, and to command an important, but initially unspecified mission. Colonel John H. Sherburne, an early biographer of Paul Jones, who linked together very perceptively a large volume of important biographical material that he had collected, adjudges that at this point in his career Paul Jones had 'entered upon a very hazardous enterprise against Whitehaven'. What exactly would be the outcome?

Keeping Sherburne's words in mind, let us return to the *Ranger*, as necessary preparations were made for the imminent attack. It is doubtful if John Paul Jones gave even a passing thought to his past as he concentrated on bringing the *Ranger* into position for the night approach to the blithely unsuspecting port; its township very attractively and only recently developed around its harbour, its quays bustling with trade. Something of a novelty, Whitehaven was in fact the first model town built in Britain since the Middle Ages. It was of course an ideal choice of target for Paul Jones because he knew its features well enough to navigate in and out at night. He had considered that the town as well as the shipping might go up in flames, and as a deserter would soon assert, it seems probable that from the outset he had intended the conflagration to spread into the town.

At that critical point, his mind was undoubtedly preoccupied, not with the rights and wrongs of the attack, but with immediately practical matters. The night was dark enough, but the dying wind was causing real concern. In fact, as Paul Jones says, it '… became very light, so that the ship could not in proper time approach so near as I had intended'. This failure of the *Ranger* to close with the coast as anticipated was an ominous start to the night's events. It jeopardized his plans and eventually compelled him to leave the ship prematurely, rowing on in open boats for longer than planned and against the tide. The situation was not helped by the attitude of the crew.

Since setting sail from New England six months before, *Ranger* had taken three prizes; but several small vessels, all potentially meat for the prize pot, had been sent to the bottom to the disgust of the crewmen. They had enlisted to make a lot of money out of prizes, the easy pickings from commerce raiding being the stock-in-trade of the fledgling American navy. In those days American ships did not often take on British warships by choice, and certainly not fortified shore installations. The British were enraged at their expensive depredations amongst merchant shipping, and it was perhaps no wonder that they regarded American ships as mere pirates or at best privateers, and in contrast to their attitude to captured soldiers, regarded any captured crews as common criminals rather than prisoners of war. As a properly commissioned officer by his lights, to be described as a pirate or even a privateer annoyed John Paul Jones intensely; and what he was about to do was definitely not an act of piracy or privateering: it was a calculated act of war.

The crew could not have agreed more, and were appalled at the prospect of such a financially pointless stroke. They voiced their opposition in no uncertain terms. At this point, it has to be said that the captain of the *Ranger* was not the only American sea captain to have trouble with his crew. In the land of the newly and gloriously free, discipline was a constant problem aboard naval vessels, and Paul Jones himself, in the midst of his current operations in the Irish Sea, sensed the heady brew of democratically inspired mutiny. Mundanely, it stemmed from the fact that making no money, and disdainful of glory and its accompanying danger, the men were fed up. They considered that they had been at sea long enough and fervently wanted to get back home. To them, the Captain was the only obstacle standing in the way of prizes and a rich, long-overdue return to New England. The signal for the mutiny to get underway was to have been the action of Cullen, the Sailing Master, in lunging for the Captain. Luckily, Paul Jones had received a quiet word of warning from Lieutenant Meijer, a Swedish volunteer. When Cullen rushed to grapple with him, the Captain grimly put a loaded pistol to his head. The threatened mutiny was stopped in its tracks, but mutinous feelings were never far from the surface in the crew of the *Ranger*.

Part of the small Tollbooth gaol at Kirkcudbright, where John Paul had been incarcerated, accused of murder on his return from his second voyage in command of the John. *He was permitted to return to the West Indies to gather evidence that exonerated him.*

3

Singeing The Lion's Mane –
The 'Insolent Attack' on Whitehaven

Approaching Whitehaven during the fateful night of the raid, still with a difficult atmosphere aboard, Paul Jones had himself been piloting the *Ranger* in the familiar waters of the Solway Firth. When he called for volunteers to man the two boats, the crew showed no enthusiasm whatsoever for the Captain's proposed enterprise, still considering that an attack to simply burn the shipping at Whitehaven was pointless. There was great risk involved, but no prospect of prizes and not much realistic expectation of loot; they were being asked to hazard their lives for no good reason that they could see.

Some amongst them were no doubt aware that as well as having a functioning lighthouse, the port of Whitehaven was overlooked by a small harbour building next to the lighthouse, manned at irregular hours, much in the style of a watch-house. These important features of Whitehaven's maritime history are still extant and will be looked into later.

More to the point, as far as the crew of the *Ranger* was concerned, the harbour was protected by two batteries of guns commanding the harbour and its approaches. One of these had been built on the shore a little way outside the harbour: the openly accessible Lunette, or Half-Moon Battery; also known as the New Fort at that time. The other guns were mounted in close association with a some-what older quayside fort, often called the Old Fort. Contemplating these hazards and the reality of what they were about to do, the ship's surgeon thought the entire proposal foolhardy, and told the Captain so; echoing feelings amongst the crew when he said that in any case, 'Nothing could be got by burning poor people's property.' The first and second lieutenants, Simpson and Hall, told

Jones bluntly that being but poor men, their desire was for money, not honour. At the critical moment they cried off taking part in the assault, claiming they were 'overcome with fatigue'. Sure enough they had been struggling in a storm the night before, and the present night was lengthening sleeplessly ahead of them. But if they thought that their withdrawal from command of the boats at the last minute – and in the absence at that point of the necessary volunteer crewmen – would abort the enterprise, they were quite wrong: Paul Jones himself was going to lead the attack.

In view of the evident mood on board ship, this would seem as foolhardy a personal move on the Captain's part as surgeon Green thought the whole enterprise to be. But Jones was determined to take his chances. He reassured the crew that he was 'perfectly acquainted with the town and harbour of Whitehaven', and, significantly in view of later developments, 'all the places adjacent'. He had a considered objective in burning the shipping tied up there, and of course, had his burgeoning reputation at stake. Glory was beckoning; he must have felt compelled to follow it. He simply had to achieve more military success in British waters than he had managed so far.

Reconstruction of events at Whitehaven relies mainly on Paul Jones's own official report to the American Commissioners in Paris, his later memoirs (which differ somewhat from this report), the official report of the Whitehaven authorities to the British Government and the accounts in local newspapers and periodicals. There is also the promptly elicited affidavit and subsequently reported words of a 'traitor' – a deserter from the *Ranger* in fact, to whom the towns-folk soon became well disposed. Jones's accounts are very much to the point, but not lacking in dramatic effect despite their terseness. Fleshing out events from other sources in order to give a fuller and more rounded picture gives rise to some puzzling anomalies, even controversy, as will be seen.

Becalmed around midnight, much further from Whitehaven than he wanted to be, Jones prepared to man and then prematurely launch into an adverse tidal flow the two boats earmarked for the hope-fully spectacular enterprise. According to the eventual deserter, he stressed vehemently that the crew would 'receive the same reward for burning and destroying the ships as if they had taken them'. Paul Jones had indeed, as mentioned earlier, approached Congress on this very matter; but it was an unfamiliar arrangement to put to the men. They may well have found it hard to swallow as they lay that night uncomfortably far from Whitehaven, and an ocean away from New England and Congress. Their Captain added earnestly – desperately even – that all he wanted out of the exploit was the honour; any money or valuables they came across in Whitehaven would be for the men accompanying him in the boats.

His exhortations at last drew, he says, 31 volunteers, including the eventual deserter. However, the Carlisle Journal of 31 January 1905, reporting the recent 'interesting discovery' of the log of the *Ranger* amongst the archives at Douglas Castle on St Mary's Isle, says that according to the log – since then unfortunately burnt in a house fire – 40 volunteers accompanied Paul Jones. Be that as it may – and the inhabitants of Whitehaven agreed with Jones on the matter of numbers – the Captain personally took charge of one boat, with the clearly trustworthy Swedish Lieutenant Meijer, aspiring to an army commission in America, as his second in command. The other boat he entrusted to Lieutenant Wallingford of the Marines, with midshipman Ben Hill as his mate.

When questioned soon after his defection, the deserter said that the captain 'fully explained his design to the men' before embarkation, so both boat crews were party to their Captain's plans. He asked them to stand by him, saying that he would be the first ashore and the last to leave – as, in the event, he was. Each man was equipped with pistol and cutlass, and each boat with two lanterns, plenty of flint and tinder, and bundles of pine sticks and faggots wrapped with strips of canvas and dipped in a traditional witches' brew of turpentine, pitch, rosin, brimstone (sulphur) and nitre (saltpetre). These firebrands ought soon to be torching inflammable tarred rigging and blazing in the holds of the closely packed shipping.

'At midnight I left the ship with two boats and thirty-one volunteers', says Jones with probably too much precision about the time. Owing to the distance from Whitehaven, and with the tide running against them rather than in their favour, rowing proved hard and progress was frustratingly slow. They seem to have kept company for around three tiring hours and, in the Captain's own words, only managed to reach the 'outer pier' at Whitehaven as 'day began to dawn'.

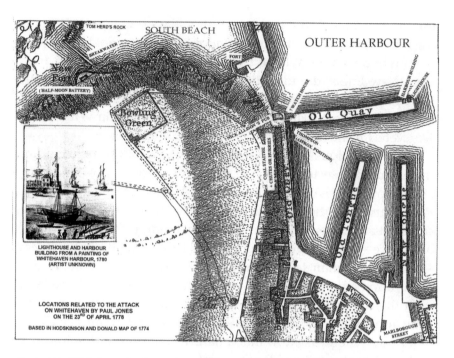

Part of the Whitehaven harbour plan, showing the South Harbour, inset into Hodskinson and Donald's 1774 map of Cumberland. The Bulwark Quay and North Harbour are off the map to the right. (Courtesy Cumbria Record Office, Carlisle)

Whitehaven's official report to the Government states that they landed about three o'clock in the morning, the *Cumberland Chronicle* opting for about two o'clock, and the *Cumberland Pacquet* for 'late last night or early this morning'.

Time of day was a peculiarly local matter in those days, and remained so until the introduction of the railways demanded rationalisation. Paul Jones, coming out of a French port, was probably not in step with the inhabitants of Whitehaven anyway. Minor discrepancies in the time of day also arose the following year in connection with the *Bonhomme Richard* expedition. Computing backwards from the present, it can perhaps be usefully said that first light at Whitehaven on the 23 April 1778 was at 04.14 a.m., with sunrise at 04.53 a.m. Low water, grounding the shipping in the harbour, was 02.29 a.m. (These figures were kindly provided by Bidston Observatory and the UK Hydrographic Office.) However, low tide, according to the contemporary local press in Whitehaven, using local time of course, was at 1.25 a.m. The tide can be affected by numerous factors, but the discrepancy here would take quite a lot of explaining. Whatever the time, the official report from Whitehaven after the raid states that as the attack got underway: 'The tide was then flowing into the harbour, but none of the ships were then on float.' The harbour at Whitehaven in those days was completely drained of water at low tide, the sea drawing back some way beyond the harbour walls, leaving the whole harbour complex well clear of the water.

The April 1778 edition of *The Cumberland Magazine*, reporting on information gleaned after the night raid, including extensive details derived from the official early morning interrogation of the deserter, stated that initially, '... the boats attempted to land near Saltom, with intent to come round by the half-moon battery, but were prevented by the rocks, which occasioned a delay of near half an hour'; though prolonging delay would be more accurate.

If this statement in the *Cumberland Magazine* is correct (relying as it did on the account from the deserter) the original aim was to come quietly ashore just south of the town and take over and put out of action the easily accessible Half-Moon Battery on the way into the fringes of the seaport itself. There the battery in the Old Fort could in turn be dealt with, putting the attackers in a secure position to undertake in concert the main fire-raising business of the raid. A change of plan was probably dictated on the spot by the topography and perhaps the state of the tide, no longer to the attackers' advantage as it would have been at the time of their foiled attack a few days previously, when they were thwarted by the sudden squall. In the uncertain days of sail, plans were always subject to the vagaries of weather and tide, and captains often had to use their own initiative. The clearly resourceful John Paul Jones would have been not much disconcerted by the turn of events.

In fact, staying firm in his endeavour despite the initial setbacks, Jones dispatched the boat under Wallingford and Hill to burn the shipping in the northern section of the harbour, separated from the southern section by a stone pier he described as 'about a ship's height'. The Bulwark Quay fits the description and has this dividing function nowadays. Paul Jones went with the party in the larger boat, to ensure all possible safety for their eventual departure and to burn the shipping in the southern section of the harbour.

Whitehaven Harbour 1789, by Askew. The two buildings remain virtually unaltered, with, as yet, no extension of the Harbour Building. (Courtesy Cumbria County Library Service, Carlisle)

According to the subsequent official report, and the local *Cumberland Chronicle* (25 April), ten men were in Wallingford and Hill's boat, whilst Paul Jones with twenty men 'landed on the battlement near the head of the Old Quay'. Maybe they had little other choice of a landing spot because of the state of the tide; and Jones certainly wanted to find the merchant ships grounded. First, Jones himself scrambled onto the quay to reconnoitre. The rest of the party then followed, probably climbing up onto the 'battlemented' quay by means of an extant stone stairway set into the side of it, uncomfortably close to the little building next to the lighthouse, perhaps by then actively functioning as a watch-house.

On landing, the Captain's first act was to hurry his boat party stealthily along the stone flags of the quay, in the shadow of the 'battlement' (rather like a high parapet), to engineer an entry into the unsuspecting Old Fort and, assuming all went well, get at its guns. The fort came dimly into view some little way off – at the foot of the New Quay on plan – as they turned right towards it on leaving the cover of the Old Quay parapet. Had the state of the tide been more favourable, they might have been able to land under the very walls of the Old Fort, alongside which there seems to have been a way down onto the beach. That they do not appear to have used this approach is evidenced by the *Chronicle*, which presents a different scenario, as does the Official Report of the Justices: 'Captain Jones and his party landed in the Harbour of Whitehaven' – not on the beach south of it. John Paul Jones' account of the assault on the Old Fort in his Report to the American Commissioners in France is short:

> I was successful in scaling the walls, and spiking up all the cannon in the first fort. Finding the sentinels shut up in the guard house, they were secured without being hurt. Having fixed sentinels, I now took with me one man only (Mr. Green), and spiked up all the cannon in the southern fort; distant from the other a quarter of a mile.

In a later memoir account he expands on things more vividly:

> We took the fort by storm, [but] lacking ladders we had to climb it by mounting on the shoulders of the largest and strongest men, and entered it in this manner through the embrasures.

Some of the remnants of the Old Fort at Whitehaven, after surviving partial demolition for substantial harbour modification, and subsequent conversion to use as a lime kiln.

I commanded this operation and was also the first who entered the fort. The morning was cold, and the sentinels had retired to the guard-room; they were not expecting such a hostile visit. No blood at all was shed in securing their post; we spiked thirty-six cannon of the fort and battery.

By 'the battery' the Captain doubtless meant the open Half-Moon Battery. As soon as they had succeeded so effectively at the Fort, Paul Jones, after posting sentinels as he said, hurried off to the easily accessible and clearly unguarded battery just a short way around the curve of the foreshore. Being accompanied only by midshipman Joe Green to help him spike the powerful guns there, he clearly anticipated no opposition.

The guns at Whitehaven are recorded as including in 1763 (at the end of the Seven Years War with France, 1756–1763), formidable 18-, 24- and 42-pounders. However, these defensive armaments, the details of which Paul Jones would have remembered from his Whitehaven days (which took in the latter part the Seven Years War), had been downgraded after the war ended, with some guns moved and others put into storage. After the raid the official report from Whitehaven refers to the fact that, on landing, the Americans '… immediately took possession of a Fort adjoining to the Harbour and spiked all the guns which are 32 pounders and some which carry 42 pounds'. Paul Jones is unspecific as to poundage, referring generally to the 'heavy cannon' that he found at Whitehaven.

The bold and totally unexpected intruders were not challenged up to this point and no alarm was raised. Paul Jones, without the dangerous scuffle that might well have broken out, had neatly secured his first key objective: the complete disabling of the harbour defences. This would safeguard the *Ranger* when she came within range to pick them up, as well as ensure the safety of their own open boats when making their escape. One suspects that Paul Jones knew pretty well the lax defensive situation he would find at Whitehaven. The defences had never been tested and the townsfolk thought they never would be. They were nearly right because the defences were never tried – except this once. Still, the Americans were lucky, as things might have turned out differently.

In William Brownrigg and Henry Ellison's signed official account of events at Whitehaven on 23 April, which formed part of the report to the government signed by a multitude of Whitehaven's worthies, the two Justices of the Peace made a statement contradicting Paul Jones's account. After announcing at the outset the capture of the Fort by the Americans, they then explain that this ensued from 'the people of the town being then in the greatest security and no guard or watch being then kept either in the Fort & Batteries, or in the Harbour.' Neither party in this contretemps could afford to get its facts wrong on such a serious and publicly sensitive matter as to whether the defences were manned or not. The crew of the *Ranger* knew quite well what transpired in Whitehaven, and the townsfolk knew the defensive situation there. There must be some reasonable explanation for the differing accounts.

It is most unlikely that Paul Jones found vagrants or squatters in an active military establishment, with an arms and ammunition store, or that he would take them to be the 'sentinels'. However, if the people of Whitehaven had wanted to save money after the Seven Years War, they might have dispensed with a full cohort in favour of some 'caretaker' option, with gunners on a retainer perhaps, or some such less expensive and therefore more popular arrangement. Simply having a gunner and gun crews available when needed might suffice. Such a situation is plausible and would explain the ease with which the Fort was overwhelmed. Of course, it would involve Paul Jones promoting caretakers to 'sentinels'. Caretakers would be expected to be asleep at night-time, whereas sentinels would not; at least not usually. Cannily, Paul Jones does not say how many 'sentinels' he found, though his use of the plural means that there was more than one! In his official report to the Commissioners he states, ambiguously: 'Finding the sentinels shut up in the guard house, they were secured without being hurt'. Is a 'guard house' different to a 'guard room', the term he uses in the later and more dramatic account in his memoirs, written after reflection? Who exactly were the persons in the original 'house', or 'room'? Did Paul Jones ever see them? Did he simply shut 'them' in, under pain of death if they made a sound?

The Half-Moon Battery was another matter entirely. Evidently the most recently constructed, but on an open site, it was found unguarded by Paul Jones, as he clearly expected it to be. Both the Fort and Half-Moon Batteries – whatever their state of manning might have been – were fully operational physically, as is evidenced by the inhabitants of Whitehaven rushing to use them, only to find the guns spiked, when the Americans were making off in their boats. The Half-Moon Battery is labelled 'New Fort' in the near-contemporary 'Plan of Whitehaven' incorporated into Hodskinson and Donald's 1774 Map of the County of Cumberland. This plan seems to be the best available for placing locations and events, and a detail from it is provided on page 32, courtesy of Cumbria County Archives, Carlisle.

After his successful spiking foray to the Battery, just out of sight of the town around the base of the coastal cliffs, the eager Captain of the *Ranger* was presented on his return with a disconcerting scene in the harbour. In his official account of the expedition in a long letter to the Commissioners in Paris, written after his eventual return to Brest and dated 27 May, he says: 'On my return from this business I naturally expected to see the fire of the ships on the north side, as well as to find my own party with everything in readiness to set fire to the shipping in the south.' And in a fuller, later account:

> ...to my great astonishment, I saw that the boat sent to the northern part had returned without having accomplished anything. Those who had gone in it pretended to have been frightened by certain noises which they had heard, but I told them that these noises existed only in their imagination.

More to the point, they said that at the critical moment, when they were starting to set fire to the ships, their candles had burnt out. Moreover, his own men, who had performed well in capturing the Old Fort, were themselves unprepared to set fire to any shipping. 'By the strangest fatality' says Jones, sardonically, 'my own party were in the same situation, the candles being all bunt out'.

Standing in the midst of the then assembled crews, Jones must have been pretty exasperated; he would have been enraged had he been aware of the reason why the boat party commanded by Wallingford and Hill spent so little time fire-raising in their allotted section of the harbour. A *Cumberland Chronicle* Extraordinary published hot on the heels of events and reproduced in Lloyd's Evening Post (Vol. XLII, no. 3252) after reporting the landing of Paul Jones and his party, 'near the head of the old quay', stated: '... another boat came into the harbour, and landed ten men at the Old Quay slip, when they proceeded to Nich. Allison's, a public house on the Old Quay'. In other words, it would seem that the smaller boat party under Wallingford and Hill soon abandoned their task – or did not even start it – and, fancying a quick drink, made straight for the nearest pub! According to the *Chronicle*'s 'Extraordinary', they rousted the sleeping publican and his family out of bed to serve them, and thereupon '... made very free with the liquors and would not permit any of the family to stir out'. There is little reason to doubt this colourful incident, confirmed by the *Cumberland Pacquet*, although the Official Report does offer another explanation, saying that to obtain a flame the intruders 'were obliged to break into a watch house on the Key [sic] where a small family lived who were all in bed'. A pub and a watch house are unlikely to be confused.

To have landed ten men 'at the Old Quay slip' would have been touch and go so early in the proceedings at near low tide; though the tide had by then turned and the sea was flowing in. Certainly the Old Quay slip – as well as any other slipway for that matter – would have been inaccessible by water for some time after low tide, with all ships and boats lying helplessly aground. The *Chronicle*'s reporter would not personally have witnessed the events, and a question mark hangs over this point – especially as he implies that Wallingford and Hill's boat came in directly to the Old Quay slip without going to the North Harbour at all. This is unlikely, since Paul Jones directed them to go there and would have seen, at least initially, that they were acting according to instructions; and he makes no later criticism on this point: Quite the contrary in fact, as we shall see. Once the raid was underway Freeman – the deserter – would have lost some overview of events, resulting perhaps in an incomplete narrative.

The *Chronicle* was the source of the pub story and the Old Quay slip element. After stating that the Captain's party landed at the head of the Old Quay, the *Chronicle* went on to say that it was 'another boat' that came in at the slip, whose crew proceeded straight to Nicholas Allison's. The implication of this – if correct – is that it was the northern boat party only that barged its way into the pub. One hopes, in a way, that the *Chronicle* got it wrong, and that the Captain's own boat party did not miss out on some liquid refreshment whilst waiting at the Old Fort for the Captain to return from his work at the Half-Moon Battery! Paul Jones was obviously not present, and neither was Joe Green, who was helping the Captain to spike the guns at the Battery. Apart from the apparently ineffective foray to the North Harbour and the successful spiking foray to the Battery, nearly all the action centred on the Old Quay, with Nick Allison and his family presumably kept under close guard in their pub by those lucky enough to be detailed to do so. In reporting the American landing the *Cumberland Pacquet* avoided the tabloid sensationalism of the *Chronicle*: 'A number of armed men (to the amount of thirty) landed privately at this place, by two boats, from an American privateer, as appears from one of the people now in custody.' It can be taken that the main source of the reports was the deserter.

The truth about the burnt-out candles is hard to judge. They may well have gone out, as the journey from the *Ranger* had been a very long one. This fortunate burn-out might have seemed an ideal excuse for diving into the pub by seamen unenthusiastic for the enterprise anyway, and without much faith in the promised financial inducements. On the other hand, the suspiciously coincidence of the flames going out for both parties might suggest more deliberate obstruction of Jones's object. This is strongly supported by the fact that Lieutenant Meijer, whom Jones had on good instinct left at the quayside in charge of the boat under his own command, said later that the rest of the boat crew told him bluntly that they intended to leave the captain behind, abandoned to whatever fate had in store, and asked for his assistance. When he loyally and dutifully refused this and kept a watchful eye on the Captain, they had to think again.

The obvious – though perhaps not the only – bad apple in the crew, a David Smith, suspiciously eager to volunteer for the attack, now turned into David Freeman the deserter. Once in custody Freeman said – no doubt choosing his words carefully in a life-and-death situation for himself – that he was Irish by birth but at five years old, 'never having known his parents', was taken by Thomas McMillan, a blacksmith, to America, where he grew up in the man's service. Eventually, according to his account, when travelling with his master towards New York – just captured by the British – in order to join the King's troops, they were both taken by the rebels and put in prison. McMillan soon escaped, and a year later Freeman also escaped, joining the crew of the *Ranger* to avoid renewed imprisonment, and in hope of getting back to his native country, which, he claimed, he had not seen since leaving as a child. Those of the Irish diaspora are proverbially sentimental about 'Auld Erin's Isle', a river of nostalgia in full flood every year on St. Patrick's day – not least in America – and Freeman's declared motive should not lightly be dismissed, even though his name is not obviously Irish, and he sounds like an orphan or a foundling with no-one to return to in Ireland.

At the earliest opportunity once ashore, maybe when Wallingford's party dived into the pub, Freeman had quietly detached himself from his companions, divested himself of his weapons and, as reported in Whitehaven, went along Marlborough Street, a very short street between the quayside and the town. According to the *Cumberland Pacquet*, he started rapping at the doors 'a little after three o'clock', warning the townsfolk of the impending firestorm, and perhaps able by then to point to a blaze in the harbour. Though Paul Jones scoffed at any sound as being all in the mind, the rumpus created by Freeman might have been the source of the unidentified noise that scared the boat party; ensconced inside the alehouse and unable to hear well enough to gauge the real significance of it.

Judging from what Paul Jones had to say later, nobody had any idea what Freeman was up to. For his part, Freeman obviously wanted to get as far away as possible from Jones and the rest of the crew before he raised the alarm, preferably – and actually as it turned out – in a respectable part of the town near the harbour. There are only a few houses left on Marlborough Street now by which to judge what the residents might have been like then, but Freeman must have been reassured that he would be taken seriously and not turned over to the mercy of the angry crew by dwellers in the warren around the harbour. Instead, once the town was alerted, having already thrown away his arms as soon as he was able, he trustingly 'delivered himself up to a Man in the Streets'.

Freeman, a young man of twenty-two, was questioned at about eight o'clock in the morning Whitehaven time, before magistrates and other prominent people assembled in Haile's Coffee Room. When he was apprehended, just after alerting the town, he was initially viewed with suspicion. According to the *Cumberland Pacquet*: 'Whether he was left by accident or escaped by design, is yet

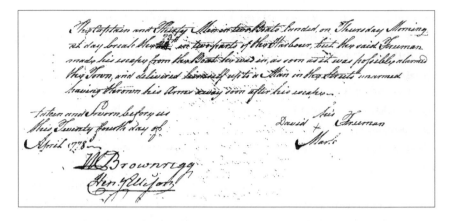

David Freeman's 'mark' on the affidavit 'taken and sworn' before the Whitehaven Justices – William Brownrigg and Henry Ellison.

uncertain', nevertheless, 'the alarm was immediately spread, and his account proved too true'. The very detailed revelations spilling out about Paul Jones and the *Ranger* during his interrogation later secured for Freeman the benefit of the doubt. Luckily for him, Freeman's personal account of himself was also accepted, and he was soon favourably regarded as the saviour of the port. Like most, Freeman was illiterate, and the relevant essentials of what he had to say would in the normal way have been written down and read back to him. On 24 April he attested to the contents of his affidavit, with an X appended with the usual style and form of words: 'David Freeman his mark'. Freeman talked about many matters, either recorded specifically in his affidavit, or more generally in Whitehaven's Official Report to the Government, as well as in local newspaper reports. His information included details of the ship, her place of origin and armament, her relationship with the French, the officers and crew, Paul Jones himself and his activities and plans – all of which would be of interest to the British Government and the Admiralty of course. He attested that, as part of his exhortation to the men prior to embarking in the boats, the Captain informed them that he 'hoped to destroy all the ships in the harbour, and to set fire to the town'. Since so much of Freeman's reported information is correct – and there is plenty of it, both official and unofficial – there is no reason to doubt him on this point; and Jones confirms it. As a participating eyewitness, we can trust Freeman's account of an initial aborted landing attempt, whether planned or resorted to in order to shorten the rowing marathon; a detail passed over by Jones as immaterial to his bold exploit.

Freeman's revelations were reported at length by the newspapers. Whilst the *Cumberland Magazine* related '... the principal part of the information communicated by Freeman', and the *Cumberland Pacquet* referred to 'the purport of his affidavit', all the newspapers in one way or another relied heavily on Freeman's words. Had they existed in the eighteenth century, he would no doubt have been a target for the paparazzi.

Standing resolutely on the quayside in the midst of the raid, the diminutive John Paul was undaunted by the turmoil which was developing rapidly from Freeman's hammering. 'The day too came on apace' he wrote later, 'yet I would by no means retreat while any hopes of success remained.' He weighed up the situation, placed men to cover the party on the quay from the assembling townsfolk, managed to secure a light from an isolated house nearby, and soon lent a hand himself in holding back the growing crowd. He says in his report on the raid that 'a fire was kindled in the steerage of a large ship, which was surrounded by at least an hundred and fifty others'. According to the *Chronicle*'s 'Extraordinary', this ship was in fact the *Thompson*, described as 'a coal loaden vessel, lying opposite to Allisons'. One wonders exactly where she was lying, if 'loaden' means fully loaded. Perhaps she was lying alongside the coal wharf, or at the root of the Old Quay pier, still 'opposite to Allisons', in order to release loading space at the coal chutes to another collier. She would be one of a vast number of colliers trading in coal, mostly to Ireland, from Whitehaven. The loading of coal at Whitehaven was very advanced for its day, and five vessels at a time could tie up stem-to-stern for loading by gravity feed down thundering coal chutes, known as 'hurries', from the Staithe (or Staithes), an enormous wooden structure kept supplied along wooden waggonways from the pits. Five ships could probably be loaded simultaneously on one tide. Paul Jones was well aware of Whitehaven's coal trade with Ireland, and did in fact specifically talk later about disrupting it. Perhaps this was a secondary motive when he carefully stoked up the fire on the *Thompson*, especially in view of where she was.

The *Thompson* was a fine ship; brand new, and built in Whitehaven. An apprentice sleeping aboard was hauled out of his bunk in only his shirt, tied up, gagged with a handkerchief, and deposited on the quayside, along with a couple of others, under threat of being shot if they made a false move. The fire aboard the *Thompson* at first proved too lazy for the raiders' now urgent need. But not to be thwarted, Jones found the solution: 'After some search a barrel of tar was found and poured into the flames, which now ascended from all the hatchways.' With the fire apparently raging beyond control the situation was rapidly improving for the raiders; but only under the Captain's personal supervision. Crowds gathered: 'Individuals ran hastily towards us. I stood between them and the ship on fire, with a pistol in my hand, and ordered them to retire, which they did with precipitation.' He was able to do this because the crowd was not gathering around him but approaching along the quay in front of him.There would usually be few or none in the workaday stretch behind him at night-time; and none that night, as the Captain was backed up by men armed to the teeth, lit up by the lurid glow of the flames from the *Thompson*. Paul Jones comments with evident satisfaction that by then, 'The flames had already caught the rigging, and began to ascend the mainmast.' Since the *Thompson* was, as reported after the raid in the *Cumberland Pacquet*, '… lying close to one of the steaths, there was the greatest reason to fear that the flames would, from it, be communicated to the town'. In other words the *Thompson* was well placed to cause considerable havoc in Whitehaven, and maybe fortuitously to the coal trade (storage and shipping), and more specifically to Nick Allison's property, as the ship was said by the *Chronicle* to be lying close to his alehouse on the Old Quay. Unusually for a newspaper, the *Cumberland Pacquet* in its 'Extraordinary' of 23 April exhibits frustrating restraint at this point: 'The scene was too horrible to admit of any further description.'

Time was pressing for the raiding party, and the rapidly swelling crowds on the quayside were becoming angrier by the minute and less controllable by Jones and his armed seamen. The townsfolk now realised how dire a threat to their livelihoods and homes was posed by these dastardly fire raisers. Paul Jones hoped that the flames blazing out from the hatches and rapidly threatening to engulf the *Thompson* would spread amongst the forest of vessels lying aground, closely packed around the stricken vessel; as well as to nearby buildings, including the coal Staithe and of course the unfortunate pub on the Old Quay.

Paul Jones would have liked to have superintended more of the fires which had been initiated, but had to settle for stoking up the one already raging for as long as was feasible. He estimated that there were another seventy ships also lying aground and close packed in the northern section of the harbour, just across the stone pier separating it from the southern section. However, in the rapidly evolving situation, any further action of real consequence amongst the ships in either portion of the harbour had become impracticable. Though the Whitehaven authorities reported that there were some 200 ships in the harbour, the necessary element of surprise was long gone, and it would have taken far too long to get fires blazing. In addition, the angry crowds, which Paul Jones then estimated (unrealistically) at 'thousands', could not long be successfully fended off by his cut-throat crew and piratical self (as the inhabitants naturally viewed the intruders). The sun by that time, as Jones noted later, 'was a full hour above the horizon'; which would mean the time was around 5.45am. Jones in his later memoirs says that it 'was almost eight o'clock in the morning'. The *Pacquet* and the *Chronicle* say that the Americans had gone by four o'clock (Whitehaven time of course). This is a major discrepancy, but whatever the actual time, it was high time to go!

John Paul says that his assault party, all members of which must have been very eager to leave by then, retreated in good order to their boats and embarked. The Justices in their official report say that the intruders beat 'a very precipitate retreat, leaving their work unfinished'. This means they left in good order but at the double! Before he finally left Whitehaven, John Paul Jones would have been clearly visible from the town quayside, standing alone and unruffled to observe the scene: 'I stood upon the pier for a considerable time, yet no persons advanced. I saw all the eminences around the town covered with the amazed inhabitants,' which sounds plausible. Later he embellished the description. He presented himself more graphically, as one might well do in a memoir, especially one such as Jones. After the crews had embarked for their return to the *Ranger* he recalls:

> I still remained for some minutes on the outside mole to observe
> at my leisure the terror, panic and stupidity of the inhabitants,
> who in numbers of at least ten thousand remained motionless
> like statues or ran hither and thither like madmen to reach the
> hills on the other side of the town.

Stemming from his typically excellent Scottish grounding at the village school on the other side of the Solway Firth, Paul Jones had a
way with words that set him apart from most of his naval colleagues.
His words here, though, are out of tune with local descriptions and
with his earlier account; indeed, they seem to carry more than a hint
of sneering disdain for the rudely awoken townsfolk of Whitehaven.
Maybe what he felt to be an unjust local summary judgement of
himself still rankled; as local Whitehaven historian Daniel Hay puts
it: 'Open talk of his murder of Maxwell poisoned the minds of the
inhabitants of Whitehaven and his native village of Kirkbean.'

Some guns, either overlooked in the flurry of events and unspiked,
or manhandled from ships, were hastily loaded. In 1928, in an article on Whitehaven in the June edition of *Sea Breezes* magazine, it is
recounted – evidently quoting Hutchinson's *History of Cumberland*
(mentioned earlier and not infallible of course) that three of the
spiked fort guns '… were soon cleared and several shots were
fired; a few of them were observed to fall between the two boats
but not to take effect'. The *Cumberland Pacquet*'s 'Extraordinary'
puts it slightly differently: 'By this time some of the guns at the
half-moon battery were loaded, two of which were fired at the
boats, but without the desired effect.' Presumably the guns were
loaded by some, whilst others struggled to wrench out some of the
hammered-down spikes. Obviously, where the hastily loaded guns
could not be unspiked – dangerous to attempt one would think
– they could not be fired. Not too concerned about where precisely
the shots came from as he left the stage at Whitehaven, Paul Jones
imagined the frustration of the English when, 'streaming' towards
their forts, they 'found at least thirty heavy cannon, the instruments
of their vengeance, rendered useless'. In the later memoirs, he
increases the number spiked from thirty to thirty-six. The Old Fort
had a gun platform annexed to it, with the fort building in effect a
small separate entity housing powder, ammunition, and personal
weapons as well as personnel.

Like other locals, with Brian Scott-Hindson prominent amongst them, David Bradbury casts serious doubt on the number of guns Paul Jones claimed to have spiked at the Fort and Half-Moon Battery, with detailed supporting evidence including a plan of the fortifications predating Paul Jones's attack, showing eight gun embrasures at the Half-Moon Battery. It is most unlikely that the Old Fort had the twenty-eight necessary to bring the sum up to the thirty-six Jones claims there were; and the relevant plan shows only ten embrasures. After the attack the defences were substantially improved, and according to J. Howard's 'Town and Harbour Plan' of 1790, the Half-Moon Battery had by this date fourteen embra-sures, not eight. In the town's report on the Paul Jones attack to the Government, there is an ambiguous reference to 'batteries', as if there were others in addition to the Old Fort battery. However, between the words 'Fort' and 'Batteries' there is a small sign which occurs nowhere else in the package of documents, except it seems linked to another unusual character further down the page, the combination there clearly meaning 'et cetera'. It looks as though the interposed linking sign could be an older form of the ampersand. Unfortunately, the professional archivists whose help I sought could not be sure after examining the document.

In Whitehaven's official Report, the fort seems to be set apart by the enigmatic little sign from its own adjoining battery as well as from the Half-Moon Battery. Fortunately, we can resolve the puz-zle by quoting the *Cumberland Pacquet*'s 'Extraordinary', published on the day of the raid. 'The incendiarists had spiked most of the guns of both our batteries' – clearly meaning that there were two: the Old Fort Battery and the New Fort (Half-Moon) Battery, with the Old Fort building itself not meriting a separate mention. The Whitehaven newspaper would know the facts. Of course, though it was quite small, there would probably have been some guns in the Old Fort building itself, forming part of its overall battery and the *Pacquet* might well have seen things this way. None of this pre-cludes there being perhaps other guns in the environs of the Old Fort. For the sake of thoroughness in ensuring a safe departure, Paul Jones would have spiked anything he could lay his hands on, even stored guns for good measure perhaps. But, though he does mention unspiked guns lying on the beach, he does not specifically mention any 'casual' spikings, nor anything which would account for the unrealistically high total, nor the discrepancy in numbers between his two statements. In the flurry of fast moving events, did he actually count the spiked guns? It is more likely that he relied largely on his memory of how many were there during the crisis period of the Seven Years War and on what improvements he might have known were planned towards the end of that period. After all, his object at Whitehaven was to burn out the massed shipping and set fire to the town, not to count the guns.

The war ended in 1763, around the time John Paul returned to Whitehaven from his last voyage to America in the *Friendship*, only to find Younger bankrupt, and himself at the age of seventeen out of a job; until he sailed for Africa aboard the *King George* in 1764. After that date he lost touch with Whitehaven. He would most likely have known that the total number of guns at Whitehaven was about eighteen (eight at the New Fort and ten at the Old Fort). But being intelligent, ambitious and interested in such things, he might also have been aware that, as David Bradbury says, it was planned towards the end of the war to improve the defences by putting double the number of guns in double the number of batteries. Doubled, the number of guns would be thirty-six: Paul Jones's second figure. David Bradbury has difficulty in getting the number of guns above eighteen, that being the number of embrasures in both forts combined. Brian Scott-Hindson thinks that Paul Jones's claim to have spiked thirty-six cannon in the Fort and nearby Lunette Battery 'would appear to be highly exaggerated, as it seems that the Fort usually had eight or nine and the Lunette Battery nine, although of small calibre'. Whitehaven's official report on the American raid does not mention any figures for the number of guns, simply asserting that on landing in the harbour Paul Jones 'immediately took possession of a Fort adjoining the harbour and spiked all the Guns which are 32 pounders and some which carry 42 pounds'. That particular Fort would seem to have packed a punch regardless of how many guns there were, and Paul Jones confirms this when he mentions the 'heavy guns' he found.

Paul Jones might very well have been unaware that the planned improvement of the defences soon faded once the Seven Years War war was over; and that far from being augmented, the guns were partially dismantled after the war; leaving Paul Jones with an embarrassingly high guesstimate.

Jones did acknowledge some directionless shots plunging into the sea astern of his two boats as they were leaving Whitehaven, and speculates that, as well as guns from ships possibly, the townsfolk 'used one or two cannon which lay on the beach at the foot of the walls dismounted, and which had not been spiked'. Instead of causing damage these shots proved a 'diversion' for his men, who eagerly 'discharged their pistols etc. in return of the salute', clearly relishing the situation. In the later account in his memoirs Paul Jones cuts out the horseplay, saying that he replied to the ragged and ineffectual fire from the town with 'several swivel guns which I had placed in the stern of my barge'. The townsfolk reported no damage.

The boats made hastily for the hovering *Ranger*, which had by now come in closer, having been standing off at a distance of about two miles, and succeeded in picking them up without mishap. No doubt she was flying the Stars and Stripes in mocking defiance of the spiked and impotent guns of the batteries. The bold American warship then turned and soon headed out into the Solway Firth. 'I was pleased that in this business we neither killed nor wounded any person', said Paul Jones after the event, though the outcome could have been otherwise.

This American raid on Whitehaven was the last time that attacking enemy forces set foot on the English mainland. Not so the family of John Paul Jones, though. Tongue in cheek, the *Cumberland Pacquet* on 3 September 1782, about five years after the raid, recounts: 'Our late Lammas fair was honoured with the presence of two of Paul Jones's sisters,' presumably from Dumfries. Less bold than their brother, the *Pacquet* says they concealed their identities – as well they might!

Whilst on the quay, John Paul was recognised by some of the inhabitants; acquaintances from earlier days, who quickly made the connection between the John Paul they knew of old and the John Paul Jones attacking Whitehaven that day. In fact one eyewitness recognised 'Jack' Paul (as he knew him) at very close quarters when the resolute Captain personally held off the townsfolk at pistol point.

Paul Jones seems to have felt little affinity with Whitehaven, even though he had known the town and some of its inhabitants from a very young age, albeit intermittently because of his long voyages.

One such person was Mabel Waugh, a widow of eighty-one by 1832, when she clearly recalled making three shirts for the young John Paul at Whitehaven in the days of her youth. Before he left Whitehaven to work out of other ports, in the West Indies as well as Kirkcudbright and London, he probably spent little time socialising there, being mostly aboard ship and in foreign parts. Perhaps because of this he was devoid of affection for this hub of British seagoing trade. Alternatively, as one local commentator has surmised: 'Embittered by the events which had clouded his career as a merchant seaman he was prepared to wreck the entire merchant fleet at Whitehaven'; a motivation that perhaps coloured the higher purpose with which he justified his actions.

It was raining as the American intruders left, and with the help of the elements and their two fire engines, which were quickly brought to the quay, the inhabitants of Whitehaven soon put out any fires in the harbour, including the great blaze aboard the *Thompson*, which, fortunately for the townsfolk, did not engulf the ship as Paul Jones had planned. The newspapers reported that '… by an uncommon exertion the fire was extinguished before it reached the rigging of the ship, and thus, in a providential manner, prevented all the dreadful consequences which might have ensued'. Paul Jones in his report to the Commissioners says specifically that as they were departing the flames had 'already caught the rigging, and began to ascend the mainmast'. This discrepancy aside, the *Thompson* was certainly very badly damaged. It was reported that, 'Her cables and almost everything in the cabin and steerage were burnt, and the decks have suffered much.'

When the authorities had taken immediate stock of the situation after the raid, they stated in their report that the intruders had with them a large stock of varied and closely described types of firebrand. They considered these to have been made in France rather than on board ship, which they thought an inappropriate place for such an activity. David Freeman confirmed that the incendiary devices had not been made up on the *Ranger*. The Government was informed of this putative French connection. It was observed: 'Many of these faggots and other combustible substances they had disposed in the holds of eight ships, that lay towards the middle and in the most crowded part of the harbour.' Though they set fire to only one ship, the Americans 'made some attempt to kindle some in other ships; which failed thro' their great hurry'. It was the opinion of the signatories of the report that 'had two or three ships been set on fire all the ships in the harbour must have been consumed, with some part of the town'. It is clear from the evidence in Whitehaven that there was indeed some kind of attempt to spread the fire widely about the harbour, 'towards the middle' and 'in the most crowded part', in which Wallingford and Hill's party might well have played some initial part. Damage done at Whitehaven was in fact of little local consequence, but it is said that insurance rates immediately doubled in British ports, resulting in the loss of many uninsured ships.

On 28 April the *Cumberland Pacquet* reported: 'The guns at the port are all cleaned and put into order; some are also planted on the north wall,' pending improvement of the fortifications, assisted by voluntary subscription. Nicholas Allison, one of only two subscribers listed on the Old Quay, gave a guinea (twenty-one shillings). James Young, the other subscriber on the Old Quay, gave two shillings and sixpence. A certain William Brownrigg, living on more affluent Lowther Street, and apparently one of the two Justices of the Peace closely involved in investigating and reporting the affair at Whitehaven, gave five guineas (five pounds five shillings).

Captain Jones can only have been bitterly disappointed at the damp squib that his planned incendiary spectacular had turned out to be. The elements – the wind, the tide and the rain – had conspired against him, as had his officers, the unenthusiastic crew, and the deserter who raised the alarm.

With hindsight, the train of events at Whitehaven could be seen as a fiasco. Even looked at in this way, though, John Paul Jones himself emerges from the affair with great personal credit, having proved himself tenacious of purpose, undaunted by events, resourceful and intrepid. He may not have burnt out the great huddled mass of vulnerable shipping at Whitehaven, nor fired the still-pristine model town, but he had effectively disarmed the defences of a major British port, and had gone about his business there with galling impunity and panache. He may have felt his lack of pyrotechnic success, but in Britain the effect of the 'insolent attack', as one Whitehaven resident put it in a letter to the newspapers was, as Paul Jones had anticipated, extraordinary. The descent on Whitehaven was mortifying to a proud nation whose forces were already facing grave difficulties in their rebellious colonies, as well as in dealing with the French yet again. The Government and its navy were lambasted in the press, and lax coastal towns were galvanised into improving their defences, as at Whitehaven. Despite the determined opposition and contrary behaviour of the *Ranger*'s ungallant crew of dedicated privateers, the American navy had started to look less piratical and more warlike in its purpose. John Paul Jones himself took his first – some would say extraordinarily lucky – steps along the path not merely to glory, but to a kind of folk hero status.

Two days after the raid, on Saturday 25 April, the *Cumberland Chronicle and Whitehaven Public Advertiser* contained an insight into the state of affairs aboard the *Ranger*, gleaned probably from the deserter David Freeman, or perhaps from the keeper of the alehouse and his family who might have either heard the crewmen talking together as they drank, or had conversed with them. 'The Captain of the *Ranger*, the article ran, 'is said to be a very passionate man, and the crew much dissatisfied with his conduct.' It appeared that trouble might well be brewing on board.

At Whitehaven, the harbour and the quayside today are very much as they were in the days of Paul Jones. The Half-Moon Battery, shown on the plan reproduced here, stood close to the beach behind Tom Hurd's Rock, a very prominent local feature. In 1872, this battery was buried under a huge landslide, but earlier, in 1734, Tom Hurd's Rock itself was connected to the shore almost directly below the Battery by a substantial breakwater, long since lost to the sea and sand.

The Old Quay is weatherworn and was until fairly recently rank with weeds. At its seaward end, recently restored, is the old harbour lighthouse, sometimes described as a 'watchtower' or 'lookout', and a distinctive feature of Whitehaven which, with its affixed sundial, would have been very familiar to Paul Jones. There was provision on top for flying a flag during daylight; though the light and the flag were only shown when the water in the harbour was at least nine feet deep. The lighthouse seems to have been renovated rather than built around 1730 and according to the plaque fixed to it in 1971, used 'for general surveillance of sailing vessels in the harbour'. This might appear puzzling because the outlook in 1778 seems to have been only out to sea, with no over-view of the harbour, except of course for the all-round view from the roof. The function of the tower might well have varied somewhat over its many years of usage, and it might easily have combined more than one function (though it is very cramped with no floors, except the space the light would fill). Close beside the isolated 'lighthouse' there stands what has been claimed to be the house, perhaps a 'watch-house' by then, where the light to rekindle the candles was sought. In his book *Whitehaven Harbour*, Brian Scott-Hindson states that, towards the end of the nineteenth century at any rate, the Old Quay 'had a house on it and two watch houses'. Three buildings are shown on the Old Quay in Hodskinson and Donald's town plan of 1774, but there is no indication of usage for any of them.

Unfortunately, Paul Jones is not helpful in resolving the matter of securing a light, as he refers merely to 'a house disjoined from the town' as his source for the flame – and there are other possibilities. The building next to the lighthouse as it now stands is clearly not as it originally was, as confirmed by pictorial and documentary evidence. Part of the stonework of the small, slate-roofed building now existing is of a piece with that of the lighthouse, no doubt associated with the functioning of the lighthouse in some way. This original structure is now joined to another small building to form an incongruous whole, both parts similar in size but quite different in materials and construction. This addition to the original is of a much later date, not being shown in plans and portrayals of the harbour around the time of the American attack in 1778; in fact it is not present in a painting of the harbour dated to 1780, by an unknown artist; nor is it shown in Askew's later painting of Whitehaven harbour, dated to 1789. Both these paintings do, however, show the Old Quay pretty well. An almost identical view by Askew, also from 1789, was reproduced as an engraving in *The History of the County of Cumberland* by William Hutchinson, published in 1794 (page 34). In these harbour illustrations the lighthouse is shown on the Old Quay, with its flag flying, and ships sailing in the harbour. Next to the lighthouse, in all these depictions, there is the original single small building; but how different it looks.

Instead of the conventional double-sloped slate roof – as tops the linked pair now – there is an unusual and attractive peaked roof, quite unlike the roof of a normal house, and the building has generous provision of window openings overlooking the harbour.

Judging by the illustrations of it and its form of construction, the smart little building had a fine view of the whole harbour from its upper storey. It also had a ground floor windowed room, as well as an outside stone stairway leading to the room above. Despite appearances (it is similar in style and materials), this building is not in fact contemporary with the lighthouse, being on record as built in 1764 for storing harbour materials such as hawsers, capstan bars, and the like. It was provided with a room for the 'resort of the Pier Master and Harbour Boatmen to attend the Tides and assist ships as required'. This building seems to be one which, on the face of it, might better bear the 'watch' plaque, with a separate one for the lighthouse. These unique and prominently situated relics of Whitehaven's maritime past are in need of urgent conservation. (Though the lighthouse's bowed window has been restored.) Its more recent use was as a mortuary for those recovered from the sea. In the 1861 Ordnance Survey map of Whitehaven the lighthouse on the Old Quay is labelled 'Inner Light' in a much enlarged harbour, and the building alongside is rectangular; having doubtless been extended by then into the joined pair now extant. In his book *Whitehaven Harbour*, Brian Scott-Hindson describes this pair as 'a building which was once a public house, and also provided accommodation for the Harbour Master and stores'. This leaves specific usage somewhat vague, and undated. Judging from earlier plans, modification seems to have taken place much earlier in the nineteenth century, but there was only the building with the unusual roof at the time of the American attack. Did Paul Jones get his urgently needed light from the small building next to the lighthouse? Writing in 1943, Lincoln Lorenz identified Jones's 'house disjoined from the town' – in tune with the town's version of events – as 'a watch-house on the quay'; though he mentions nothing about occupancy, and like the town's official report he does not say where this building was situated on the quay. Various possibilities and combinations of these have been suggested, but the building next to the lighthouse well fits the description, 'a house disjoined from the town'. Its general functions, including its tide-related function when created in 1764, perhaps with the family of a 'keeper' living on the job, might merit the description of 'watch-house'. It would also reconcile with rousting out Nicholas Allison's sleeping family to supply booze and with the official report's statement that to obtain a flame Paul Jones had to 'break into a watch house on the Key where a small family lived who were all in bed'.

As mentioned earlier, In their official report to the government after the raid, the Justices said: 'there was no guard or watch being then kept either in the Fort & Batteries, or in the Harbour'. But 'no guard or watch' in the harbour would not by 1778 preclude use or occupation of the building near the end of the Old Quay by someone regularly attending to the light and the flag, and sundry harbour duties. So there might well have been some anxiety for Paul Jones when he landed at the head of the Old Quay to weigh up the situation there, being (as he said he would be) the first to step ashore, if indeed he did land at that spot as the sea was flowing back into the harbour. The scraping of the boat against the quay, the clink of weapons and the tread of boots mounting the very narrow stone stairway set into the quayside, could have proved disastrous. Surely Paul Jones, venturing so close, knew just what the situation was regarding usage of the little building in 1778.

David Bradbury seems to have got a handle on an intriguing possible secret intelligence connection between Whitehaven and Benjamin Franklin in France, though one which is difficult to research further. Benjamin Franklin visited Whitehaven in 1772, a year after the Boston Tea Party and three years before real hostilities, as part of a tour of northern England. He showed interest in the mines and coal trade arrangements, which were ahead of their time. It would be interesting to know whom Franklin met at Whitehaven. In addition, in June 1777, the year before the raid, it was found that five of the eight cannon at the Half-Moon Battery had been spiked!

Just after the raid there was some scandal when Sarah Alkin, the landlady of the 'Grapes' in Marlborough Street (now a restaurant) alleged that slanderous remarks concerning her relationship with Paul Jones were made about her. She was said by her postman John Birkhead to have received a letter addressed to Paul Jones, care of herself. She was appalled at the implication and the hapless Birkhead was obliged to recant his allegedly scurrilous remark in a letter to the *Cumberland Pacquet*, published on 27 April 1778, only the fourth day after the raid. But it is still said in Whitehaven that Paul Jones once lodged at the 'Grapes', and that his relationship with the Landlady was not platonic.

To the P U B L I C.

Whitehaven, April 27, 1778.

WHEREAS I, JOHN BIRKHEAD, (Letter Carrier to this Post-Office) have reported that I delivered to Mrs. SARAH ALKIN, at the Grapes in Marlborough-ftreet, a LETTER directed to Capt. Paul Jones (to the Care of the faid Mrs. Alkin) and which Report has been circulated through this Town, to the Prejudice of her Chrracter and Bufinefs,

I do therefore, in Order to remove any Prejudice that might arife to the faid Mrs. Alkin, in Confequence of this Report, DECLARE, " That I never did deliver any fuch Letter to the faid Mrs. Alkin, and that my Affertions with Refpect to this Matter are abfolutely falfe.

In Proof of which I hereby fet my Hand , in Order that the fame may be made Public.

JOHN BIRKHEAD.

John Birkhead's somewhat mealy-mouthed retraction in the Cumberland Pacquet. *When she read it, would Sarah Alkin, landlady of the 'Grapes' where Paul Jones is said to have once lodged (on more than friendly terms with Mrs Alkin), have felt her honour to have been fully restored?*

The fort where John Paul led the gun-spiking party through the embrasures has long since been partially demolished to extend the harbour, though another now-ruined building, a lime kiln, was constructed using stones and some upstanding remnants of the Old Fort walls. One of the cannons from the original battery does apparently survive – perhaps personally spiked by Paul Jones in 1778! When I first set foot in Whitehaven, many years ago now, it was planted, muzzle-down, deep into the quayside to function as a somewhat insignificant mooring post, painted orange but heavily rusting. It is said that this was probably done at the end of the eighteenth century, when all the guns became 18-pounders. Visiting Whitehaven on a more recent occasion I found it had been uprooted as part of a scheme to breathe new life into the old port, and was told that it was undergoing conservation prior to being displayed to better effect. Nearly opposite the Harbourmaster's Office two old cannons are set on the quayside, on authentic replica carriages.

Both are from the era preceding Napoleon; one is thought to come from one of Whitehaven's batteries, and the other is considered to be a ship's gun.

Nicholas Allison's alehouse is an alehouse no more, being long demolished in fact – though there are plenty of other interesting old pubs in Whitehaven. Naturally there is one alehouse dubbed 'The Paul Jones', with (when I first visited the town) the thoroughly piratical-looking figure of the man himself glaring villainously out from the swinging inn sign, wearing an eye patch. Nowadays the once-reviled 'Scotch renegade' is considered more of a tourist attraction than a pirate, and the inn sign now displays a portrait of a thoroughly respectable and uniformed Paul Jones, every inch the professional naval officer. Progress in the rehabilitation of the Captain since his 'official pardoning' by the Town in 1999, can be seen in plates 17, 18 and 19. Jones was sometimes even shown with a piratical eye patch, but this may be accidentally authentic. It was reported in the *Cumberland Pacquet* on 9 May 1780, barely two years after his attack on Whitehaven, that Paul Jones (only in his mid-thirties) was thinking very seriously of retirement 'having lately had a defluxion [discharge] in his eyes, which has almost deprived him of his sight'; so he may well have worn an eye patch for a time.

The actual location of Nick Allison's pub on the Old Quay has been a matter of much speculation over the years, a problem that seems to have been satisfactorily resolved by David Bradbury. It was near to the foot of the seaward extension of the Old Quay. Its sign may have been a 'jolly sailor' (see Appendix V). Judging by its position it probably catered mainly for seafarers, harbourmen and colliers, and Allison's generous contribution towards the harbour defences indicates good business. Visitors to Whitehaven in the nineteenth century, however – admittedly seventy years later – noted the 'squalor and filth' and overcrowding on Quay Street, and generally in the harbour neighbourhood: 'Sallow looking women covered with rags, thrust their heads and half their bodies through the windows to look after you, and as they do this, they seem to gasp for fresh air'. Clearly there was vice as well as squalor around the Old Quay, but was it quite so insalubrious in 1778?

A curious tradition in Whitehaven has it that there was more than one desertion from the *Ranger*. These men, it is said, 'hid in some whins [bushes] in the neighbourhood of Solway View'. Paul

Jones mentions no such desertions, though there had indeed been a number of worrying defections before they set sail from Brest, and the log of the *Ranger* mentions forty, not thirty-one, participants in the raid. Jones was concerned only about Freeman, supposedly fallen unwillingly into enemy hands to be imprisoned as a felon. 'Coming off in a hurry,' says the *Ranger*'s log as tersely as usual, 'left one man [not nine] at Whitehaven, David Smith. At 7 o'clock saw much smoke at Whitehaven.' Again a local tradition claims that Freeman in fact settled down in Whitehaven and eventually died there. This is a distinct possibility, because after all, he had helped to save the shipping and the town, and was favourably regarded in consequence; and he really had no material connection with Ireland.

What of the abortive landing attempt to which Freeman alluded after being taken into custody? This was a sorry mischance which compounded delay, and which was reported – or interpreted – by the *Cumberland Magazine* to be 'near Saltom'. Freeman, though a stranger to Whitehaven, actively participated in events until his defection and was surely unlikely to be wrong about the fact of an attempted landing outside the harbour, even if he could not per-haps have named the actual location; especially since Paul Jones, according to Freeman, had 'fully explained his design' to the boat crews before the raid, thus ensuring that they knew how they were going to carry out the enterprise. But does 'near Saltom' mean the vicinity of Tom Hurd's Rock, close to the Lunette Battery and the breakwater beyond South Beach and very close to Saltom Bay; or the vicinity of Saltom coal pit and its huddle of pit buildings and dwellings, a little way along the base of the cliffs from Whitehaven and connected to it then by a track low on the cliffs for hauling coal to the port, not much more than a ten minute walk through a totally deserted scene? Saltom could refer to an area rather than a place. Each of these landing points, though attractive in terms of secrecy, would have presented serious practical difficulties.

Tom Hurd's Rock is so-named because, after his boat foundered on this prominent feature towards the end of a pleasure jaunt with his sweetheart (who was tragically drowned there), the grief-stricken Tom soon drowned himself at the same fateful spot. The story is an old one, predating Paul Jones's attack, and the loca-tion is dramatic. Standing beside the great bulk of Tom Hurd's

Rock – treacherously masked at high tide but lying fully exposed when the tide is low – and surveying the current coastal scene, it is tempting to see the immediate vicinity of the Rock as material to the initial American plan of attack. Though the nearby Half-Moon Battery has vanished under the landslip, and the breakwater is long gone without any trace, the contemporary map reproduced here shows both of them in relation to Tom Hurd's Rock. At low tide dangerous outliers break the surface menacingly around the massive feature, and there are other dangerous rocks, submerged and never seen. The menace of the Tom Hurd's Rock area fades as the tide steadily rises above the hazards; the depth of water at high tide on 22 April had been around four metres (about 13 feet). In contrast, low water during the night of the Americans' arrival was, as pointed out earlier, at 2.29am (1.25am Whitehaven-time); a bad moment for a night landing in such a place.

Tom Hurd's Rock marks an abrupt and dramatic change in coastal topography. Stretching towards the nearby harbour, and hazardous to approach at low tide because of the rocks, there is a wide and largely shingle beach – the South Beach. In the opposite direction, towards Saltom, the coast stretches away in a seemingly endless jumble of very large boulders and rocks, cruel at any stage of the tide.

John Paul's intrepidity and local knowledge could well have led him to opt for a bold landing on the shingle close to the Half-Moon Battery in the vicinity of Tom Hurd's Rock, assuming similar topography then and plenty of water, especially if he had a good idea how lax the manning of the batteries was likely to be, with no-one actually posted at the Lunette Battery. In view of the fact that he was not averse to rowing at the crack of dawn straight into the lion's jaws of the harbour itself, landing with scant regard for any watchtower, and tackling the batteries full on, this does not seem an unlikely scheme for a seaman who confidently said that he knew Whitehaven and 'all the places adjacent'. The low state of the tide would have been very problematical around the time of their arrival. However, Tom Hurd's Rock is very near Saltom Bay, which stretches inaccessibly away southwards from its immediate vicinity. Did Paul Jones give the South Beach a try before heading for the harbour? There seems to have been very good access from the beach to the harbour, by means of a narrow path alongside the

Old Fort, which would have afforded an easy and direct approach to their main initial objective. The nature of the beach at that time is unknown.

Lost to very active coastal erosion hereabouts, only the fragmentary start of the Saltom coal track can now be recognized, set above the base of the cliff behind Tom Hurd's Rock. Where 'near Saltom', could Paul Jones have safely landed along this boulder-locked stretch of coast, near low tide and at night-time, in order to use such a convenient and admirably discreet track? Could he (though this is not what the *Cumberland Magazine* proposes) have landed not 'near Saltom' but at the Saltom pit complex itself, with its pit buildings and dwellings tightly enclosed behind an encircling sea wall, not breached by the sea until 1852? The shaft at Saltom was sunk in 1751. The pit complex, along with its innovatory undersea workings, is now mostly lost to the sea; and crucially, from surface plan drawings forming part of an 1864 survey, seems not to have had a docking facility, relying instead on transport of coal by road to nearby Whitehaven. Only the gaunt ruin of one pit building now remains, and the adjacent beaches are heavily strewn with rocks.

Given favourable tidal conditions, the South Beach near Tom Hurd's Rock would seem the better start point for an attack. Maybe on 23 April, Paul Jones was trying to make the best of a plan devised for the storm-blighted attempt of 18 April, nearly a week before, when the state of the tides would have been critically different and perhaps very favourable to his bold enterprise, using a discreet access point from the beach directly alongside the Old Fort; and with quick access to the Lunette (Half-Moon) Battery.

Surveying the scene now from Tom Hurd's Rock, one can see how any initial plan might have been aborted because in one way or another, a landing was 'prevented by the rocks', thus delaying the eventual attack by 'near half an hour'. Paul Jones said in his report on events to the American Commissioners:

Had it been possible to have landed a few hours sooner, my success would have been complete. Not a single ship, out of more than two hundred, could possibly have escaped, and all the world would not have been able to save the town.

As Freeman implied, if things had gone according to plan, with Paul Jones in full and timely personal control of unfolding events from the outset, the outcome might have been spectacular. Unfortunately, the record passes over details of any abortive landing attempt. The actual approach to Whitehaven was clearly from a southerly direction, if we give credence to the *Cumberland Magazine*'s report of Freeman's information about the landing attempt being somewhere just south of the harbour.

The boats were rowing against the tide, which always ebbs in a generally southward direction, subject to modification locally by the coastline of course. As noted earlier, Paul Jones says they cast off from the *Ranger* and started rowing into the tide around midnight, pulling their oars northwards against it for the better part of three hours, before finally reaching the harbour wall. By that time the rowing would have been getting easier for the no-doubt exhausted crews.

As Paul Jones says nothing definite about his landing point, we can only rely on Whitehaven's official report, and the newspaper report in the *Cumberland Pacquet*, both of which were based on Freeman's evidence, since no-one else is mentioned as having witnessed any landing.

On 18 August 1778 Paul Jones wrote an interesting letter from Brest to the Marine Committee in America regarding the *Ranger*'s difficult crew; or more specifically, those members of it who took part in the landing at Whitehaven. Jones had the backing of the American Commissioners in Paris for this approach to the Marine Committee. Surprisingly one might think, in view of what actually took place during the descent on Whitehaven, it is a letter beseeching the Committee to

> ...recommend the men who landed with me at Whitehaven, to the bounty of Congress. That service being unprecedented in latter wars, accounts for the extreme difficulty which I found prevailing with the handful of men who, at last, reluctantly undertook it. The men have in my judgment well merited a reward.

He is revealed as something more than merely benevolent when he goes on to say about such a bounty that:

… bestowing of it liberally on so few would, I hope, have a happy effect in prompting others to attempt still greater enterprises, with such spirit and unanimity as will generally ensure success, and lead to the most glorious victory.

The last words were prophetic of course as to the outcome of the war, and is there not also a faint gleam here of the future magnificent shrine at Annapolis?

At Whitehaven now, Paul Jones, divested of his crudely piratical image, is strikingly represented by a sculpture near the site of the Old Fort (plate 23). Along the quay a life-size tableau is strung out, comprising a small 'battery' of three cannons and the cast bronze figure of a young and gritty looking Paul Jones, his sword at his side and a hammer raised high to drive a spike into the touch-hole of one of the guns.

4

Breakfast With The Countess –
An Odd Diversion

The *Ranger* left the vicinity of Whitehaven early on a wet April morning, but before lunchtime on that same day had cast anchor on the other side of the Solway Firth, off the Scottish coast in Kirkcudbright Bay, not far from John Paul's own birthplace near Kirkbean. The next card up the enterprising captain's sleeve was about to be played, and it was a bizarre one. He planned to kidnap a local bigwig, the Earl of Selkirk, hold him hostage as an unwilling mediator and, according to a rather odd letter which he later wrote to the Earl's wife, thus compel the British government to agree to the general exchange of naval prisoners in Britain and America. The British treated captured American soldiers as prisoners of war, but at that time, owing to their unfortunate experiences of American privateers early in the war, regarded captured American seamen as pirates – criminals in effect – and would have had no qualms about treating the crew of the *Ranger* as such if they were taken. Paul Jones himself might well have been hanged: British seamen were apt to taunt the Americans wherever they might encounter them by alleging that their captain was fighting with a noose around his neck, referring to what they considered his shady past in the West Indies. The British Government would no doubt have taken other matters into account in dealing with this outrageous renegade.

How did the notion of kidnapping the Earl originate? Paul Jones certainly knew of the Earl and his estate from his boyhood days and his youthful employment in Whitehaven, and would have passed by the peninsula of St Mary's Isle on numerous occasions on his way to the quayside at Kirkcudbright. So his local knowledge of navigation and especially of the fact that the Earl's house was readily accessible by sea would have been important in making his decision.

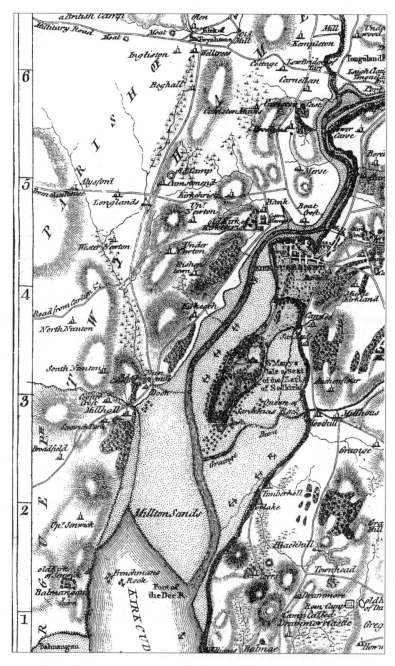

Ian Gillone's map of the Parish of Kirkcudbright (1792), showing Kirkcudbright, Kirkcudbright Bay, and St. Mary's Isle on which, where the paths cross, is the 'seat', the mansion or house, of the Earl of Selkirk. (Courtesy Dumfries and Galloway Libraries, Information and Archives)

But was the actual decision forced on him by unrest aboard ship arising out of the fact that no-one on board the *Ranger* had gained anything at all from the attack on Whitehaven, or was it planned in advance? If it was, Paul Jones had got the wrong idea about the value of the Earl in his scheme; unless he was to be used as a plausible smokescreen for some surreptitious brigandage, to keep the crew happy for a while.

As a properly commissioned naval officer, moving in fashionable social circles, and very conscious of his honour, Paul Jones is at pains to rule out any such base object in his long justificatory letter to the Countess of Selkirk. His position is backed – if it is not just a later response to unfolding events – by a statement in the *Cumberland Pacquet* dated 28 April 1778, nearly a week after the Whitehaven attack, and after the attempt on the Earl became known there:

> David Freeman who may, in some respects, be considered as the saviour of this town, says that 'The captain of the *Ranger* declared that the destruction of Whitehaven was his first object, seizing the person of Lord Selkirk was the next thing he wished, after which he would sail for Brest, and on his passage, sink, burn, and destroy whatever fell in his way belonging to Great Britain.'

The latter part of this statement is wrong, since Jones's object was to capture anything worthwhile which he had the capacity to man, not to destroy it, as becomes more evident in due course. Whatever the real truth about his motives in disturbing the tranquility of St Mary's Isle, Paul Jones would have wanted to present his strange visit – strange even in terms of a prisoner exchange deal – in the best possible light, and of course within the very wide scope of his written instructions from the American Commissioners. Despite their latitude, these specified that his actions must be 'consistent with the Laws of war, and the terms of your Commission', according to 'the Rules and Discipline of War'. Paul Jones would undoubtedly have wished to be seen as a gentlemanly follower of those rules.

In his eventual Report on the cruise of the *Ranger*, Jones refers the Commissioners to an enclosed copy of the long letter he wrote to the Countess of Selkirk on 8 May 1778. This letter is concerned with justifying his conduct in the expedition and any future actions thereafter, blaming the British for 'this cruel and destructive war' which he hopes will soon end, and as 'the feelings of your gentle bosom cannot but be congenial with mine', entreating the aid of the Countess and her husband in stopping it. 'Who can resist the power of such an advocate?' he addresses her gallantly, whilst assuring her less romantically that her endeavours would be 'an act of humanity which will afford you golden feelings on a death-bed.' He includes personal hopes and reflections, as well as philosophical ruminations, whilst addressing the Countess familiarly through-out, almost as though he knows her personally, and in the spirit of chivalry informs her: 'I wage no war on the fair.' Less gallantly, he provides copies of his letter to a number of people other than the Commissioners, as though he wants his viewpoint and sentiments to be bruited in society. Is the letter for her or for the public at large? Midshipman Fanning, whom we shall meet aboard Jones's next ship, says Jones asked him to make a copy, and regrets not keeping one for himself: 'It appeared some time after he wrote it in several of the English Gazettes.' The fulsome justifications of the letter sit uneasily alongside the factual account of events for the American Commissioners, which would in due course be communicated to Congress. Plainly, the letter is intended to be read together with the report; hence the inclusion of a copy, with specific reference to it (although not a word from it) within the body of the report itself: 'The motives which induced me to land there [St Mary's Isle] are explained in the copy of a letter which I have addressed to the Countess of Selkirk.' It seems clear that at the outset of his actions, knowing that he would be castigated and reviled, he wants to put his case and justify himself in the eyes of society. Looking at the letter in this way explains its contents and tenor.

In the letter he explains his motives in attempting to abduct the Earl in the following rather incongruous terms: 'I wished to make him the happy instrument of alleviating the horrors of hopeless captivity,' he tells her disarmingly, whilst admitting that 'It was, perhaps, fortunate for you, madam, that he was from home; for it was my intention to have taken him on board the *Ranger* and to have detained him until, through his means, a general and fair exchange of prisoners' [in Europe and America] was effected.' The Earl could have been forcibly parted from his wife for quite some time by the sound of it, especially as he was a studious type and although he had

Portrait of the 4th Earl of Selkirk, unfortunately hanging in an awkward place for the photographer! On his own admission the Earl was at odds with the Government regarding British policy and actions in America, as Paul Jones may well have known. The Earl was lucky to have been away from home when events so rudely overtook his wife that day in late April 1778. (Courtesy Sir David and Lady Hope-Dunbar)

social connections of course, they were not in the right establishment circles and without the political influence assumed by Paul Jones, as the Earl himself was later at pains to point out in a letter to him.

Not long after their arrival off St Mary's Isle at around mid-morning, with the ship swinging quietly at anchor in the rain, arrangements for landing had been finalised. Since he was familiar with the landmarks and winding channels in the Bay, Paul Jones took personal control of the enterprise, as he had done at Whitehaven, employing 'one boat only and a very small party'. This party of twelve included two officers: Master Cullen in blue; and Marine Lieutenant Wallingford, wearing the mostly green jacket, white waistcoat, and white britches of the marines under a blue greatcoat of some kind, presumably for discretion. They rowed their boat towards the peninsula of St Mary's Isle, where the Earl's modest mansion was situated amongst verdant gardens and woods. They successfully negotiated the shallows and came up to the beach. However, Paul Jones says in his letter: 'When I was informed by some men whom I met at landing, that his lordship was absent, I walked back to my boat, determined to leave the island.' According to Lorenz, the Earl was in London, while Morison (see bibliography) has him attending the then fashionable spa in Buxton. Quite probably he went to Buxton on his way to, or from, London. Whatever the case, the Captain was foiled in his kidnap attempt, as there could be no prospect of the Earl coming home that day.

When Paul Jones turned back for the boat, the rest of the party did not let him get very far, protesting vigorously against leaving. Wallingford and Cullen were at the forefront of the protestations, the latter undaunted by the fact that he had already had the captain's pistol at his mutinous head. Considering the rapacious conduct of the British in America and their meagre gains so far, the men saw no reason why they should not loot the mansion before leaving. 'I had but a moment to think how I might gratify them,' Jones said in his letter to the Countess, 'and at the same time do your ladyship the least injury.' Jones realistically appreciated their bitterly angry feelings, and according to his letter, not wishing to commit a crude act of armed robbery he reluctantly backed down and compromised. After all – no matter what the British thought of him – he was a commissioned American naval officer, not a mere brigand. He conceded that the party could relieve the household of its silver plate but must take nothing else, and must stay outside the house, behaving with civility. He did not go with them. Continuing his walk back onto the beach, and waiting there for their return, no doubt with some anxiety, he relied on Cullen and Wallingford, and the good sense of the boat party, to carry things off punctiliously.

After parting from the Captain, the armed band continued on its way along some half-mile of pleasant, leafy pathway to the mansion. To account for their presence as they walked purposefully through the estate armed to the teeth – and to scare off the estate workers – they perpetrated a deception on landing. They told those they encountered that they were the press gang, out looking for likely lads to force into the harsh life of the Royal Navy. This unwelcome 'news' caused major consternation among the estate workers. Word spread like wildfire, and all potential targets started vanishing from the estate like flushed partridges; though some of them might not have been suitable press gang material, as the Countess pointed out on her initial encounter with the convincingly deceptive party.

All went well from the outset. When the boat party reached the main door, the household and some guests were finishing breakfast. The officers asked for the Countess, who came to speak with them. Those in the house were at first wary of the supposed 'press gang', but instantly became very alarmed when it was disclosed who the armed and rough-looking intruders really were. They must have been reassured a little when, according to a contemporary account by someone strolling around the estate at the time, Wallingford unbuttoned his blue greatcoat to display a 'very handsome American uniform, green turned up with white, and trimmed with silver'. However, the more practical Cullen, getting down to the business in hand, told the Countess to produce the family silver 'directly'. Heavily pregnant with her twelfth child, she rose calmly to the occasion, saying afterwards that the affair, '… was far more dreadful to those at a distance than to us at hand'. The silver plate was collected and bagged up, with only the two officers entering the house, the rest dutifully waiting outside as Jones had instructed. There was a short dispute over certain items from the silver service, but the problem was resolved by the calm intervention of the Countess, who did not want any complications. The silver teapot, almost overlooked, was taken from the breakfast table still with wet tea leaves inside it as it went into one of the bags, which the party had to request the Countess to provide. This indicates that they had not come prepared for looting; a point in favour of Paul Jones's account of events. He said in his letter, penned in the aftermath of the coming fight with the *Drake*, that he would purchase the silver himself in order to make financial provision for his men, and return it to her in due course.

From the outset the Countess was unimpressed by the appearance of the party. 'The principal one was in blue' she said later, having Cullen in mind. Observing that he 'seemed by nature a very disagreeable, and one may say bad man', she added that he had 'a vile blackguard look'. Although Master Cullen stayed pretty civil throughout the proceedings except for his blunt speech, the Countess suspected that 'he might have been rough enough had he met with provocation, and that was one reason I never left him'. In fact, there was no provocation. Weighing up the situation nicely, the Countess calmed the atmosphere with admirable aplomb, offering Cullen and Wallingford a glass of wine each. After a little polite conversation, including excited questions about America from one of the female members of the household, the boat party left courteously enough for the beach, marching off down the path in an orderly fashion, the seamen fearsomely armed with a musket and bayonet each, a pair of pistols, and a cutlass. The Countess was pleased that no one in her household had blurted out in anger 'what was at all their tongue's ends'. Writing to her sister after the raid, the Countess of Selkirk recounted:

> The plate they got; it was needless to expostulate as it was impossible to resist. I must do them the justice of saying they behaved very civilly; tho' the doors were open no man offered to enter or ask for anything.

Wallingford made quite a good impression, the Countess noting sympathetically that, unlike Cullen, 'he seemed naturally well bred and not to like his employment'. In another letter later she described Paul Jones, whom she did not meet of course, as being 'as great a villain as ever was born'. Again, writing to a neighbour of hers, she recalls: 'He killed a man in a sort of duel, but I believe it was understood an unfair stab', indicating that the killing of the 'ringleader' in Tobago was certainly known about in Scotland before the raid, and seen as a very different incident to the one described by John Paul in his letter to Benjamin Franklin. In yet another letter, however, she says magnanimously of Paul Jones, 'We should give the devil his due', readily acknowledging that in controlling his men, 'he behaved well at my house'.

Paul Jones, thankful when the two officers and their men reported back that the thing had at least been carried off as decently as possible, piloted them back to the *Ranger*. After initial relief at the outcome, the Captain must have retired to his cabin to contemplate another frustratingly unsuccessful enterprise. He had failed in his strange attempt to capture the Earl of Selkirk. Instead, more like a thief than a kidnapper, he had carried off a mere bagful of tableware, albeit valuable silver.

In fact, he would almost certainly have been little better off if he had captured the Earl, who was more of a family man than an influential political figure, with a twelfth child imminent, reportedly a man of mild temperament. Regarding his 'influence with the King' as assumed by Jones, and his negotiating abilities, the Earl, living far from the political vortex of London, says in a letter to him: 'Now, Sir, nothing can be more erroneous than these ideas, for I have no influence whatever with the King, and am scarce known to him.' Neither does he have any influence with the King's Ministers he says, having '... generally disapproved of most of their measures' and especially 'of almost their whole conduct in the unhappy and ill-judged American war'.

As to his negotiating an exchange of prisoners he says: 'I am altogether at a loss how any man of sense could entertain such an idea.' He asserts that he has hardly ever in his lifetime been to London, and tells Jones bluntly, 'Your intention of taking me was certainly absurd', recognizing, however, that Paul Jones had simply made a mistake, perhaps under a misapprehension stemming from his younger days.

Of course, if he had been at home, the Earl would have become a prisoner, and might perforce have had to function as a mediator of sorts, especially as there was no question of a ransom. On his own admission, the Earl did have views on the war in America which would have given encouragement to Paul Jones in his endeavours to enlist his aid in respect of captured seamen. Maybe Jones was aware of his leanings in this respect. But as the Earl points out, the only effect of his abduction would have been to distress a family that never injured any person.

The *Ranger* already had some prisoners on board to act as not very effective pawns, including three men from Whitehaven who had not been turned loose when they left. Amongst them, for some reason, was George Jefferson, formerly master of the *Isaac and Barbary*, who had gone down to the Quay at three o'clock in the morning with the intention of doing some fishing, but had ended up captured. A few of the captives, one of whom was a customs officer, might have been useful in an exchange, though as yet there were no Royal Navy personnel. Paul Jones had not, apparently, got around to thinking along these lines when he played for the Earl of Selkirk.

In his long, florid, but still very interesting letter to the Countess, John Paul apologises for carrying off the silver plate, explaining the circumstances which made it necessary. True to his word in this letter, and despite rather drawn-out complications (with accompanying publicity), when the war with Britain was over he did in fact manage to return the family silver to the Countess, after 'purchasing' it at an independent valuation – at no little expense – in order to reward the crew financially. Regarding the crew, he enquires in his letter about their conduct whilst at her house, with a view to punishing any miscreants if there was justification for doing so, he says. The Selkirks had no complaints; and the returned teapot is still in existence (see plate 26).

When I visited St Mary's Isle a few years ago now, I found that the invitingly leafy path from the beach still exists, but that following two disastrous fires, one of which destroyed the original log of the *Ranger* which had ended up in the library there, the house itself has become a sprawling pile of over-grown rubble, sprouting substantial trees. An attractive modern bungalow, with friendly and informative occupants taking tea outside when I turned up out of the blue that day, occupies part of the site, and the only remnant of the original complex is a detached service block in squared stone.

Owing to its sheer oddity, some have tried to divine some ulterior motive for John Paul's visit to St Mary's Isle, over and above his explanation in the letter to the Countess about using the Earl as an intermediary. Upon leaving Whitehaven, perhaps he was pressured at the very outset into a looting expedition to satisfy the disgruntled crew, and just happened to know quite a bit about the mansion on St. Mary's Isle and its inhabitants from childhood. Alternatively, not knowing quite what he would find when he got to the Earl's house at around breakfast time and not wanting to witness what went on because it would directly impugn his honour, he returned alone to the beach when the worthy purpose of the enterprise was thwarted by the Earl's absence. If they had captured the Earl, would the silver had been left alone? We shall never know.

Author Thomas Chase, no doubt also somewhat baffled by the puzzling circumstances of the raid on St Mary's Isle, presented a case in 1859 for the Earl of Selkirk being John Paul's natural father; one since effectively refuted, along with other equally unlikely paternity theories referred to later. Such a scenario might have added some poignancy to his unheralded visit, but it seems unlikely that Paul Jones would have gone with a band of armed men to seek out his natural father in order to harness his (hopefully sympathetic) assistance in negotiations over the status of American prisoners. In a letter penned close to the events the Earl said: 'We were perfectly unacquainted with him till his landing at my house.' Paul Jones also denied any connection: 'I never had any obligation to Lord Selkirk except for his good opinion nor does he know me or mine except by character.' Is there an implication in these statements that the descent on St. Mary's Isle had set people gossiping? Perhaps so, but dates and facts undermine any real scandal, as does the tenor of the Selkirks' correspondence with Paul Jones, and with their friends and acquaintances.

In immediate reaction to the raid, the Earl thought the kidnap scheme quite harebrained and though giving him his due in some ways, considered Paul Jones an 'odd fellow' as well as 'dangerous and worthless'. Like others, Lady Selkirk was puzzled as to Paul Jones's real motivation in intruding into the seclusion of their tranquil peninsula, and in a letter to her sister soon afterwards, before she received Jones's letter, she said: 'As to the expedition here I know not what to say,' supposing that, 'just having a few hours to spare he wished for a little private booty.' The eventual tortuous return of the silver plate at Jones's expense gives the lie to this. Paul Jones had been under pressure, and although she was unaware of it at the time, the crew of the *Ranger* were already pretty upset that they would get nothing out of the abortive Whitehaven attack – not even any incidental loot promised to the boat parties whom Jones had persuaded to volunteer. It is surprising that his men even allowed Paul Jones to begin walking back to the boat – as he says he did – before they forcefully brought up the matter of looting the mansion. They were not to be frustrated again and return to the *Ranger* empty-handed! Despite the fraught circumstances, on 4 August 1784, some six years after the silver was bagged up whilst the Countess of Selkirk entertained Cullen and Wallingford with a glass of wine each at the end of breakfast, the Earl of Selkirk was able to write a very understanding letter to Paul Jones in Paris. He unreservedly extolled the conduct of the boat crew, saying that they 'would have done credit to the best disciplined troops whatever', and concluded with the following words:

Some of the English newspapers at that time having put in confused accounts of your expedition to Whitehaven and Scotland, I ordered a proper one of what happened in Scotland to be put in the London newspapers, by a gentleman who was then at my house, by which the good conduct and civil behavior of your officers and men was done justice to, and attributed to your order, and the good discipline you maintained over your people.

The Earl was right; but little did he know of the alarmingly volatile relations aboard the *Ranger* at the time!

The whole affair on St Mary's Isle could be considered swashbuckling but honourable, or quixotic and pointless. Although inconsequential to the conflict, the intimate and colourful personal details have a romantic, almost chivalric character that in due course added piquancy to the nascent folk hero persona attaching to the still young John Paul Jones (he was by then only thirty years old). Judiciously circulated after careful composition, the letter addressed in the first place to the Countess of Selkirk was part of the growing legend, and with the extensive correspondence associated with it, certainly fed that legend mightily.

All this was not evident to John Paul at the time, however, as he uneasily evaded a small cutter shadowing him out of Kirkcudbright Bay. This vessel was in fact the dogged and admirable *Hussar*, which had correctly identified the *Ranger* this time, and sped back to her home-port of Whitehaven with the news.

It was certain that the Royal Navy would soon be fully alerted, and out in force looking for the American corsair in the right locality. Although on this score Paul Jones still felt fairly secure, something would have to be done promptly to turn the cruise of the *Ranger* in British waters into something more than an empty propaganda spectacular, the flamboyance of which masked near failure. Viewed in the cold light of day, it had an air of farce about it. It was a bleak thought, and at this desperate and sobering moment, John Paul must have clutched like a drowning man at the memory of the powerful British warship *Drake*, lying anchored off Carrickfergus, not far away across the Irish Sea. There was no need for reflection. The *Ranger* was immediately set on a fateful course for Belfast Lough.

5

Twisting The Lion's Tail –
The Fight With the Drake

The crew, as well as the officers, were appalled at the dire prospect of slogging it out with a British man o' war, especially as their captain again boldly proposed tackling her in broad daylight. They could be forgiven for sensing that his distinctly unhealthy desire for glory had turned into a raging thirst for this heady and dangerous commodity. They would not have been happy to know that their under-strength complement of men was substantially outnumbered by the crew of the *Drake*, which had recently been augmented by freshly press-ganged Irishmen; though these were raw conscripts who not surprisingly were reluctant to fight and not up to it anyway. One of the main functions of the *Drake* was 'recruiting'. Although the crew of the American warship did not know the crewing details of the *Drake* they would have doubtless taken comfort from the fact that the *Ranger* had an advantage over their potential adversary in firepower, with a main battery of eighteen six-pounders compared with the British sloop's twenty four-pounders; some compensation at least for the daunting reputation of British warships. Though the reality was different this time. The Americans would have been further comforted had they known that all was not as it should have been aboard the *Drake*, more of which in due course. They were not to know either that whilst their own ship was brand new and very strongly constructed as a purpose-built warship, the vessel which they had so recently closed with in the dark of night, but could only see as a vague mass, was in fact a converted tobacco freighter. She was a good deal older than their own ship, built originally in Philadelphia but captured by the British early in the war and handily converted into a warship.

As they approached the wide entrance to Belfast Lough, the crew of the *Ranger* probably thought that with any luck there would be no encounter. The *Drake* might well have upped anchor and left Carrickfergus, probably in hot pursuit of the *Ranger* if news of the Whitehaven raid in the early hours of the previous day had reached the British captain – as it undoubtedly would, and sooner rather than later.

The *Ranger* actually entered Belfast Lough once again, in search of the *Drake*, early in the morning of 24 April. As it turned out, the crew were unlucky in their heartfelt hope, and John Paul had been needlessly anxious about the whereabouts of the British warship. To his relief and satisfaction, but to the consternation of his crew, the sloop was still riding quietly at anchor there. She had recovered the anchor and cable so recently cut in haste by the *Ranger* to avoid an encounter botched by drink; her captain, having no inkling of what was going on, had been totally mystified by the strange event, which he could only shrug off. However, urgent dispatches had arrived at Carrickfergus from Whitehaven the night before, so by that morning he was at least aware of the presence of a hostile American vessel in the Irish Sea.

He did not give Paul Jones any impression of suspicion when the *Ranger* confidently sailed deep into Belfast Lough, flying British colours, and once more in the convincing guise of a merchantman, with her gun ports concealed. Burden, the captain of the *Drake*, may well have been inclined to accept her as a merchant ship, because he would probably have found it difficult to imagine what on earth an American commerce raider of the usual type would have found of interest in such a hazardous place as Carrickfergus. The massive bulk of Carrickfergus Castle, which was garrisoned until 1928, dominated the town's small harbour and its battery of guns guarded the approaches to Belfast along the Lough; or at least they were supposed to. The reality was that, as elsewhere in the British Isles, the guns were in a sad state, lacking in the most basic repair and readiness.

A commerce raider would not have been aware of this situation, so no wonder Burden was not alerted to the possible danger. Even had he correctly deduced the identity of the vessel involved in the so recent and very odd night-time incident, he would certainly not have expected her to return. He would have found it hard to believe that she was interested in a British man o' war, a type of vessel to be avoided like scurvy by the usual commerce-raiding warships at that formative period of the American Navy. He may have thought she had slipped her cable in some sort of panic to get away, upon realising that his vessel was in fact a ship of war with a powerful sting, not a vulnerable merchant ship ripe for plucking. On the other hand, maybe the wily old salt hoped to lure an unwary privateer into an encounter. Unfortunately for Burden, whatever his thoughts, John Paul Jones was a new phenomenon.

He may have been puzzled, and he certainly seems to have been from the record, but as he observed the approach of the enigmatic vessel, the Captain of the *Drake* was in full command of a disciplined crew (apart from the raw, pressed men) and some welcome volunteers he had just taken aboard. Paul Jones was in a different situation. Even if the *Ranger* succeeded in retaining some element of surprise, her crew, in contrast to that of the *Drake*, was seething with discontent and mutinous talk. Even as their vessel sailed into a battle situation, which they could now see as unavoidable with Paul Jones in command, a plot was being hatched to seize the Captain and either clap him in irons, or fling him over the side. The hasty plan was that the ship would then return to America with one of the officers, the popular and prize-hungry Lieutenant Simpson, in command. Luckily for him, Paul Jones still had his finger on his crew's pulse and again discovered what was afoot, successfully forestalling trouble at this critical juncture: 'The mutiny almost reduced me to the necessity of putting some of them to death,' was his cool observation later.

Simpson was proving a problem to Paul Jones, and it was not just a question of grating personalities. After arriving in Europe, Simpson had in fact been led to expect that he would take over command of the *Ranger* when John Paul had, as was planned, taken command of *L'Indienne* ('The Indian Woman', rendered in some sources as *L'Indien*), under construction in Amsterdam for delivery to the United States government when Paul Jones was crossing the Atlantic. She was a brand new and much more powerful warship than the *Ranger*; long and slim, with thirty 36-pounder guns on one deck. This enviable vessel was a 'reward for his zeal and the important services he had performed in vessels of little force' said the Marine Committee. She was a frigate of advanced design and superior armament, but for reasons beyond his control – and to his great disappointment – this command did not materialize, and Simpson was thus frustrated in his ambition. Paul Jones must have been even more galled when *L'Indienne*, about to become the veritable jewel of the fledgling United States Navy and placed under his command, was, after a complex chain of dealings, leased to Alexander Gillon of South Carolina (whom we shall meet later) and, under the command of someone else, ignominiously captured by a pack of British warships off the American coast. Jones's problem started when the British learned from their spies in France that *L'Indienne* was being built for the Americans. (She was in fact to be bought by the French *for* the Americans, who were short of financial resources at the time.) The Dutch firm Boux, the British intelligence report ran, was 'going to build many frigates on the same plan', which was a prospect of no little concern. The publicity generated by the British embarrassed the Dutch, who were allied to Britain through the treaty of Utrecht (1678), and diplomatic pressure from London scotched the plan for *L'Indienne* as far as the involvement of John Paul Jones was concerned. Jones accepted things more philosophically than might be expected, and writing to the Marine Committee in America asserted: 'my unfeigned thanks are equally due for the intention as for the act.'

However, at that moment in Belfast Lough, both Jones and Simpson had been thwarted in their ambitions and were not on friendly terms. As far as the *Ranger* was concerned, Simpson was the darling of the crew; who much preferred an affable New Englander of his type as their captain, rather than the alarming Scotsman then in control of their destinies. They must have been as disappointed as Simpson and Paul Jones by the unhappy turn in command arrangements! Not long afterwards, on their way back to France, Simpson was held responsible for what Paul Jones deemed an act of gross insubordination which finally finished him as far as his Captain was concerned; but for the present Paul Jones steeled himself and concentrated on the task in hand: the sinking, or preferably the capture, of a British man o' war.

From afar *Ranger* approached the *Drake*, which was warily standing out now from Carrickfergus Bay. Jones had concealed his crew below deck, where, unbelievably, they continued their mutinous talk, egged on by Simpson. For the present the American ship was still flying the British flag, hoping to retain the element of surprise – by which Paul Jones always set great store – until the last possible moment. Naturally, he would stay out of range of any shore-based gun battery, but the *Drake*, now coming on promisingly, had not been tied up within the harbour anyway.

In due course Captain Burden put out a gig from the *Drake* to investigate more closely the strange ship proceeding along the Lough in front of them. As he drew ever nearer, the lieutenant in charge of the gig, spyglass in hand, was kept in ignorance of the gun ports (which were camouflaged anyway), by subtle movements of the *Ranger* that kept her stern towards the approaching vessel. The lieutenant must have been either reassured or uncertain as to the identity of the American vessel, because he still came steadily on. Once close by, he was politely invited aboard an ostensibly friendly ship. As soon as he started to ask questions, however, he was told that he was a prisoner of the United States Navy. The crew of the *Ranger* could hardly believe that the British could be so gullible as to fall for their ruse, and were so reassured by the quirky turn of fate that they were suddenly spoiling for a fight, and the capture of a very valuable prize. As Paul Jones himself explained, enlightened by his salutary recent experiences of them, the incident 'tickled their caprice and soothed them again into a good humour'.

The *Drake* fired a gun to recall the gig, but there was no signal in reply. Insolently, the *Ranger* took the gig in tow. She now became a lure, trailing behind the *Ranger* and leading Burden angrily on, out of the Lough, with alarm smokes rising into the air and pleasure-craft and other small boats heading out for a ringside view of the fight that was now imminent. 'At length,' says Paul Jones 'the *Drake* weathered the point, and having led her out to about mid-channel, I suffered her to come within hail.' As she came on into the open sea in the wake of his ship, Paul Jones was getting the measure of the British ship. No doubt the captain of the *Drake* was doing exactly the same to the *Ranger*, though at a subsequent court martial investigating the conduct leading to the loss of the *Drake*, her Master John Walshe, in charge of the ship at the end (the Captain being dead and the next in line mortally wounded), made the serious allegation that in his view the ship was not properly cleared for action at the commencement of the engagement – meaning she was not fighting fit when Burden was in command.

Clearing a ship for action was a complex business, and perhaps the *Drake*, mainly a recruiter now, was out of practice. Although this aspect was vitally important, clearing for action meant much more than having an efficient servicing system from the secure magazine down below to the gun batteries, involving 'powder monkeys', young lads of ten or so servicing cannon and small arms with ammunition. Clearing ranged from having grenades in special containers in place at the allotted stations around the ship, to ensuring the decks were properly free of tables and other objects and sanded to soak up blood and prevent the crew slipping in the gore, and stowing hammocks so that they might intercept lethal wood splinters. Under questioning, Walshe said that they were handicapped by a serious shortage of ammunition for both 'the great guns and small arms', stating somewhat damningly that 'we were making musket cartridges as we went out', and with makeshift paper, not regular cartridge paper. As well as the ammunition deficiency that affected the operation of the main batteries, there turned out to be serious mechanical problems affecting possibly as many as four of the guns after firing; their muzzles tipped downwards. There were numerous deficiencies later disclosed, or alleged. Had he not been killed, Captain Burden would have been the prime person examined at a court martial investigating the loss of the *Drake*. By the end of the engagement, Walshe was in unexpected charge of the ship in a chaotic battle situation.

In contrast to the *Drake*, the *Ranger* was well primed for action. In accordance with Paul Jones's tactical plans, many of her guns were already loaded with grapeshot for lethal anti-personnel fire at the start of the imminent battle. Grapeshot consisted of bundles of small iron balls, not much more than the size of small apricots and up to a dozen or so in number, sewn together quite rigidly in a canvas-wrapped bunch enclosed in a tight string netting. It was suitable for quick and easy insertion into the muzzle of a cannon, as a single compact entity on a round wooden base, or sabot. The name grapeshot, as can be seen in the illustration on page 190, arises from the resemblance to a bunch of grapes rather than to the size of the balls. Grapeshot could be sewn up and tight netted on board ship ready for use. When fired, the balls were sprayed across enemy decks with the main object of killing or wounding in a murderous hail of shot.

Amazingly, in view of the persistent and dangerous dissension on board, *Ranger* was, in fighting terms, perfectly ready to engage the *Drake* when Paul Jones gave the order. She was properly cleared for action.

The two sloops manoeuvred until they eventually came within pistol-shot of each other. The *Drake* had an effective crew of 175 officers and men, with long tradition and a steadfast spirit underpinning their resolve. The *Ranger* mustered 123 men of somewhat sullen and certainly rebellious disposition, who would be of doubtful reliability - one would have thought – in a bloody sea battle to which they were not at all accustomed and which they had most definitely not wanted. However, after the fight with the *Drake* John Paul Jones acknowledged magnanimously that their conduct throughout the action had been 'truely Gallant'. The vaunted backbone of the British Navy did not on this occasion carry the day.

Drake, now at close quarters, hoisted her English colours, whereupon *Ranger* downed her British flag and ran up the Stars and Stripes, the 'American stars' as Jones put it, unfamiliar as yet to English ships, and quite unknown to the crew of the *Drake*. It was pretty obvious now, however, whom the *Drake* had encountered, and the Americans had the *Drake*'s gig trailing in tow to dispel any lingering doubt. Nevertheless, Burden stolidly put the customary question 'What ship is that?' Master Cullen, prompted by Jones, stated at some length – perhaps in order to gain a last-minute tactical positioning advantage – the obvious reply:

> This is the American Continental ship *Ranger*; we are waiting for you, and desire that you come on; the sun is now little more than an hour from setting, it is therefore time to begin.

Paul Jones immediately swung his ship so that she passed across the bow of Burden's vessel. The *Ranger* fired a first devastating broadside of mainly grapeshot, sweeping the deck of the *Drake* with a lethal hail of iron balls. This beginning had gone exactly as Paul Jones planned, employing the ready-loaded grapeshot in the hope of reducing the numbers on the deck of the enemy ship. After this opening gambit the details of the action are obscure, but it lasted for just over an hour, and *Ranger* was handled brilliantly, with minimal damage. Paul Jones could not allow the English to grapple his ship and board her, as they were superior in numbers, and anyway he had something else in mind. After cruelly raking the *Drake* at the outset, the *Ranger*'s tactics were to operate at a distance and concentrate destructive attention on men, masts and rigging. After all, if things went well they wanted a worthwhile prize, with as little damage to the hull as possible. Sinking a ship was not primarily the object of most battles under sail, and it was difficult to sink wooden ships. Paul Jones wanted to smash up the sails and rigging so much that the *Drake* would become unmanageable in the water. He later described the battle as 'warm, close and obstinate'.

The colours of the *Drake* were shot away twice and ended up trailing in the sea. Confirming the lamentable ammunition situation, which included the shortage of cartridge paper, one of her midshipmen stated at the court martial that in the heat of the action: 'The people stationed at small arms called out for cartridges ... the armourer went down and came up with his hat full of balls and two horns of powder.' So the armourer himself could get no cartridges for the muskets, only powder and balls with which to make them – in the heat of battle! This was disastrous organization in any battle, but especially when confronting Paul Jones, who made a feature of bringing intense small arms fire to bear on the deck of an enemy ship, in particular from his purposefully enlarged fighting tops, commanding firing platforms fixed high on the masts.

The American battle tactics were successful, in that the *Drake* was kept at a distance just far enough to prevent a boarding attempt but close enough to maximise the impact of cannon fire. In fact as Walshe (still the Master at that point) said during the court martial: 'we were not above half a pistol shot distance from her all the time of the engagement'. The *Drake*, again according to Walshe, 'fought to windward and to leeward', meaning that both sides of the British sloop were engaged by her skilful and determined adversary, as the Americans attacked with devastating effect. Just as Paul Jones hoped and planned for, critical damage to the masts and rigging of the *Drake* was brought about early in the action and in due course she did become completely unmanageable, probably because of the crippling damage inflicted on her by bar shot (two balls connected by an iron bar); and chain shot (cannon balls connected by a length of chain), fired with dramatic effect into the mass of spars, sails, rigging and masts.

After the battle, Jones described the sails and rigging of the *Drake* as 'entirely cut to pieces', with 'her masts and yards all wounded, and her hull also very much galled'. The British midshipman mentioned earlier, also giving evidence at the eventual court martial, said tellingly that towards the end of the action, because of the damage to the spars, rigging and sails, '... we could not bring our guns to bear'. He was asked if the American ship was damaged or disabled, and simply said, 'No.' He continued that towards the end of the engagement, 'She went round us like a Tope and had done so for a considerable time before'. The tope is a variety of small shark (weighing up to a hundred pounds) found in British waters. The image of the *Ranger* circling the *Drake* like some calculating predator is a powerful one, and probably reflects quite vividly the reality of the battle.

Towards the end of the engagement the captain of the *Drake* was killed. The unfortunate man was on the very point of retirement after long service, and left a wife, Rachel Hannah, and four children. Through naval channels, she approached the Admiralty for a pension of seventy pounds a year. A letter in support of this outlined the basic facts of Burden's reaction to the masquerading visitor in Belfast Lough: 'Captain Burden immediately weighed, and gave chase, when an engagement ensued, in which he received a musket ball through the head, of which he instantly died' (though Paul Jones says he lingered for a little while). Unfortunately for the *Drake*, Burden's second-in-command, Lieutenant Dobbs, was also mortally wounded. Dobbs, who was on leave from a top-rank British warship and had volunteered to assist in a crisis, was in no position to command, and died two days later.

When he took over the stricken *Drake*, Walshe considered her no longer capable of effective handling, and with Dobbs mortally incapacitated, described her as, '... an entire wreck and under no command'. Very quickly he reached a decision, under intense but legitimate pressure from others, including the helmsman who could no longer get the ship to respond at all to the helm. Walshe bluntly asserted at the court martial that by this time the ship had '... not the least prospect of repulsing the enemy or getting away from them'. As was his prerogative, he made the decision. Over the terrible din of battle, he called out: 'Quarter'.

Gunfire stopped on both sides, and John Paul sent the captured gig over with a boarding party. On climbing aboard they were confronted by a scene of ruin and carnage. Rigging and tattered sailcloth were trailing in the sea or strewn around, and the deck of the *Drake* was found to be running with blood and rum, a large keg of which had been blown apart by a cannon ball. Walshe was taken on board the *Ranger*, observing, as he commented at the court martial, 'She had received very little damage [and] had the use of all masts and sails.' From the evidence of such battle damage as the *Ranger* could be seen to have suffered, Walshe says he '… learnt that our shot had not force enough to go through her sides'. He could see the *Drake*'s four-pound cannon balls lodged firmly and visibly in her timbers. From his personal observations aboard the *Ranger* he also concluded, 'She was much better constructed for action than the *Drake* was'; confirming that a converted old tobacco freighter had been no match for a brand-new, purpose-built – and very strongly built – warship. How the ships were handled is another matter.

Burden left no account of the fight of course, but no doubt he would have had something to say about the Master's allegation that the ship was not properly cleared for action, a very serious matter, at the start of the engagement. In the event, the court martial laid no blame for the loss of the *Drake*, concluding it was legitimately brought about by the vessel being rendered unmanageable – in effect by being reduced to a sitting duck. Paul Jones stated the casualties on the *Drake* as forty-two killed and wounded, though only a few of these were in fact killed. He stated his own losses as two killed (one of whom was Wallingford) and six wounded, including one who lost an arm and another who died later. He was sad about the fate of Dobbs. In his long letter to the Countess of Selkirk, which he wrote at leisure a short time after this battle, he reflected in a stiff, quasi-literary vein: 'Humanity starts back from such scenes of horror, and cannot sufficiently execrate the vile promoters of this detestable war', meaning the British government of course. He was only too aware, he said with more humanity, 'of the uncertainty of human prospects, and of the sad reverse of fortune which an hour can produce'.

Regarding the fight with the *Drake*, the entry in the log of the *Ranger* for 24 April 1778 recorded in the usual curt style: 'after one hour and five minutes engagement obliged her to strike to the

United States'; a few simple words that contained geopolitical significance. The victory was well deserved and it was in fact the very first time that a British warship had been defeated by one flying the Stars and Stripes of the United States of America. In different ways, much was made of the historic event in America, France and Britain, as we shall see.

At the end of the engagement, the *Drake* was incapable of being sailed on her own, and the *Ranger* took her in tow. Fortuitously, they soon encountered a brigantine, the *Patience* of Whitehaven, which unluckily for her sailed a mite too close to the *Ranger*. Paul Jones, in a more relaxed frame of mind now, and with glory enough for the moment, had no hesitation in slipping the tow for a while to capture another easy and welcome prize. She was not in the same prestigious league as the *Drake*, however. The captured British sloop was worked on intensively at sea until before long she was put into makeshift but reasonable sailing condition. She was entrusted to the care of Lieutenant Simpson, who was instructed in writing to support the *Ranger*: 'The Honour of our Flagg is much concerned in the preservation of this Prize, therefore keep close by me and she shall not be given tamely up.'

They enjoyed an uneventful passage back towards Brest, prudently sailing down the western coast of Ireland, without even a sighting of the numerous enemy warships now scouring the seas around the British Isles in search of the American sloop of war. The *Heart of Oak* was close behind them into Belfast Lough, but in vain: the bird had already flown.

They had successfully made their way down the west coast of Ireland, with the *Drake* in tow again, and were getting close to the French coast when another likely looking prize hove into sight. Jones cast off the towline and by hailer ordered Simpson, in accordance with his written instructions, to follow him. Simpson did not do so. After a chase, the vessel turned out to be a neutral Swedish ship. Paul Jones was livid that Simpson, as he saw it, had deliberately ignored his order and had simply continued on his way to Brest, as he had indeed been instructed to do, but only in case of separation by accident or bad weather. The prize crew of the *Drake* backed the congenial and prize-oriented Simpson, saying that he had misunderstood an order shouted indistinctly from the *Ranger*. Brooking no doubts, Jones placed him under arrest – probably with some personal satisfaction – though eventually he magnanimously agreed to Simpson taking *Ranger* back to America; and with a bonanza of prize vessels taken on the way!

On the evening of 8 May the cruise of the *Ranger* reached a fitting climax. The victorious American warship entered Brest, proudly flying the Stars and Stripes, and accompanied by the *Drake* also flying the American flag, with her English colours ignominiously turned upside down below. On board the *Drake* were some two hundred prisoners, a substantial bargaining counter and one far more persuasive than the Earl of Selkirk would have been in John Paul Jones's unremitting struggle for prisoner-of-war status to be granted to captured American seamen, no matter how devilishly piratical the fortune-seeking New Englanders might seem to the British.

The hapless *Drake* was a bedraggled symbol of the stinging humiliation of Britain by the upstart colonials, as she limped into Brest with bodged-up rigging. To add to the humilation, she bore the name of a man famous in the annals of British naval history; Sir Francis Drake: a peppery man of small stature like John Paul Jones, and animated with the same intrepid and indomitable spirit. This point was not lost on the mythmakers. A ballad recounting some of the highlights of the cruise of the *Ranger*, so reminiscent of Drake's legendary style of action, very soon made its appearance – and in England at that:

> You have heard o' Paul Jones?
> Have you not? Have you not?
> And you've heard o' Paul Jones?
> Have you not?

So ran the opening verse, in true folk-hero style already. Of course they had heard of him. The stirring fight with the *Drake* and the incident involving the Countess of Selkirk, were strands woven into the verses of the ballad. Sometimes the popular image was that of a demonic pirate, sometimes that of a more romantic figure with distinct overtones of Robin Hood. His generosity, in terms of money and in kind, towards the Irish fishermen who revealed the identity of the *Drake* and whom he had temporarily detained for the sake of secrecy when he first entered Belfast Lough, was the stuff of popular folklore. 'The grateful fishermen were in raptures' says Jones in his report on the cruise, and they heartily cheered the *Ranger* as they passed by her quarter in a 'good boat' which he had given them to get ashore, their own having foundered in a storm whilst with the *Ranger*. He also gave them the clever PR gift of one of the *Drake*'s sails, which he thought '… would sufficiently explain what had happened to the volunteers', as he described the detained but co-operative fishermen.

However, *Ranger*'s triumphal return to Brest was marred by a mundane problem. She desperately needed supplies to refit the ship and to cater for daily subsistence. The situation seemed increasingly deadlocked, with Paul Jones using his own money as a stopgap. He rounded off his report by remonstrating very strongly with the French authorities and with the American Commissioners about supplies. Towards the end of the report he says scathingly in reproof: 'I know not where to find tomorrow's dinner for the great number of mouths which depend on me for food', and indignantly asks the Commissioners 'if I have deserved all this?' He thinks not, and concludes in the same indignant vein: 'I am unwilling to think that you have intentionally involved me in this sad dilemma, at a time when I ought to expect some enjoyment.' When he felt it necessary, Paul Jones did not mince his words. He had spent a deal of his own money before the matter of supplies was sorted out satisfactorily by the Commissioners. Thus ended the cruise of the *Ranger* on an unexpectedly tawdry and discordant note.

6

Dalliance In France –
Affairs and Affaires

Cruising in British home waters with an almost breathtaking disdain for the Royal Navy, John Paul Jones had plucked glory from a series of events that might have easily added up to nothing more than a comic, if deadly, fiasco, rather than the brilliant naval exploit which is portrayed in the historical military record of the United States. He sailed proudly into Brest with much to show for the cruise: an audacious attack on a British port and the disarming of its defences, the capture of a British man-o'-war in convincing style after a well-fought sea battle, and two more valuable merchantmen taken as prizes. He could reasonably have expected a grateful, even euphoric, acknowledgement of his services from the American government, but he did not get it. He languished in France for nearly a year before being given another command.

He wanted to have the whole of Simpson's conduct on the voyage exposed and judged by court martial, including the allegation that he was one of those eager to throw the captain overboard before the engagement with the *Drake*, and that earlier he would have left him on the quay at Whitehaven to the tender mercies of the angry inhabitants and the incensed authorities. Dealing with Simpson was complicated by the fact that he was very well connected in New England society. He socialised with people who also socialised with Paul Jones. However, even in France, where he had the run of the quarterdeck of the *Drake* for his easy confinement, he fomented discontent in the prize-crew, and had to be moved to a cabin on a French prison hulk, where he again created so much trouble that he ended up in the disgusting confines of a French naval prison. Partly perhaps because he was keener on prizes than glory, the officers and men of the *Ranger* seem to have genuinely

liked Simpson – or at least many of them did – and supported
him against the captain, whom they criticised and even blamed
as the cause of the disaffection on board the *Ranger*. 'His mode of
Government is so far from ours that no American of spirit can ever
serve with cheerfulness under him', declaimed the 'Jovial Tars', a
group comprising seventy-two crew members – over half the crew
– who wrote a complaining account of the cruise of the *Ranger* to
the American Commissioners in Paris.

However, to his credit, Jones was demonstrably solicitous of the
basic welfare of his seamen. The problem seems to have been his
perfectionism and quick-tempered criticism of faults, combined
with his idea of discipline, which related more to the strict life
of duty on board a warship than to the more free and easy lifestyle possible on board a privateer intent on very profitable easy
pickings rather than on the bloody hazards of war. Whilst most
American sea captains, as remarked upon earlier, seem to have had
trouble with their crews, only very few could have had such a bad
experience as Paul Jones aboard the *Ranger*. Indeed, in spite of his
favourable comment after the fight with the *Drake*, he did say later
that if he had been fortunate enough to have had any of his previous crews with him on the voyage, he would have certainly burned
two hundred ships at Whitehaven. Despite the initial opposition of
his captain, Simpson was eventually given the command of *Ranger*,
to take her back to America. Once there, Congress commissioned
him as a captain, to the disgust of Paul Jones.

Some pointed remarks in a letter by Benjamin Franklin, exasperated at Jones's conduct on one occasion, are worth quoting in the
attempt to cast more light on the personality of John Paul Jones:

> Hereafter, if you should observe an occasion to give your offic-
> ers and friends a little more praise than is their due, and con-
> fess more fault than you can justly be charged with, you will
> only become the sooner for it, a great captain. Criticising and
> censuring almost everyone you have to do with, will diminish
> friends, increase enemies, and thereby hurt your affairs.

However, an English gentleman who went aboard his ship out of a
mere curiousity 'to see this famous adventurer', says that he 'found
the vessel as clean and sweet as any British man-o'-war, his men in

the greatest order', and noted that Jones '… carried his command without an oath, and appeared to be very well bred, and a man of few words'.

Life in France was not all tribulation. Despite the rather stinging rebuke quoted above, Paul Jones always greatly admired and enjoyed the company of Benjamin Franklin, in effect a diplomat representing the United States Government in France. Franklin, who was based in Paris of course, was normally friendly and basically well disposed towards John Paul. He was a man of many parts, world-renowned in his own day and described more recently as 'the apostle of modern times'. In the words of an admiring contemporary, the French economist Anne-Robert-Jacques Turgot, he 'snatched the lightning from the skies and the sceptre from tyrants', a neat conjunction of Franklin's experiments with lightning and electricity (flying conductive kites into thunderstorms), and his role in wresting power from the hands of King George and transferring it to the United States Congress. Franklin enjoyed the company of women, and had already advised John Paul Jones that the most congenial way to learn French was in bed with a woman, jokingly referred to by him as a 'sleeping dictionary'.

Unlike Franklin, Paul Jones never married, but his affairs with women are at times quite well documented. He had, for example, an affair with the Comtesse de Nicolson, a young married lady of Scottish Jacobite descent, whom he always referred to romantically as 'Delia' (a name taken from a song, not her real name). Almost as soon as they met in France they spent a rapturous but discreet five days together. 'Delia' wrote passionate love letters to Paul Jones. In her first letter, written just after this short and clearly memorable interlude, she calls him, in French of course, 'my only love', 'my angel' and 'my adorable Jones'. She goes on: 'When will we meet never again to be parted? … Nothing ever gave me so much pleasure … I feel that I have never lived but during those five days which have passed, alas, like a dream … *Je t'aime avec idolatrie et pour toi seul* (I love you to distraction, and you only).' She says she would be happy in a hut with him, would give up everything to be with him. In a later letter she even offers to sell her diamonds to pay the crew! However, John Paul was gentleman enough to turn down the offer, even though he was at that time in fact having difficulty in extracting the cash to pay his men. 'God, I die of desire to be with you and never leave you', she writes. Things did not, indeed could not, remain at this distracted level of absorption. In a later missive, she refers to a sword belt that she has made for him, complains that he has not written, and says that if she does not hear from him by Tuesday, she will never write again; she does of course: 'Six posts and no news. I try to have courage, but what must I think of such forgetfulness? Are you ill? Have you stopped loving me? Heavens! The very thought chills my heart! I cannot believe you so cruel.'

Asked on one occasion, by a susceptible and wide-eyed young woman, if he had ever been wounded, he replied disarmingly: 'Never at sea, but I have been hit by arrows that were never discharged by the English!' Jones did actually lead a charmed life; he never was wounded at sea beyond a mere scratch. Another lady, obviously quite charmed by him, wrote: 'To be sure he is the most agreeable sea wolf one would wish to meet with.' According to the memoirs of one of his crew members, he was surprised in 'a very loving position' by the Irish husband of a young married Frenchwoman; she was about seventeen. On another occasion he arranged for the (elderly) husband of this same young lady to be unavoidably detained, safely on board his ship, whilst he enjoyed a lengthy interlude ashore with the woman.

Abigail Adams, the fiercely intelligent and admirable wife of president-to-be John Adams, (the man who would broker the peace with Britain in Paris in 1782) described her first encounter with the intrepid Paul Jones. 'I expected to have seen a rough, stout, warlike Roman.' But she found that instead:

> I should sooner think of wrapping him up in cotton wool, and putting him in my pocket, than sending him to contend with cannon balls. He is small of stature, well proportioned, soft in his speech, easy in his address, polite in his manners, vastly civil, understands all the etiquette of a lady's toilette as perfectly as he does the mast, sails and rigging of his ship. Under all this appearance of softness he is bold, enterprising, ambitious and active.

Her husband, more prosaically, considered Paul Jones to be the most ambitious officer in the American navy. The thoughtful John Paul composed a special cipher for another lover; '... so that you will be able to write to me secretly and without risk'. He enclosed a lock of his hair, with the following honeyed words:

> I beseech you to accept the within lock. I am sorry that it is now eighteen inches shorter than it was three months ago. If I could send you my heart itself or anything else that could afford you pleasure, it would be my happiness to do so.

The love life of Paul Jones certainly had its lighter moments. An amorous midshipman was once ushered into a room in a brothel, where the previous brief sojourner had been his Captain, Paul Jones. Unfortunately, the Captain had left his gold watch behind. It was instantly recognised by the midshipman, who, in cahoots with a couple of his friends, pawned it for a dozen bottles of wine and sent the pawn ticket to Paul Jones (without any acknowledgement of course) so that he could redeem the pledged timepiece. We will meet Midshipman Fanning, the source of this tale, in due course

John Paul had an apparently more meaningful relationship with Therese Townshend, considered with some justification to be an illegitimate daughter of King Louis XV, and whom Paul Jones referred to in his papers as Madame T—. She lived with him in Paris and is said to have borne him a son. However, both Therese and any son seem to have disappeared without trace during the course of the French Revolution. In a letter Jones referred to her as 'the person whose happiness is dearer to me than anything else'. He left her to further his career in Russia, lost contact with her for some reason, and tried in vain to find her later.

Whatever his feelings for 'Madame T—' it was fairly asserted by one of his earliest biographers:

> The only mistress to whom Paul Jones was ever devoted with all the powers of his heart and mind was Glory, in pursuit of which he made no scruple at any time to set his foot on the neck of the gentle Cupid.

In my long-ago student days, we often took part in a change-your-partners dance called 'The Paul Jones'. It was a regular 'old time' feature, and anachronistic (even then!) at a student dance. The women formed an outward facing circle, moving to the music in an opposite direction to the men, who faced inwards looking towards them. When the music stopped couples facing each other became partners for a while. With any luck one might find a partner for 'The Moonlight Saunter', a much slower and more intimate dance that invariably followed later in the evening with the lights turned down low. It was a mode of encounter that appealed to students of course, and which might well have appealed to John Paul Jones himself, after whom the dance appears to have been jokingly named by the British as a commentary on his notorious, perhaps secretly envied, love life!

Putting aside affairs of the heart for the present, we return to John Paul's immediate predicament in France. He concerned himself, of course, with necessary matters such as the sale of the prizes, the infuriating Simpson affair and the care and future of the prisoners taken during the cruise; but he fretted all the time for a new command. Franklin was reassuring, saying that he would get something worthwhile in due course. In the event, he did not get it from America.

On 5 July 1778, the French Minister of Marine, Monsieur De Sartine, after discussions with Paul Jones, approached the American Commissioners in Paris with a written request: 'As I find myself, sirs, in a situation to have need of Captain Jones for a special expedition, I should like to have him remain here'. The Commissioners agreed, and a small task force evolved out of this decision. These developments (which would soon cause a great deal of frustration and anxiety for John Paul), saw him given command with the status of Commodore (an evolving rank at the time). The proposal looked good on paper. Very importantly as far as he was concerned, the planning of the expedition was to be at his discretion, and it was provided that he would have freedom of action and would use his own judgement in carrying those plans through to conclusion.

However, once the matter was agreed with the Commissioners, a task force had of course yet to be assembled for this unformulated expedition against the British. There was to be a lot of discussion, in which Paul Jones was intimately involved; a lot of vital preparations had to be made under his supervision before the task force was a reality and before he was in command of anything beyond a shifting idea, based initially around one ship.

This one ship, once settled on, would be purchased with money provided by the French Government. Commodore Jones would have liked a new and very fast ship, so that he could better, as he put it, 'go in harm's way' and if necessary force an engagement upon a reluctant enemy. However, a such a new vessel was not to be found, so he spent some time looking for a likely ship amongst existing vessels available on the market. He found one at last, in the port of Lorient, one which in due course became the principal vessel in a larger squadron. She was the merchant ship *Duc de Duras*, built in 1766 for use in the East India trade. This ship was by no means ideal, but she was the best that Paul Jones had come across. He was anxious that the purchase be expedited, for fear of losing the vessel. Things were conveniently arranged through the French government, which purchased the ship for the king. He assigned her for use by the Americans, but bore the cost of fitting her out himself, as well as taking responsibility for her payroll. She was to be crewed by volunteers taken on by Jones rather than regular sailors. Chaumont was given a free rein in organising the outfitting, but Paul Jones handled the practical matters, such as finding suitable guns and selecting the crew. It was agreed that she would sail under the American flag, as would the task force in due course. Paul Jones changed his new ship's name from *Duc de Duras* to *Bonhomme Richard*. He did this as a tribute to Benjamin Franklin, who used this pen name, meaning 'Poor Richard', for a popular annual publication of wise sayings, which he culled from every available source both ancient and modern, and which never seemed to run out, or fail in pithiness. John Paul's most pressing task was to find the guns to turn *Bonhomme Richard* into an effective warship. He could not get exactly what he wanted, but was eventually satisfied with six nine-pounders on the forecastle and quarterdeck, sixteen new twelve-pounders and twelve old ones as his main battery on the covered gun deck, and the six old eighteen-pounders already installed in the rear gun room (the *Duras* had been in the process of being fitted out as a privateer). He would have liked more eighteen-pounders, but the old ones proved defective anyway, and would seriously endanger the ship in the midst of battle.

Other ships gradually made up a squadron of seven vessels. One of these was a new warship, the *Alliance*, built in New England and sailing under captain Pierre Landais, a Frenchman made a citizen

of Massachusetts and granted a commission as Captain in the US
navy. She was armed with twenty-eight twelve-pounders and eight
nine-pounders. Landais was destined to prove a much bigger liability than the dangerous eighteen-pounders that nearly demolished
the *Bonhomme Richard*.

There was also a frigate (*La Pallas*) carrying twenty-six nine-
pounders and six four-pounders. A corvette of twelve guns (the
Vengeance) and a cutter of eighteen guns (the *Cerf*) were both more
lightly armed but useful, the latter being particularly nimble and
fast. The force had in their company two privateers, one of which
(the *Monsieur*) was almost as powerful as the *Bonhomme Richard*; the
other was the *Granville*. Paul Jones tried hard, but unsuccessfully,
to enlist the aid of an American privateer, the *Mifflin*, which had
suddenly appeared on the scene in France. The *Monsieur* had been
particularly sought after, as she greatly facilitated the interception of valuable convoys with an escort of warships, a more risky
proposition, but a more richly rewarding one, than the usual easy
but still profitable chase after single vessels. The task force was to
be accompanied – eventually – by a substantial body of 137 French
marines.

Under sail, inevitable changes of plan were often the responsibility of captains far out at sea and out of touch. Paul Jones was
deadly serious about intercepting convoys when the opportunity
materialized, assuming plans were not scotched by factors outside
a captain's control – not merely the weather of course. For example, just before the task force eventually sailed, John Paul wrote
informing Benjamin Franklin that he had received intelligence that
the British Jamaica Fleet, with a powerful escort comprising a fifty-
gun warship and two frigates, might be intercepted on its way
home. 'Should we fall in with that force,' he said, 'we will certainly
engage and I hope overcome it; but in all probability our ships
will be so much cut to pieces in the action that we shall be unable
to prevent the escape of the convoy'. He adds persuasively that
if he had the *Monsieur* under his command things would be very
different, and he got it soon afterwards. But the particular Jamaica
Fleet referred to was successfully attacked, by other American warships, off Newfoundland. Coincidentally, the *Ranger* was one of
the attacking vessels. Another small fleet of eight ships, which
Paul Jones knew about in advance, also escaped interception by

the task force, this time largely owing to delay caused by adverse weather.

Whilst the task force was being formed and fitted out, there was a deal of confidential discussion (though secrecy was not always maintained), regarding possible courses of action. Naturally, Paul Jones, as the Commodore who would be in command of the expedition, was asked for his opinions on various matters, not least plans of action, by the French Ministry of Marine, who would be largely financing the expedition. Paul Jones was never short of ideas. His suggestions ranged widely, from a raid on the coast of West Africa, which he knew from his slave trading days, and the interception there of British East Indiamen; to the destruction of the Greenland and Newfoundland fisheries with an attack carried into Hudson's Bay, another area with which he was familiar from his earlier seagoing. Closer to the seat of British power were proposals to raid again into the Irish Sea, to attack the east coast of England and Scotland, and to prosecute a raid up the Clyde into the port of Glasgow. He discussed a project for an 'unexpected blow' by a squadron of five ships and 400 troops. He also put forward proposals to intercept several merchant fleets: from the East Indies, the West Indies and, significantly as it turned out, the often very large escorted convoys from the Baltic. A pointer to his intentions was his statement: 'I shall endeavour to make my cruise a busy one rather than a long one.'

There was a governing political dimension to any planning which weighed heavily with Paul Jones. By the middle of July 1779 the Marine Committee in the United States had become desperate, following an equally desperate resolution of Congress, to retaliate for British attacks on civilian targets in America. London, Bristol, Glasgow and Edinburgh were spotlighted 'as the first objects of national retaliating resentment'. The Committee suggested Paul Jones, if he was available, as the appropriate instrument to 'attempt the destruction of some of their Towns by a naval surprise', with his force augmented if necessary. Sentiments of this nature were already familiar to Paul Jones, and some of the targets had been already mulled over. He may well have become aware of this latest authoritative and dramatic expression of them before he sailed on 14 August. The only written record is a long and anguished draft letter of the Marine Committee, destined for Benjamin Franklin in

Paris. Franklin, for his part, seems from his collected correspondence not to have received the actual letter, and to have been anxious,
in April at any rate, that Paul Jones should refrain from setting fire
to defenceless towns, stating firmly: 'Although the English have
wantonly burnt many defenceless towns in America, you are not to
follow this example, unless a reasonable ransom is refused,' adding
that sufficient time must be given for the evacuation of vulnerable
inhabitants, the old and the sick, women and children. It can be
seen that it might be difficult, if not impossible, for an essentially
hit-and-run force, relying largely upon surprise and speed, to comply with such humane instructions in the heat of the moment and
in enemy country.

The task force of seven ships would soon set sail together under a
cloak of secrecy. But what plan of operation had in the end resulted
from all the discussions? In fact, the final objective of the task force
was not at all as originally conceived. Three successive schemes
had been settled on in turn, the final one emerging from the shadow
of the second.

The first plan was based on the 'unexpected blow', with a large
body of troops involved. The proposal was for a large-scale amphibious attack on the port of Liverpool, with Paul Jones as Commodore
in command of the task force, and the Marquis de Lafayette, a debonair and charismatic French officer who was already giving good
service in America to the United States Army, in command of the
ground assault troops. 'There is enough honour to be got for both of
you if the expedition is conducted with a prudent unanimity', wrote
Benjamin Franklin. Relations between Paul Jones and Lafayette,
who was a fellow Freemason, were very cordial and all boded well.
However, by some means the Liverpudlians managed to get wind
of the enterprise, and scotched it by making a public outcry. They
forcefully demanded that the government get on with the construction of a permanent fortress commanding the approach to Liverpool
up the river Mersey. Rapidly completed, this fortification was based
around a formidable half-moon breastwork with guns mounted in
open embrasures. Inside the fortification were large barrack buildings and the main ammunition store for this and ancillary gun batteries. These ancillary batteries were constructed at the entrances
to George's and King's Docks. Liverpool became almost overnight
a difficult nut to crack. Unfortunately, the *Bonhomme Richard* had

been specially adapted for the purpose of the Liverpool expedition, with special consideration for the accommodation of troops, and with a roundhouse built on deck to accommodate Lafayette and his military staff. In the future, this roundhouse proved to be not only superfluous but something of a nuisance, and the vessel not as fast and manoeuvrable as she might have been had she been radically re-adapted specifically for chasing ships, as Paul Jones had very much wished. Benjamin Franklin's confidential secretary, Dr. Edward Bancroft, a fellow of the Royal Society and a Member of the Royal College of Physicians, may have been the source of the leak to the Liverpudlians, since as well as being a friend of Paul Jones, he also was a British spy in receipt of a princely one thousand pounds a year for his very valuable services. However, Bancroft was not the only British spy in the employ of the American Commissioners in Paris. Whoever the source, Paul Jones had already complained bitterly to Benjamin Franklin about careless talk of supposedly secret matters, which ended up as common knowledge for discussion at dinner parties!

The second plan, devised after the Liverpool raid was scrapped, relegated the function of the task force into a supporting role in a much more ambitious enterprise: no less than a full-scale inva-sion of England based on a combined French and Spanish fleet of sixty-four ships of the line – a second Armada in effect. This force was deemed more than adequate to overpower the British Channel Fleet of thirty-eight similar ships. John Paul Jones was to mount a diversionary attack with his task force around the northern coast-line of the British Isles; hopefully to draw off forces from the South, and pin down those already in the North. The main thrust of the invasion was to be provided by forty thousand French troops assembled and poised ready to cross over into Britain. The whole extravagant and massive enterpise would come to naught, though not before Paul Jones and his task force had set sail on their expedi-tion, minor in comparison, into northern seas. The British Fleet very wisely refused to engage with the Combined Fleet, even though the enemy at one point anchored en masse in Plymouth roadstead, showing every sign of going through with a landing. Instead of responding to this provocation, the British warships simply hov-ered like a baleful presence in the general vicinity of the much larger enemy fleet, ready to intervene in concentrated force at what they considered an opportune moment of vulnerability, such as when their enemies were actually attempting to get troops ashore. The British commanders were right to be wary, because the main thrust of the invasion attempt was directed not against Plymouth, but against the Isle of Wight. Operations in the Plymouth area had been specifically devised as a means of diverting British efforts away from this main theatre of proposed operations – a ruse which failed. The Plymouth diversionary feint, which was envisaged as transformable into the main effort in favourable circumstances, had the advantage of being under the direct control of the commanders of the invasion fleet. There was really little point in the nominally diversionary enterprise in Britain's northern seas. In the event, nothing was to come of the threatening situation along the south coast of England because after some initial dithering and failure to provoke a full British attack, the Combined Fleet was devastated by the outbreak of disease: the rapid spread of a virulent smallpox epidemic. This very soon affected virtually all the ships, with deadly results, and ruled any invasion out of the question.

Sketch of the Bonhomme Richard, *artist unkown. Exact information about the ship is hard to find and any representations of her were made after her sinking.*

How the remarkable events on the South Coast of Britain after the two fleets sighted each other at daybreak off Deadman's Point near Falmouth were understood by the public can be ascertained from the following pieces. The first is a letter from a citizen of Plymouth threatened with invasion, dated 17 August 1779:

> The bloody flag was hoisted yesterday about twelve o'clock: in the evening the French etc. drew up in a line, and continued in that situation all night, which was a night of confusion indeed! … About noon I was looking from my window, and saw the signal for an engagement hung out, and almost instantly heard the noise of cannons like the repeated peals of thunder. This continued about two hours when the [minor] engagement ended.

Another piece, published on 31 August and more personal in tone, had visions of 'wives and daughters ravished by pig-tailed Frenchmen' and 'dreadful apprehensions of their property being lost'. Others were more nonchalant: 'Several gentlemen and ladies set out yesterday afternoon for Portsmouth, in order to have a view of the engagement, which is expected off that place'. They must have been disappointed when the anticipated sea battle did not take place. However, it was no doubt with great relief, tinged perhaps by at least some pity, that by 18 September people could read in newspapers around the country that the danger of invasion was past, and that 'a great sickness has prevailed amongst their sailors, the French having thrown overboard above one thousand men'.

So as well as being the focus of the Government's attention and of the activities of the Royal Navy, the Great Armada unsurprisingly held the attention of the newspapers. Unfortunately, any advance diversionary function that Paul Jones's task force might have fulfilled was nullified by a serious delay in departure, brought about by an accidental collision between the *Bonhomme Richard* and the *Alliance* during a preliminary cruise in the Bay of Biscay. This was an accident for which Paul Jones and Peter Landais strenuously blamed each other; a portent.

When Paul Jones was eventually able to leave Lorient with his squadron, the combined Franco-Spanish fleet would already be approaching Plymouth. But it was limping back into Brest, racked and exhausted by disease, by the time the task force was stirring things into a ferment far away in the north

Because of the delay before it eventually set sail, this American task force, originally part of a greater strategy, seems to have become transformed into an entity in its own right and with its own dynamic. It was now not so much a third plan as an evolving inevitability built around several of the elements which Paul Jones had been suggesting during the formative stages of the expedition, but which seem to have been disclosed only gradually to the other captains as the cruise progressed. This was in accordance with his original brief that he could make untrammelled use of his discretion and judgement; but it was often to the consternation of those captains, especially Pierre (sometimes referred to as Peter) Landais of the *Alliance*.

The months leading up to the final departure of the task force were full of exasperation for Paul Jones: he had to overcome or accommodate procrastinating, meddling – even hampering – individuals, and at times bitter disappointment. The changing circumstances meant that the ship that he had obtained and adapted with the transportation of troops for the Liverpool expedition in mind, was not at all the fast ship he would now have chosen; for an operation such as eventually emerged he would have liked to cut the *Bonhomme Richard* down by one deck and rely on a single powerful battery of thirty eighteen-pounders on an open gun deck. At one point he had been incensed at being offered the command of a privateer as a sop to his impatience, saying – prophetically perhaps – that he would not serve '… in any private line whatever, unless where the honour and interest of America is the premier object'. To De Sartine, the Minister of Marine, he forcefully complained: 'I have already lost near five months of my time, the best season of the year, and such opportunities of serving my country, and acquiring honour, as I cannot again expect this year.' De Sartine, stung by his tone and exasperated with him anyway by this point, suggested to Benjamin Franklin that perhaps the best course of action would be to send Paul Jones back to America.

This did not happen of course, and at the beginning of July 1779 Paul Jones received fresh orders, in which there was no explicit mention of any diversionary purpose, or land-based operations; he was simply instructed to attack British commerce. Sartine and the French Ministry of Marine drafted the orders in French, and Benjamin Franklin had them translated into English and sent them to Paul Jones in the form of a short letter:

> Being arrived at Grois [now Groix], you are to make the best of your way, with the vessels under your command, to the West of Ireland; and establish your cruise on the Orcades [meaning the Orkneys], the Cape of Dirneus [something of a puzzle], and the Dogger Bank: in order to take the enemies property in those seas.

It will be useful to bear these orders in mind when the expedition is underway and differences of opinion and individual actions start to manifest themselves amongst the participants. For one, though the matter was blurred later, the task force was in these orders clearly seen to be under the command of Paul Jones, 'the vessels under your command' is perfectly unambiguous.

Groix, designated as the start point for the assembled ships was the Ile de Groix, an island off the French coast near the naval base of Lorient. The orders indicated a direct crossing from Groix to the vicinity of Cape Clear (Clare), the southernmost tip of Ireland, and from there a steady sail northwards off the west coast of Ireland, steering westward of the Hebrides, well beyond Cape Wrath at the north-western corner of Scotland, into the general vicinity of the Orkneys. There were no plans to enter the Irish Sea, but the British – unfortunately for them and despite their well-placed spies – did not latch onto this fact, and their attempts at interception suffered in consequence, with a lot of wasted effort.

The objective is plainly stated to be 'to take the enemy's property in those seas'. On the face of it this might mean nothing more than capturing enemy ships – including warships of course – at sea, and might well be seen as excluding land-based operations such as attacks on ports, although taking 'the enemy's property' would be a legitimate aspect of such action. The orders given to Landais were subtly different.

The main area of operations was clearly intended to be the general area of the North Sea, and there were three specified operational indicators: the vicinity of the Orkneys, the Cape of Dirneus, and the Dogger Bank. These markers encompass a wide, wild and mainly watery environment where British men o' war would be expected to be few and far between.

The Orkneys is clear enough, but Franklin's 'Cape of Dirneus' is not now identifiable by that name on the map. It was taken by Rear Admiral Samuel Eliot Morison USN, in *John Paul Jones: A Sailor's Biography*, to mean 'The Naze', a promontory at the southern tip of Norway marking the entrance into the Skagerrak, the narrowing channel leading the way into the Baltic Sea. The Norwegians refer to this feature as 'Lindesnez', but the British familiarly call it 'The Naze' on maps of the area. 'Dirneus' and 'The Naze', are not very far apart phonetically, which lends credence. A Naze, which is a geographical feature well known and much used as a reference point amongst seamen (usually in the form, 'Ness'), is a distinctive 'nose' of land – or nez in French.

However, in the absence of certainty, and partly because the task force never in fact approached the Norwegian coast, Dennis Head (or Dennis Ness as it is alternatively known), has been suggested as another possibility. This feature is situated, more obscurely, at the north-eastern tip of the Orkneys, being a promontory – with a light even in those days – jutting out eastwards from the northern end of the island of North Ronaldsay. However, Franklin's instruction 'to establish your cruise on the Orcades', followed by a separate reference to the 'Cape of Dirneus', would seem to make a specific reference to Dennis Head or Ness superfluous as an operational area boundary indicator. In any case, the cruise extended well to the north of the Orkneys, with sighting of the island of Foula, close to the southern mainland of the Shetlands, and later of Fair Isle, roughly half-way between the Shetlands and the Orkneys.

There are many projecting land features in both the Orkneys and the Shetlands referred to as 'Head' or 'Ness', but the word 'Cape' does not appear at all. However, the term 'Cap' is the French version of 'Head'. Since 'Cap' in topographical terms translates directly into English as 'Cape', the cruising instructions prepared by the French Ministry of Marine, as translated by Franklin in giving his orders to Paul Jones, could plausibly have referred to Dennis Head or Dennis Ness in the reference to 'Cape Dirneus'

To complicate matters even further, the closest written resemblance is between Dirneus and Durness, a remote location in the very north of Scotland. In Scottish pronunciation the two words would be virtually indistinguishable. Durness is a very ancient place of settlement quite close to Cape Wrath. The actual place of that name is situated at the root of a very substantial and distinctive promontory of land jutting out from the mainland, with the long and winding Kyle of Durness on one side and the vast sea-filled Loch Eriboll not far away on the other. This Loch was the place from which Charles Edward Stuart, 'Bonnie Prince Charlie', was eventually spirited back to France by a French warship after the failure of the Jacobite Rebellion of 1745. Paul Jones, with an expeditionary force in such an evocative location, might well have induced nightmares amongst the British establishment, or at least a restless night; especially at a time when the Bonnie Prince was still alive (though infirm and lost in the grip of alcohol); and when a very powerful Franco-Spanish invasion force was hovering menacingly off Plymouth with similar diabolical intent to the first Armada of 1558. It is worth remembering that before 1745 there had been no less than five attempts to restore the Stuarts in Britain. At least three of these had serious potential, involving foreign (usually French) assistance, with diversionary action built into the plan to interfere with any British response. Such attempts at distraction were similar in principle to that uneasily unfolding in 1779 – though this one was marred by the delay arising out of the collision in the Bay of Biscay involving Landais and Paul Jones. There would be no comeback for the Stuarts. Their cause was by then burnt out, as the French doubtless realized, but they were quite prepared to hint at it through the American diversion – anything to throw the British off balance.

Durness might have once been related through its name to the conspicuous 'nose' jutting out northwards from it. Its name now, Faraid Head, is English, and could involve a quite common place-name duplication (i.e. Far Head Head). Its name and context now suggest that the promontory might once have been known as the Cape of Durness, or simply Durness. One can imagine the British puzzling mightily over scraps of intelligence they might have gleaned on the location of the 'Cape of Dirneus', as they tried to work out Paul Jones's place in the Franco-Spanish invasion plans! And a final complication: a prominent feature at the northern end

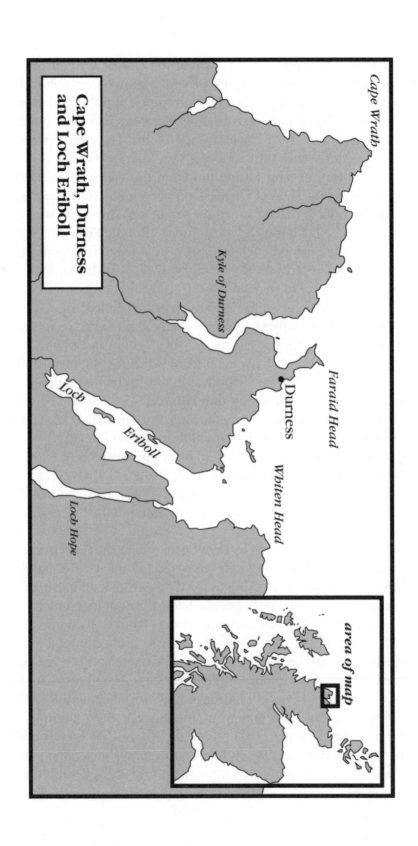

Cape Wrath, Durness
and Loch Eriboll

Cape Wrath

Kyle of Durness

Faraid Head

Durness

Whiten Head

Loch

Eriboll

Loch Hope

area of map

of Fair Isle is known as The Nizz, and Fair Isle is well placed to function as a point of reference for an enterprise involving the Shetlands as well as the Orkneys.

The task force was in due course to linger in the vicinity of the Shetlands for nearly three days, taking two small prize vessels. The eventual course of the cruise, carefully plotted from the logbook of the *Bonhomme Richard* by Admiral Morison, was in fact to take the task force between Fair Isle and North Ronaldsay, the northern-most of the Orkney Islands. Positively identified, the location of the elusive 'Dirneus' would have a bearing on the interpretation of the differences which blew up during the course of the operation in these northern parts. The Naze, at the entrance to the Skagerrak on the southern tip of Norway, in its geographical relationship to the Baltic trade would be material at that time to the instruction to 'take the enemy's property in those seas', which was the stated object. It might also have played a part in a change of plan in the Orkneys mentioned, but not explained, by Paul Jones in his subsequent account. In the instructions translated by Franklin, 'Cape Dirneus' is distinct and separate from the reference to the 'Orcades' which it follows, so this Cape ought to be an operational indicator quite distinct from the Orkneys, and a sufficient distance away to consti-tute a defining point of reference, together with the third defining operational indicator, the Dogger Bank, which is an unambiguous demarcation.

The Dogger Bank is an area of very extensive shoaling, roughly about a third of the way across the North Sea between England and Denmark. It is a fishing-ground of prime importance, and in some parts only about six fathoms (thirty-six feet) deep. The Dogger Bank is a long way south from 'Cape Dirneus', whether this means the The Naze in Scandinavia, The Nizz on Fair Isle, Dennis Head on North Ronaldsay, Durness in the vicinity of Cape Wrath; or some other feature in these northern seas: South Ness at the southern tip of the island of Foula, for example, which marked the turning point of the cruise from northward to southward. These three locations were clearly intended to broadly delineate the general extent of the area to be actively scoured for prizes by the squadron. Reviewing all the options, the 'Naze'on the southern tip of Norway seems the most logical choice as the Cape of Dirneus. Evidence to back this identification will emerge in the narrative.

Chance encounters would be the normal expectation along much of the proposed route, but trawling for the property of the enemy in the seas between the Norwegian Naze and the Dogger Bank could really mean only one thing: an attack on one of the British Baltic Fleets. This was a project Paul Jones had considered, and suggested. The Baltic Fleets were regular, often huge, convoys of British merchant ships under the escort of Royal Navy warships. Such a fleet would make its way out from the Baltic Sea via the Skagerrak and down through the wide expanses of the North Sea to gradually hive off to various British ports. Significantly, the orders translated in Benjamin Franklin's letter instructed that prizes were to be sent, according to proximity, to Bergen in Norway as well as Ostend in Holland and Dunkirk in France.

It was planned that the task force would eventually end up at the Texel, a Dutch naval base, by a date that was changed as a result of unavoidable delay, or perhaps because of intelligence about ship movements. The latter suggests itself because, despite all the mishaps, delays and vagaries of weather, the task force managed to be 'hanging around' in about the right place – Flamborough Head – at about the right time for the interception of a large British Baltic Fleet, towards the end of the voyage.

After having arrived at the Texel, hopefully after a very success-ful cruise yielding rich rewards, the squadron was supposed to escort a French Baltic Fleet down the coast to Brest. This French fleet was penned up in the Texel by the Royal Navy, whose ships had been for some time doggedly lying in wait off the Dutch coast to give it a thorough mauling if and when it moved out, and, by way of prizes, profit greatly.

Returning to the task force as it assembled off Groix, it is crucial to note that the status of this aggressive assemblage of ships was very important to Paul Jones, and changes to that status from the orginal concept can be seen in the orders and written arrangements regulating the voyage. There had been a persistent rumour in well-placed circles in Philadelphia, as well as in Paris and Holland, that the task force was becoming nothing more than a crude attempt to make money: a huge privateering exercise masquerading as some-thing more than that under the auspices of the Stars and Stripes. With the purpose of the expedition set down so bluntly, 'to take the enemy's property in those seas', it is not difficult to see why the rumour might have got about. Had they been informed about it, people might have commented that the departure of the task force seemed to have been very poorly timed; it was now too late if the primary object was an effective diversion of British effort away from the operations of the Combined Fleet, which had been on the verge of putting into effect its own diversion anyway. Admittedly, there had been unavoidable delay as explained earlier; but doubters would have looked even more askance had they known that John Paul Jones's latest written orders, countersigned by Franklin, omitted any reference whatsoever to a diversion of British sea-power, or to any other higher purpose. Of course, some diversion of effort would have been implicit in any response by the British to hostile action, but the orders were terse and on the face of it baldly profiteering in tone. Franklin himself was of a very entrepreneurial disposition. He had numerous business interests, and his nephew was one of those accused by name of mere profiteering in connection with the expedition. Maybe, owing to bad luck in the Bay of Biscay and consequentially changed circumstances, the diversionary plan really had perforce turned into a tawdry smokescreen for legitimised greed.

However, greed might in its turn have masked a higher purpose that was tacitly understood by Paul Jones, who had all along been party to the formative discussions. Franklin was most certainly no fool, and the framing of the orders by the French Ministry of Marine could have been sensibly politic, showing in their simple wording a commendable regard for the secrecy and deception so essential for the element of surprise; as we have seen a military advantage greatly valued by John Paul Jones, and which was vital in the type of operation which he now undertook. He was well aware of spies and the possible consequences of careless talk, and might well have preferred some things to be implicit rather than explicit. For his part, Franklin, who had taken a prominent role in framing the American constitution, was always – now urgently – seeking to negotiate peace with the British on behalf of the United States, whatever exemplary and persuasive show of force might be imminent. He was, after all, a diplomat. But he was also very well thought of by the French, who were now openly and seriously at war with the British. In short, Franklin was in a tricky position and had to tread carefully.

John Paul Jones was not a diplomat; he believed in even and direct dealing, and practised it. He was genuinely incensed at the very idea that he could be thought of as merely out for filthy lucre, as an affront to his honour. Even after the squadron action had come to an end, the rumour persisted. In a letter to Benjamin Franklin in August of 1780, after the cruise had ended, Paul Jones wrote:

> Mr. Gillon of South Carolina has taken much pains to promulgate that you wrote him a letter with an assurance that the *Bonhomme Richard* was a privateer. This has already done me much harm; and as it is not true, I beg your Excellency to contradict it.

Franklin did so, saying that the tale arose out of Gillon's undue curiosity prior to the cruise, and that his own dissembling, politic reply was a necessary smokescreen, implying that Franklin was complicit in some secret purpose underlying the ostensibly privateering adventure, a purpose of which Paul Jones must have been aware. Franklin's letter to Gillon, and Landais's comments on it, fill in much of the background to the forthcoming expedition (see Appendix II). As recently as 1991, the privateer label still persisted: a local historian of the development of the defences of the port of Liverpool (Ken McCarron) asserted that the provision of effective fortification there was first catalysed by 'fear of attacks by American privateers such as Paul Jones'. Jones made much of the fact that he was a commissioned officer of the United States government, lest his actions be misconstrued; he saw himself not as a privateer but as an instrument for the prosecution of American policy; and acted thus.

Actions speak louder than words, and the course of events soon to unfold would amply demonstrate that despite setbacks and changes of plan, John Paul Jones unwaveringly saw serious, hostile engagement with Britain in order to further America's political interests as the primary objective of the expedition. As the enterprise proceeded there was no knowing, as far as Paul Jones was concerned, what developments were taking place in the planned invasion of England. As far as he knew, the troops could well be ashore as planned and the invasion successfully proceeding apace.

The expedition developed along lines curiously analagous, on a larger scale, to the cruise of the *Ranger*. Either there was a tacit understanding that commerce raiding was not the be-all and end-all of the expedition, or John Paul Jones blatantly flouted his orders in the real interests of the United States of America (as he saw them) as the events of the expedition unfolded. After receiving his orders, John Paul asks in a letter to Franklin: '... whether I may or may not attempt to avail myself of every opportunity that may seem to present itself to distress the Enemy'. In a marginal note he pens in the comment: 'I have ever made this my study'. He is seeking explicit authorisation for action outside the letter of his instructions. In a letter that Paul Jones received a couple of weeks later, on 19 July, Franklin replies in true diplomatic style: '... every opportunity of distressing the enemy should be embraced, that is not inconsistent with the execution of your general orders'. In his letter dated 26 July, in which he gives Franklin last-minute news of the Jamaica convoy mentioned earlier, Paul Jones perseveres: '... if we failed in [the attack on the Jamaica convoy] we might turn our arms against other objects which might I hope do them equal mischief'. He is angling for the green light, rather than the ambiguous amber one, for widening the scope for action, but to no purpose as far as Franklin was concerned. Of course, Benjamin Franklin had responsibilities towards the French authorities who were largely financing the task force, and perhaps he could not in all conscience overtly agree to such matters and at the same time keep the French in the dark.

It is no coincidence that, just at the moment when the task force was about to set sail, a concordat (a document setting out the terms of a written agreement) was suddenly produced for signature as though spirited from thin air, almost certainly with the intention of clipping John Paul's wings. Against his better judgement, Paul Jones was constrained on pain of losing overall command to put his name to this document by the French, who were very conscious that they were backing the expedition financially and wanted some return. One of the clauses effectively created an independent status for each ship, the vessels being 'associated' with the task force 'by common consent', though excluding the two privateers who were freelancers anyway. This proviso put the Commodore, who by virtue of his Commission and as explicitly set down in writing earlier by Benjamin Franklin was in overall command of the expedition, in an ambiguous position. Just what control could he exercise over the captains of the other ships; not so much the privateers, but those French officers who were hastily commissioned as officers of the United States Government, and with inferior rank to Paul Jones? Specifically commissioned as Commodore, he was the designated squadron commander, but did it mean anything?

Furthermore, the concordat gave the French agent, Chaumont, effective control over the prizes, making it look as though the imminent enterprise was not really being carried out under the auspices of the United States government at all, despite an outward show of this; the ships flew the Stars and Stripes and operated under United States navy regulations, but so what? It is not surprising that the whole thing could be interpreted quite easily as a major privateering enterprise, masterminded and heavily financed through Chaumont himself. But although he had financed the armament of the vessels, as carefully pointed out in the concordat, Chaumont was still in effect the agent of the French government in dealing with the Americans. He was a painful thorn in the flesh of Paul Jones, who prided himself on playing it straight; though not, it might be noted, in respect of Chaumont's young and vivacious wife, with whom he probably had a love affair or some kind of dalliance. Paul Jones suspected that Chaumont might have conspired against him because of the liaison, but the wellspring of Chaumont's machinations was more likely self-interest of a different kind: profit. The American Commissioners in Paris occupied a wing of Chaumont's house. He was their landlord as well as the agent for the French, and it was he who was most closely associated with, and insistent upon, the concordat. Paul Jones's clandestine affair with Chaumont's wife did not stop Jones complaining to Franklin and others about her husband's persistent and even perverse failure to keep secret key matters relating to the expedition. The possibility of information leaks would have certainly made Paul Jones very wary, ensuring that he would play his hand even closer to his chest; and he was well able to spring surprises at opportune moments; his original instructions when the task force was first mooted certainly allowed for that. However it originated, Paul Jones was under no illusions regarding the concordat:

At any other time and in all other circumstances, I should have rejected these conditions with disdain; I saw the dangers which I ran, but having announced in America that I had remained in Europe because the Court of France had wished me to do so in order to take command of secret expeditions, I took the resolution to expose myself to every peril.

From this it can be seen that he was a very cool player as well as being a very bold one, though he did in fact suffer during the expedition for signing up to the concordat.

The French connection was restrictive to the point of paralysis, but the financially hard-pressed fledgling republic across the Atlantic could not really do without it. The concordat would prove almost the undoing of the whole enterprise as John Paul Jones seems to have conceived it, that is, as an enterprise furthering vigorously the political aims of the American government, over and above any incidental diversionary effect which the expedition might have in relation to the actions of the Combined Fleet. However, although he may have seen the overriding aims in this light, there is no doubt that the successful prosecution of a major money-making endeavour, the capture of prizes to enrich private individuals, including himself and his crews, was not forgotten!

Hovering in the background for Paul Jones, there was another agenda to be worked through during the course of the expedition, the personal quest for glory and reputation. These were heady considerations calculated to make the backers, who were well aware of his propensities in this respect, shudder with apprehension. They were considerations that would in themselves, as far as they were concerned, have provided more than adequate justification for the concordat.

If he could not be displaced, and this may have been desired by Chaumont who finally and openly threatened it when the concordat was presented for signature, Commodore Paul Jones could at least be shorn of authority. His subordinates in name only would have a powerful say in the conduct of the expedition. They could disobey his orders with some impunity and disrupt his plans. In effect, they would have the power of veto. All these possibilities were realised during the course of the cruise of the *Bonhomme Richard* squadron, but Paul Jones gritted his teeth, survived and triumphed.

As for his crew, John Paul had been fortunate in taking on Richard Dale, a young Virginian of twenty-two, as his first lieutenant. Like Paul Jones, he had first gone to sea at the age of around twelve. He had good experience of the war at sea, and had escaped twice from English prisons. He was dedicated to his profession, loyal and faithful; and he always remained one of John Paul's best friends – one of the few, it might be said. In contrast to Dale, however, Jones was most unfortunate, as hinted at earlier, to be burdened with Peter Landais in command of the *Alliance*. John Adams, observing him once when a passenger on board his ship, wrote at that time about the Frenchman commissioned into the United States Navy:

> Landais is jealous of everything, jealous of everybody, of all his officers, all his passengers; he knows not how to treat his officers, nor his passengers, nor anybody else. There is in this man an inactivity and an indecision that will ruin him; he is bewildered – an absent, bewildered man.

A damning assessment from someone unconnected with the expedition, but one which was to prove not far off the mark as the voyage of the task force proceeded, despite the strenuous attempts of Landais to justify himself later.

The crew was a motley one, made up of Americans, Englishmen (mostly released prisoners of war who volunteered for service in the *Bonhomme Richard*), and Frenchmen; together with a sprinkling of the human flotsam of the world. But they were professional seamen who in the event turned out to be the best crew that Paul Jones – in his own later assessment at any rate – ever commanded. Maybe, in looking back, he was taking rather a rosy view, because there had been problems before the ship set sail:

> The crew was so ungovernable that I found the sole expedient by which I could control them was to divide them into two parties and to place one knave under the eye and guard of another.

The Americans and the Frenchmen started brawling, and the Englishmen became mutinous: they hatched a plot to take over the *Bonhomme Richard* and sail her back to England with Jones in irons. Quartermaster Towers, judged the ringleader, was subjected to 250 lashes of the cat o'nine tails, which normally amounted to being flogged to death, though in his case he survived at least long enough to be flung into a French prison. Some of the English volunteers were discharged forthwith, to get their numbers down to what was considered a safer level. There was another flogging before the ship set sail, involving the coxswain and crew of the Commodore's barge. They got themselves inexcusably drunk, leaving John Paul in the lurch ashore and obliged to find a fishing smack to get himself in an undignified fashion back to his flagship! In his favour however, a French officer of marines later testified:

> Commodore Paul Jones, far from commanding with haughtiness and brutality, as certain persons have endeavoured to circulate, was always – though very strict and sharp in the service, affable, genteel, and very indulgent, not only towards his officers but likewise towards the sentries and soldiers, whom he ever treated with humanity.

The *Ranger* had been crewed by mostly inexperienced local New England men looking for easy money and to make themselves rich at a stroke, whereas the *Bonhomme Richard* was crewed by good, workaday seamen – however desperate a bunch they seemed at first sight – who were more realistic about their prize money and towards life aboard a man o' war. Maybe Paul Jones changed his ways a little, as Franklin recommended, but he was, anyway, working with different human material.

On the point of departure from France, John Paul gave written instructions to the captain of each vessel in the task force. They were to have proper regard for all orders and signals. They were to keep in company with the squadron. If they lost contact with the squadron because of some emergency, they were to make for the most appropriate location listed in sealed letters of rendezvous. The rendezvous arrangements, necessarily most secret of course, and set within the general context of the orders governing their cruise, proved of great importance during the course of the voyage, though, infuriatingly, none of the sealed letters listing the locations seems to have survived.

7

Tormenting The Lion –
Marauding Around the British Isles

Weighing anchor on 14 August 1779 at 4 o'clock in the morning, the expedition was underway in pleasant summer weather with favourable winds. Little did they realise that not far away across the sea the invasion fleet, becoming increasingly stricken with disease, was on the verge of giving up the grand design, in the face of stony-faced and quite brilliantly calculated inactivity by the smaller British fleet. This approach by the British was reminiscent of the similar, highly successful treatment of the Spanish Armada nearly two hundred years previously, when strong spoiling attacks were launched at the Spaniards only at critical junctures, when they were thought likely to be attempting a landing; then, as now, a moment of terrible vulnerability. At that time of crisis the English were eventually aided by prolonged, violent gales; now their equally devastating ally was raging smallpox. They could not help but see divine providence at work on their behalf yet again.

As far as Paul Jones and the task force now crossing the open sea towards the British Isles were concerned, life was relaxed and enjoyable, with the weather remaining fair. They were quite unaware that, far from being a mere sideshow, the enterprise upon which they had just set out would in the end turn into the main event.

For the present, and not long after the outset of the cruise, their leisurely search for prizes in promising waters brought about their first encounter, with a large fleet of merchant ships. Any stirrings of greedy expectation in the crews were quickly dashed, though, when it was discovered to be a friendly convoy bound for France. This perforce amicable encounter was followed by another – equally fruitless as it turned out – with a ship bound from London for Madeira.

Unfortunately for the crew of the *Bonhomme Richard*, she proved to be a neutral vessel. Her captain was invited to dine with Paul Jones aboard his ship. The two of them would have had a mutual interest in seafaring matters, but more materially there would have been the possibility of gleaning valuable information about ship movements, as well as other news, perhaps even, as the ship was sailing out of London, some inkling of how things were going for the invasion fleet.

Just over a week after setting sail, the task force reached the southwest coast of Ireland, off Cape Clear. By this time they had happened upon their first prize. She was an easy mark, a large vessel named the *Verwagting*, laden with brandy and wine. She was a Dutch ship, but fortunately a legitimate prize because she had been seized eight days previously by an English privateer out of Liverpool. This time, the *Verwagting* was captured by the *Monsieur*. Although this latter ship too was an independent privateer, she was sailing in association with the task force. Her captain, like the captain of the *Granville*, the other privateer in their company, had not signed up to the concordat. Since the privateers were sailing in their company, however, Paul Jones saw the *Verwagting* as having been taken on behalf of the squadron as a whole, with shares in her value to be enjoyed by all concerned. The captain of the *Monsieur* saw things differently. Being a freelancer voluntarily associated with the task force for convenience, and not party to the concordat; he did not, in the final analysis, feel himself bound by mere fellow feeling. He requisitioned the prize, plundered her during the night (according to the Commodore), and on his own authority ordered her off to France under a prize crew, appointed by himself. These moves were thwarted by a furious Paul Jones. He countermanded the orders and redirected the prize, thus making the Captain of the *Monsieur* aware that despite the size, impressive firepower and usefulness of his ship to the task force, he could not ride roughshod over a duly appointed commander-in-chief and simply do as he pleased. The next day – again according to Paul Jones – after lagging behind the rest of them, the *Monsieur* deserted the task force, turning back towards France, her captain no doubt in a state of high dudgeon (though he did return the signal flags). In giving his version of events, Landais later laid the blame for the desertion or departure of the *Monsieur* – the choice

The following labels appear on the map:

NORWAY

Sighting of
Foula: 3 Sep.

Shetland
Isles

Bergen

Pallas rejoins

5 Sep. Shipboard conference
(Landais refuses to attend)

Union incident
as Alliance rejoins

Foula

North
Ronaldsey

Fair I.

6 Sep. Alliance departs, with
prizes, during prolonged
storm: rejoins over 2 weeks
later near Flamborough

Sighting of
Flannan Isles: 31 Aug.

Cape
Wrath

Orkney
Is.

8 Sep.

The Naze
(Lindesnez)

Flannan Is.

St Kilda

NORTH

Skagerrak

Alliance heads
for Foula

SCOTLAND

10 Sep.

SEA

DENMARK

Leith

17 Sep.

Glasgow

Edinburgh

Newcastle

19 Sep.

23
Sep.

Dogger Bank

Belfast

Scarborough

Pallas
disabled

IRELAND

Flamborough
Head

Hull

18:00 hours
22 Sep.

Texel
3 Oct.

UNITED
PROVINCES

26 Aug.
Storm

Shannon

Dublin

Manchester

Granville
Decamps
with prize

Limerick

ENGLAND

Amsterdam

Skelligs

Cork

WALES

Birmingham

Cologne

Barge deserts
Jolly boat 'lost'
Cerf leaves

Mayflower taken

Bristol

London

AUSTRIAN

Brussels

Rhine

Portsmouth

NETHERLANDS

Scilly Is.

Plymouth

19 Aug.
Verwagting incident
(Monsieur departs)

Cape Clear

(Franco-Spanish invasion
fleet on station more than
five weeks during Aug.
& Sep.)

Rouen

Metz

Usbant

Brest

Seine

Paris

ATLANTIC

Lorient

FRANCE

The Bonhomme Richard
Expedition around the
British Isles, 1779

OCEAN

Groix
14 Aug.

Nantes

This map of the 1779 Bonhomme Richard expedition is adapted from that of Samuel
Eliot Morison in his John Paul Jones: A Sailor's Biography. There is often an
irritating discrepancy by one day in the dates given for events, usually arising from the
difference between the calendar date running from midnight to midnight and the ship's
log date, running from midday to midday. John Paul Jones gives the date of the Battle off
Flamborough Head as August 23, the ship's log gives the 24th.

of word moot – on the unreasonable behaviour of Paul Jones. He says that after capturing the prize, the captain of the *Monsieur*, '... took on board some bales of silk goods out of her, which Captain Jones pretended to have a right to have on board the *Bonhomme Richard'*. Landais says that the captain of the *Monsieur* did not think the attitude of Jones towards him to be 'proper', and concludes his brief account by saying that by his attitude, Paul Jones 'made him and the prize depart from our company' – though Paul Jones says he redirected the prize. Midshipman Fanning of the *Bonhomme Richard* talks of 'a violent dispute' between Paul Jones and the Captain of the *Monsieur* prior to her departure from the task force. He says that Jones was furious that the *Monsieur* had been able to make off successfully out of gun range, and in 'exasperation ... struck several of his officers with his speaking trumpet over their heads'.

After the efforts he had made to have the *Monsieur* included as a valuable member of the expedition, her departure so soon into the cruise was infuriating to Paul Jones, and a blow to some of his more ambitious plans. The effect of attempting to exercise his tenuous authority as Commodore over the privateer was unfortunate to say the least, and evidently perceived as high-handed, even though he had the interests of all participants in the enterprise at heart. But would things settle now into a less fraught and more settled routine?

The *Verwagting* incident serves to highlight that despite the elation which must have accompanied their success in taking a valuable prize – and from an English privateer to boot – the seeds of dissension subtly sown by the concordat were already sprouting ominously out of this first serious encounter of the voyage.

Before going ashore in Holland at the end of the expedition, Paul Jones penned a long report for Benjamin Franklin, ultimately destined for the United States President and Congress. It forms the basis of most subsequent accounts. What Paul Jones says at the outset sets the tone, indicating much of the substance of what follows. 'Previous to my departure, I had before me the most flattering prospect of rendering essential service to the common cause of France and America'. He asserts, optimistically, that he had full confidence in every captain under his command to assist and support him 'with cheerful unremitting emulation', being 'persuaded that every one of them would pursue Glory in preference to Interest'. He continues ominously: 'Whether I was or was not deceived will best appear by a simple relation of circumstances.' We know his relation of circumstances is not the straight narrative he makes out, because after the voyage Pierre Landais also penned an account – a rather different one – of the expedition: 'Memorial To Justify Peter Landais' Conduct During The Late War', published in Boston in 1784, several years after the event. It was more detailed and very much longer than the more succinct report penned by Paul Jones immediately upon their return to the Texel in the aftermath of the expedition. Landais was anxious to defend his honour and restore a reputation shattered by the report which Jones submitted, by explaining and justifying his actions, inevitably with a different slant from that of the Commodore, and written under the immediate pressure of a threatened court martial. Landais has been generally regarded as deranged; and with good cause, as contemporaries confirmed in accounts of his behaviour on other quite separate occasions. Always a very difficult man, he may have succumbed mentally under stress with terrible consequences, as Paul Jones was quick to claim. His account has usually been dismissed out of hand as thoroughly unreliable, in contrast to that of Paul Jones, which was lauded in 1959 by Admiral Morison USN, one of his more recent biographers, as concise and to the point, a model of what a report should be.

The substance of Landais's account, however, does not convey any overall impression of madness, despite indications of paranoia, or at least of feelings of persecution – feelings that might have had some foundation in fact! There is some identifiable disinformation: for example, the allegation that Paul Jones ransomed a ship, contrary to their instructions to take prizes, when in fact the vessel in question was ransomed – though on compassionate grounds as it turned out – by Cottineau, Captain of the *Pallas*, to the fury of Paul Jones. There was a heavily pregnant woman on board whom the considerate Cottineau felt should not be subjected to the grossly unsanitary conditions of overcrowded imprisonment ashore. There is also, perhaps inevitably, sustained rancour and animosity in Landais's account. Nevertheless, it is meticulous in its detail, and well reasoned in its argument, which is well presented, well documented, and strongly backed by the crew of the *Alliance* on some crucial matters. It is also consistent on important points with the accounts of other key players in the drama: two defeated Royal Navy captains and Captain Cottineau. Like Landais, Cottineau was anxious to salvage his wounded reputation, and although it makes interesting points, his very much shorter account is coloured by indignant and irrational harangues, even a touch of hysteria. A long time before their court martial proceedings, the two British captains penned detailed reports for the Admiralty, which were also published in the newspapers for all to comment on. These accounts, and any comments that might have impugned them, were of course highly relevant to future proceedings; however, no adverse comments were made regarding either of the British naval officers, whether in the newspapers or during the court martial. Commodore Jones, the officer in command of the task force, was, as might be expected, the first to produce an account, his erstwhile subordinates inevitably responding to the substance and tenor of this, as well as to the actual events of the voyage. There were out-breaks of quite serious fighting between the crew of the *Alliance* and the remnants of the crew of the *Bonhomme Richard* when, after the enterprise had concluded, they were unhappily combined together for a while aboard the *Alliance*.

Details of John Paul Jones's account of the previous cruise aboard the *Ranger* stand up quite well when examined in the context of other, disjointed contemporary accounts and miscellaneous com-mentaries in Britain. On the other hand, we have only his studied word for it regarding the killing of the 'ringleader' in Tobago. The Countess of Selkirk referred to 'a sort of duel' and to a report of 'an unfair stab', but it was only hearsay reported as an aside in a letter to an intimate of hers. In personal letters, Jones could at times be very faux-literary, and convoluted; but in his action reports and the like he is very businesslike and to the point, with an air of mat-ter-of-fact veracity – an impression that Landais, for one, tried to undermine.

While the task force hovered predatorily off the Irish coast towards the end of August, self-serving examination of the entrails of the expedition, and the battle of the printed word which contin-ued for some time, were matters for the future. The battle in print would be given fresh impetus by a later inimical chance encounter between Jones and Landais on the streets of New York.

For the present, the routine lookout for prizes as they sailed up the west coast of Ireland went on as before. Animosity soon manifested itself again. An unsuccessful chase after a large but unidentified ship led to a successful encounter with the brigantine *Mayflower*, bound from Limerick for London with a cargo of butter and salt beef. She refused to surrender at first, but wisely gave in after a couple of educative shots had been fired in her direction. She was sent off to France under a prize crew, though Landais says that his own crew grumbled that he secured for them no share of the potatoes and other everyday provisions taken on board the *Bonhomme Richard* before the captured *Mayflower* was despatched. He alleges that instead of abandoning it in favour of tackling the *Mayflower*, Jones should have continued the pursuit of the much larger mystery ship, as the *Bonhomme Richard* 'was gaining very fast upon the chase'. Jones says simply that the mystery vessel eventually eluded them because she was to windward and they could not come up with her; the *Bonhomme Richard* as adapted for the aborted Liverpool expedition was an acknowledged sluggish sailer. Like other minor bones of contention, these matters may seem somewhat trivial in view of what was to emerge, but they are symptomatic of the niggling personal interplay that finally gave rise to the serious clash of two difficult personalities as the fateful voyage progressed. Fanning goes so far as to assert that after the bitter altercations regarding the large mystery vessel, '… a most inveterate hatred existed between these two captains during the remainder of our cruise'.

Paul Jones was trying manfully to exercise his command of a task force operating under the American flag whose French captains (excluding the associated privateers) had hurriedly been granted nominal United States commissions. It was inevitably a serious drawback that, except for the *Alliance*, their ships were owned and fitted out by the French. Pierre Landais was a Frenchman granted citizenship by one of the American states and commissioned by Congress as a naval captain in command of a brand new warship, the only American-owned vessel in the task force, with American officers and a largely American crew. Conscious of all this, Landais hotly disputed the nature of John Paul's command of his 'associates', as well as questioning the nature and true purpose of the enterprise. As far as he was concerned, commerce raiding did not include land attacks and he was very loath to risk his ship outside the strict letter of his instructions from Franklin. Issued when it was thought that Landais might have to set sail alone due to delays, they referred to 'intercepting the northern trade to England'. The instructions Paul Jones received from Franklin differed in the wording. He believed they enabled him to use his discretion – though Franklin could not be persuaded to be explicit in writing – to stretch the scope of his endeavours beyond mere prize-taking. It is certain that over a period of time Paul Jones had explored with his controllers various possibilities other than, or at any rate complementary to, the capture of prize vessels. As noted earlier, this airing of different ideas, and Paul Jones's continued and alarming enthusiasm for them, may well have been the underlying reason why those often referred to as the 'concerned' – especially the financially interested parties – considered the last-minute, wing-clipping concordat necessary.

After the voyage was concluded, Landais became embroiled in an argument with Benjamin Franklin regarding the object of the expedition. According to the account penned by Landais, Franklin stated that '... the word cruising implied as well landing as remaining at sea', which is more than he would openly concede to Paul Jones. Landais replied to him, quoting his own words: 'I never understood it so, but it was cruising about in a station given'. Franklin stuck to his guns, and according to Landais flatly 'maintained it was not'. Landais recounts that he then asked for a dictionary to be brought and showed Franklin that 'the word cruise was explained much like what I had said'. Franklin, wrongfooted and stepping outside his usual wily diplomatic character, said 'it was a mistake of the printer'. Landais, aghast and nonplussed, told Franklin: 'It was not my fault if there was such [a] mistake in the dictionary, and if he had fully explained his intention, I would have done my utmost to fulfill it'. As for being under the orders of Paul Jones, Landais says that Franklin 'insisted that I was under Captain Jones's orders'. Landais agrees that he was indeed so, as far as the preliminary cruise into the Bay of Biscay was concerned, but that he was no longer under the command of Jones after they returned to port. Franklin's view was that what he obviously regarded as a mere practice foray 'could not be called a cruise out of France, because we had cruised then only in the Bay of Biscay, which was called the French sea'. Landais holds his ground, 'I told him he might give what interpretation he pleased but there were English men-of-war and privateers to cruise for'. Landais says that his orders had not specified any particular place for cruising and that on returning from the Bay of Biscay he did not then know whether any other cruise was intended. He insisted that he had carried out his orders to the letter, but Franklin insisted equally adamantly: 'That cruise was no real cruise'. Landais's reaction was to claim: 'It appeared he was determined to find me guilty, even against his own hand writing proofs to the contrary.'

Off the Atlantic coast of Ireland in late summer 1779, things were about to take a very unexpected turn. Cruising along the rocky coast of Kerry when the wind dropped, the *Bonhomme Richard* found herself becalmed within sight of a brig on her way to Bristol with a cargo of whale oil and wooden staves. Two armed boats were sent across to take her, which they did with no trouble. However, in the flat calm, the current started to take the warship towards the Skellig rocks. The Commodore ordered that his barge, the largest boat on board, be lowered to tow the ship away from the looming danger. The coxswain was the man who had been flogged for causing the undignified return of Paul Jones to his flagship in the fishing smack, and the barge was crewed by six Irishmen. They plied the oars manfully for quite some time but as night began to fall, cut the towrope and rowed smartly for the shore. The third lieutenant Cutting Lunt, who had appointed the coxswain and detailed the boat crew, was appalled at the turn of events. Without waiting for orders he had the jolly boat lowered, and accompanied by two officers and nine men set off in hot pursuit over the deceptively placid sea. They failed to catch the deserters, getting hopelessly lost in a wreathing fog which hung over the area that night and for most of the following day. When the fog eventually lifted the next day and the jolly boat had not returned, a perplexed John Paul sent the eighteen-gun cutter *Cerf* to look for the two missing boats. *Cerf* too disappeared, never to be seen again during the voyage. In due course she found the jolly boat, but inexplicably showed English colours – she had been captured from the English – and fired a gun. Lunt in the jolly boat thought she was an enemy vessel and made off into some lingering fog, getting lost again. He and his crew were by now famished, so they landed to look for food, only to be captured by the Kerry Rangers.

There was nothing comical in this for the hapless Lunt, who did not survive his second spell in a British prison. *Cerf* made back for Lorient, claiming in due course that her mainmast had been broken in a storm on 26 August, and that she had been attacked by a British cutter. Paul Jones cast around, waiting as long as he felt able for the vessels so unaccountably missing, and twice sent out the small corvette *Vengeance* to scour the sea for them. Jones must have been quite relieved when the *Vengeance* returned on both occasions.

During the course of these extraordinary proceedings, Landais had twice come aboard the *Bonhomme Richard*. He was furious at having been forbidden to chase the *Fortune* the previous day; according to Paul Jones because the vessel was perilously close inshore and Landais was a stranger to the coast. Landais was embittered that the boats sent out from the *Bonhomme Richard* had taken the ship. He read malicious intent into the incident, asserting that Paul Jones denied him pursuit and capture simply out of spite, knowing it would further increase the discontent of his crew. But as he gloatingly observed concerning the loss of the successive vessels, 'Captain Jones paid dear with his men for having prevented me from going to take her.'

A great deal of bickering was going on between these two temperamental men. There was talk of a foray into Limerick river to take on a disarmed London privateer and an armed excise sloop which were lying there, or else into Galway Bay where a fifty-gun English ship lay at anchor. Landais said it was too dangerous to hazard his ship in the river, that it was 'inconsistent with the orders I had' and that in consequence he 'would have no hands in it'. However, he says he agreed to attack the fifty-gun ship because they would have the advantage of numbers and perhaps surprise as the fifty-gunner was at anchor and might well remain unaware of their intent until too late; also it 'would deviate but little from the course I was to keep to go on my station'. This last comment reinforces the impression that Landais does not accept that he is under the command of Jones. Eventually the enterprise was not pursued and Landais comments peevishly: 'I suppose it was proposed only in order to have my refusal, that Captain Jones [not Commodore Jones] might make a charge against me, saying that by my unwillingness he missed taking a 50 gun ship'. This comment seems either emblematic of an unstable, poisonous atmosphere, or a paranoiac symptom of the madness with which Landais came to be labelled.

Landais did not miss the opportunity of accusing Jones of incompetence in losing the boats, though he thought mistakenly that they were in pursuit of a prize at the time. When he went aboard the *Bonhomme Richard* he says that he immediately asked Paul Jones what he wanted of him; 'guessing he would try to make me say the loss he had made was not by his fault'. Landais brought up inaccurate and garbled details of setbacks observed from afar which seemed to him to compromise Paul Jones:

> … having no reason to give against what I had said, [Jones] told me 'tis a lie. As he spoke very low, I told him I hoped I had not well understood what he had said, and to repeat it; which he did a second time and repeated a third, saying 'twas a damn lie.

The situation then becomes bizarre:

> I could help my anger no longer. I got up from my seat and told him had he not been on board his own ship I would have punished him as he deserved for giving me the lie the first time, and I offered to go away. He took the key of the cabin door which laid upon the starboard cupboard, and was going to lock the door: I snatched the key from his hand as he was putting it into the keyhole; he tried to take it again out of my hand, but I pushed him off in such a manner as to intimate to him to go no further. Finding he had been too far, and that way would not answer, became as mild as a lamb, tried to exculpate himself, saying that in locking the door, he pretended only to prevent any body coming in.

Landais was having none of such blandishments: 'I told him, he had a sentry outside of the door, whom he could have ordered to let no body come in … I told him before Colonels Chamilard and Wilbert [officers commanding the French marine contingent aboard the *Bonhomme Richard*] the only two there, that I would have satisfaction of him, for his abusive language and demeanours to me', as soon as was practicable. Landais says that Paul Jones replied that '… he would give it to me as soon as we might be on shore, any way I pleased'. Landais says that at this dramatic high point: 'I went away, telling him, I would not come for the future on board his ship.' He went back on board the *Alliance*.

In his account, Paul Jones says he made efforts to correct misapprehensions which Landais entertained, stating: 'He behaved towards me with great disrespect, affirming in the most indelicate language and manner that I had lost my boats and people thro' imprudence in sending boats to take a prize', which was not the case. It was independently reported that in putting over his views, Landais used 'the most gross and insulting terms'.

Landais threatened that the *Alliance* would leave John Paul if he dallied much longer in search of his missing vessels. The Commodore endured the attitude and remarks of Landais with fortitude, as he had information that a fleet of West Indiamen was expected in the Shannon, and he was quite prepared to dally for some time in that vicinity.

Soon Landais announced that he was going off on his own to act independently; doing as he pleased in furtherance of his orders; that could only mean casting around for prizes of course. By the next morning, the *Alliance* had gone, not to be seen again for a week. John Paul had no idea what the capricious Landais had it in mind.

Landais must have believed that the Commodore's Indiamen would not materialise, if he believed that they existed at all. There was an allegation – not without foundation as Franklin eventually discovered – that Landais had been discharged from the French navy because of insubordinate conduct arising out of his quarrelsome nature. In view of his far from adequate experience, it is not easy to explain how Landais managed to get command of the *Alliance* whilst in America. In terms of personality it would have been something of a miracle if he had got along with Paul Jones, who in contrast had demonstrable experience of command and a record of effectiveness. In view of his already invaluable service to the fledgling Republic and his status as Commodore in command of the task force, Paul Jones must have been infuriated when Landais airily told him that he 'was the only American in the squadron and was determined to follow his own opinion in chasing when and where he thought proper', using the only United States warship in the whole, technically American, task force. He said he would act in a similar untrammeled way in connection with 'every other matter that concerned the Service'.

At about this time, the *Granville*, the other privateer in the task force, took a valuable prize. Just as the *Monsieur* had done, she high-tailed it back to France, but in this case with the prize firmly in her exclusive possession. Prizes were not always safe, however, as in the case of Captain Bust's ship the *Porcupine*, bound from Limerick to Bristol and taken by one of the ships of the squadron off the Irish coast around this time. A French prize master was put on board, but according to an extract from a letter in the *Galway Advertiser*, reprinted as far away as Edinburgh, 'The next day Bust threw the Frenchman into the sea, tied [up] the rest of his people, retook the vessel and brought her into Galway.' What happened to the French prize master is not recorded; could he swim one wonders, and how far from land was he when Bust threw him overboard?

Pallas broke her tiller during a storm, which dispersed the ships on the night of 26 August, the same night that the *Cerf* said she was dismasted, and had to heave-to whilst she carried out repairs. Fanning says that aboard the *Bonhomme Richard*, a lower deck gun broke loose during this storm 'and came very near being the means of sinking our ship before we could secure it'.

The dire outcome of this sorry catalogue of events was that at daybreak on 27 August, the *Bonhomme Richard* found herself alone on the ocean; the task force had evaporated. Matters were not made much better when the small vessel *Vengeance* put in a warmly welcomed appearance later in the morning. In his account, Landais says that the morning after the stormy dispersal in the dark of night he decided to make his own way over the empty sea towards Fair Isle.

In fact the expected fleet of West Indiamen did materialize; eight of them, as Paul Jones had hoped. Unfortunately, their arrival in the Shannon was later than expected and took place three days after the squadron had left the vicinity, as he later learned to his annoyance. Considering Landais's threats to leave – as he did – if they tempted fate by waiting any longer, the fact that the Indiamen were missed is not surprising. As he had said when the *Monsieur* sloped off earlier, and might well have wryly repeated now following the recent defection of the *Granville*, his tribulations were partly 'the result of being concerned with privateers, where good faith and honour are generally strangers'. However, there would be prizes enough in future for the remaining ships, if and when they regrouped at their next rendezvous to the north of Scotland; and he had little doubt that *Pallas* would catch up with them eventually.

John Paul Jones knew well enough that a good financial return on the voyage was expected by all concerned in the enterprise; the crews as well as the backers. It was a consideration quite apart from, and to many more important than, any objectives of state and the glory that the pursuit of these might entail. The privateers who had deserted the task force so early in its course were perhaps not too sure about John Paul's sense of priorities in this respect. They were right to be wary, and Landais made no bones about what he thought.

Britain was by now seething with exaggerated rumours of the actions and intentions of the demonic Scotch renegade and his piratical crews, with a lot of speculation and government attention focussed on the Irish Sea. This was not surprising in view of the discovered threat to Liverpool; a plan that, though abandoned, proved a useful smokescreen for the task force. There was speculation amongst the British about the possible use of the Isle of Man as a base for operations in the Irish Sea. The deserters in the barge and the prisoners taken from the jolly boat added their own thoughts as to what was afoot, including tales of 'large stores of combustibles' on board the ships intended 'to burn as many places as he [Paul Jones] could'. They talked of a specific intention to burn Limerick or Galway.

No British warship had sighted the task force, but the *Ulysses* and the *Boston* were sent to search urgently, though mistakenly, into the Irish Sea. This may well have been the result of earlier well-planted disinformation, including hints of a renewed attempt on Whitehaven. Paul Jones had made enough enterprising suggestions to have the British navy dissipated half way around the world if anyone reported them as items of real intelligence and if they were believed. The British concentration on the Irish Sea was very fortunate for the *Bonhomme Richard*, now sailing virtually alone off the west coast of Ireland, far away from any imminent danger of interception by the British.

However, as could be expected, the task force had been sighted and identified off the coast of Kerry, and the Mayor of Limerick, rousted out of the playhouse where he was enjoying a performance, had sent a dispatch to London. One female resident of Limerick described the effect of the sighting on the townsfolk: 'Every face was as long as my arm and as white as a sheet'. In view of the alarms and lurid tales of piracy, there must have been great puzzlement when the inhabitants along the coast heard that when foraging ashore for fresh water and food, the diabolical Paul Jones had actually paid for cattle and sheep that his men commandeered.

Reluctant though he was to desert his missing vessels, Paul Jones now judged that it was high time to leave what he considered to be increasingly dangerous latitudes. Hoping for some response, he fired off some last rumbling signals from his guns, the sound reverberating out forlornly over the empty seas. They listened as the gun-smoke dispersed, but their signals went unanswered. So the *Bonhomme Richard* put on sail and headed off northwards round the Hebrides towards the northernmost tip of Scotland.

As the days passed, the intrepid Commodore ploughed onwards, at a cracking pace most of the time, through the heaving vastness of the Atlantic, well to the west of the Hebrides, with a sighting of the remote Flannan Isles on 31 August. He must have wondered how the invasion of England by the Combined Fleet was progressing, but he was not likely to get much news about such distant events from the crews of prizes taken in these waters. He must also have been very conscious that he was now operating in command of a mere phantom force, and wondering which of his ships he might encounter at the next scheduled rendezvous.

After almost a week of sailing, as day was breaking on 1 September, when the *Bonhomme Richard* was in the vicinity of the aptly-named Cape Wrath, the stormy north-western corner of Scotland, the lookout spotted several vessels. Two of the ships turned out to be the *Alliance* and a prize that she had already taken: the *Betsy*. Once identities had been established, Landais and Paul Jones found that they were both in pursuit of the same quarry, the *Union*, though Landais seems to have been the first into the chase and played the greater part in her eventual capture. As far as the *Bonhomme Richard* was concerned, the chase lasted for about four hours, actually getting underway at seven o'clock in the morning and continuing until finally, out-sailed, their quarry hauled down her colours – or 'Curllers' as the log-keeper quaintly put it – at about eleven. The *Union* proved to be a valuable ship, carrying British uniforms as part of her cargo of mainly naval supplies. Unfortunately, before she was boarded she managed to destroy the 'public dispatches' from London to America, which she was also carrying. Paul Jones records that Landais unwisely hoisted American colours prematurely, whilst deceptive English colours were still flying on the *Bonhomme Richard*. This, says Paul Jones, is what led to the destruction of the dispatches, which were always worth securing from an enemy. Landais says that when a party was put on board the prize from the *Alliance*, the crew of the *Union*, now prisoners of course, were reported to be 'all intoxicated with liquor' and it was even said that they 'threatened to mutiny'. It was arranged, not very amicably it would seem, that whilst Landais would man the *Union* with a prize crew from the *Alliance*, the *Bonhomme Richard* would take her prisoner-crew aboard, presumably still rolling drunk and mutinous; though Landais states that the *Pallas* took them aboard from the *Alliance* later. There are many discrepancies such as this in the often much more seriously conflicting accounts. Maybe the crew of the *Union* was split up for security reasons, but there is no explicit acknowledgement of this. According to Paul Jones, Landais had said that if he manned the *Union* with a prize crew, 'he would suffer no person or boat from the *Bonhomme Richard* to go near the prize'. With a ring of truth, and also with contemptuous exasperation, Paul Jones says in his report to Franklin, and through him to Congress of course: 'Ridiculous as this appeared to me I yielded to it for the sake of peace'. Again it can be seen that the appointment of Paul Jones as Commodore clearly meant little or nothing to Landais, who, despite the terms of the concordat he had signed, relied exclusively on Benjamin Franklin's orders to him personally. This discord notwithstanding; with the capture of the *Betsy*, a pretty good prize vessel carrying twenty-two nine-pounders on her main gun deck and bound from Liverpool to Antigua laden with cargo; as well as the *Union*, things did appear to be brightening up. And one or two less valuable prizes started to accrue, with the *Alliance*, a faster and livelier sailing vessel than the *Bonhomme Richard*, playing a key part in taking them.

Unfortunately, despite the increasing prize money, Landais would still not co-operate in what Paul Jones would consider to be a reasonable manner, and things were getting worse. Paul Jones notes briefly that in the afternoon of the same day that the *Union* was taken, Landais ignored orders to give chase to another ship. Landais, who acknowledges that he was well aware of the signal, says that he had not considered it 'advisable' to pursue for various reasons, the principal one being that he had 'a great many prisoners on board, and but few men left who could be depended upon to guard them'. According to Landais, the *Bonhomme Richard* was in any case better placed in all respects to pursue the distant vessel, 'and had nothing else to do'.

> The brig *Vengeance*, a fast sailing vessel, was already three miles to windward, which Captain Jones might have with more propriety given signal to chase, but he would not, and the vessel got out of sight.

The *Bonhomme Richard* was indeed sluggish, and not what Paul Jones would have chosen for the expedition had he known at the outset that it would evolve so as to consist principally of sea chases. Paul Jones does not go into elaborate detail, tersely noting Landais's disobedience. He also notes in his concise reportage style that on another occasion soon afterwards, Landais ignored another signal: 'I made a signal to speak with the *Alliance* to which no attention was shewn'. Landais, acknowledging his awareness of that signal, says the high wind at the time made an approach 'impossible', but says also that he went to speak with Jones 'as soon as the wind lulled'. He expresses concern that in the event he was simply ordered to 'go and tell the prizes to make more sail'. Landais did this, though he considered it would have been 'more proper' if Paul Jones had ordered the *Vengeance* to carry out the task, as she was a 'fitter vessel for that purpose', and echoing his statement the day before, that she '… had nothing else to do'. He added that in his opinion, 'Captain Jones did it out of spite, to try to put an end to my patience'. In view of the fraught situation between them, perhaps he was right about this!

On 2 or 3 September – there is a discrepancy with regard to the precise date, with Landais indicating the latter – they spotted another ship and gave chase. She turned out to be the *Pallas* which, though her rudder was repaired, had enjoyed no luck with prizes since her enforced parting from them off the Irish coast over a week earlier. They were by now in the vicinity of the Shetlands, well to the north of the Orkneys, and were soon on their way to what Paul Jones calls the 'second rendezvous', attending to essential business by adding to their haul of prizes on the way. Jones does not specify the actual whereabouts of this 'second rendezvous', though he gives some indication: 'I endeavoured to weather Fair Isle and to get into my second rendezvous', which he succeeded in doing during the course of one night's sailing. The *Vengeance* had around this time captured a small Irish brigantine, homeward bound from Norway, but Captain Ricot of the *Vengeance* set fire to this prize vessel because, as recounted by Paul Jones, she 'proved leaky'. Jones was sorry to hear after the event that 'the vessel was Irish property' and that her cargo 'was the property of the subjects of Norway'.

On the evening of 5 September, after rendezvousing somewhere in the vicinity of Fair Isle (Admiral Morison indicates a location between Fair Isle and North Ronaldsey), Paul Jones sent for all the Captains to come aboard the *Bonhomme Richard*, so that they could 'consult on future plans of operation'. Paul Jones says that Cottineau and Ricot complied, but:

> Captain Landais obstinately refused and after sending me various uncivil messages wrote me a very extraordinary letter in answer to a written order which I had sent him on finding that he had trifled with my verbal orders.

Indeed, Paul Jones went to great lengths to get Landais to join them, but to no avail. He had sent Cottineau aboard the *Alliance* to reason with him. Landais says that Cottineau told him that the meeting was to discuss a land-based attack in the Shetlands: 'he told me 'twas to agree together how to land at Shetland'. Landais informed Cottineau that he would 'never go' aboard the *Bonhomme Richard*, the flagship. Landais expands further in his long *Memorial*. He says he asserted before Cottineau:

> ... that I was not under Captain Jones's orders was evident, his mission being to land as he intended to, and mine was to cruise by his Excellency Benjamin Franklin's orders to me.

Landais continued in a more conciliatory tone, with an eye to interpretation by the authorities, should there be a reckoning:

Nevertheless, if he wanted to consult me on any plan, he might do it in writing, or send an officer to communicate it to me verbally, and I would give my opinion thereupon; moreover, though I [am] not under Captain Jones's orders, if he would send them to me in writing, I would do all I could to execute them.

Having listened to this, Cottineau left. At this point in his narrative Landais quotes an exchange of short letters with Paul Jones. The first one, from Jones, is undated, and was taken aboard the *Alliance* by Mease, the purser of the *Bonhomme Richard*. It is addressed by Jones to 'Peter Landais Esq; Captain of the *Alliance*' and simply requests Landais 'to come yourself on board immediately, on business'. It is signed 'your very humble servant, John Paul Jones', with no rank indicated. The reply that Landais returned via Mease, dated 2 September, is similar in style addressed to Jones as 'Captain of the *Bonhomme Richard*' and not Commodore or Commander. The content is brusque, to say the least:

I am to answer your letter that I cannot go! You know why; if you have to ask my opinion upon any business, you'll please to send somebody who may communicate it, or send it by writing.

Landais signed off 'your very humble and obedient servant'! That brought to an end their initial exchanges.

The next communication from Paul Jones was also taken aboard the *Alliance* by Mease. The format and tone had changed, Paul Jones exerting his rank and forcefully spelling out how things stood in more formal terms, no doubt with a view to taking matters further at the conclusion of the operation:

The Honerable [sic] John Paul Jones, of the Continental navy, Commander in Chief of the American squadron, now on an expedition in Europe.
To Peter Landais, Esq; Captain in the Continental navy and of the Frigate *Alliance*, now at sea, and belonging to the said squadron.

You are hereby required and directed forthwith to come on board the ship of war the *Bonhomme Richard*, for which this shall be your order.

Given on board the ship *Bonhomme Richard*, at sea, the 5th day of September 1779.

                                                  John P. Jones

Unabashed, Landais immediately replied, denying Paul Jones any command superiority:

> To Paul Jones, Esq; Captain in the Continental navy, and of the Frigate *Bonhomme Richard*, now at sea.
>
> I shall not go on board the *Bonhomme Richard*, as I told you in my last letter: you know the reason why, for which this is my answer.
>
> Given on board the Frigate *Alliance*, at sea, the 5th day of September 1779.
>
>   P. Landais

This was the end of the extraordinary ship-to-ship correspondence. But Landais, as a precaution, not long afterwards prepared 'certificates' for signature by some of his officers and crew members testifying that he did fall in with Jones's plans to the extent of following in line behind the *Pallas* towards the Shetlands, and having boats, men and equipment ready for any landing.

However, Landais was never put to the test on this, because the next day, before any of these certificates had been prepared, Paul Jones spoke with a pilot boat from Shetland and received information that, as he says, '… induced me to change a plan which I otherwise meant to have pursued'. He does not say exactly what this plan was, nor does he say why he abandoned it, but its nature can perhaps be deduced from the exchanges. Maybe his conversation with the pilot persuaded him that a land attack was not worthwhile, or maybe the pilot passed on interesting information gleaned from other vessels regarding a better prospect. As the date fits perfectly, it is extremely likely that this encounter with the pilot boat is that involving 'a frigate and a sloop' observed for 'two hours' on 6 September by curious watchers in Lerwick in the Shetlands, 'by the help of exceedingly good glasses'. In a letter to a friend, who communicated it to the *Edinburgh Courant,* one of the observers says: 'They carried away a boat and four men from the island of Mousa.' He doesn't say what happened to them.

At this juncture, Landais queries in his *Memoir* the source of Paul Jones's authority to command 'the American squadron', asserting that it did not come from Franklin or Congress as far as he could see, but solely from the concordat. Franklin in due course strongly disagreed, with obvious irritation. Landais claims he was wary of entrapment into disobeying the orders of Franklin by obeying the orders of Jones. 'Seeing into his plan to ensnare me thus', he says, is why he wanted any orders put in writing, as a safeguard for himself later. He claimed: 'Captain Jones always took care not to give me orders in writing to follow him at Shetland.'

Paul Jones could have no illusions by now about exerting control over Landais; it was a hopeless prospect. There was little further opportunity for friction however, because on 7 September the squadron was struck by a gale that, as Jones noted, '… continued for four days without intermission'. Though battered, *Bonhomme Richard*, *Pallas* and *Vengeance* were still together when the gale blew itself out. Contrary winds continued to delay their progress. According to Landais, the *Alliance* lost sight of the rest during the gale and could not make contact again. Paul Jones says: 'In the second night of that gale the *Alliance* with her two little prizes again separated from the *Bonhomme Richard*.' They saw neither hide nor hair of the *Alliance* until more than two weeks later, in the vicinity of Scarborough, many leagues away down the English coast. She was still in pursuit of prizes, as 'the concerned' would have no doubt noted with approval. For the period between his parting from the rest of the squadron until he reached the vicinity of Scarborough many days later, Landais's published *Memoir* – apart from noting a gap which had opened up between his cutwater and the hull – is pretty much a blank.

An independent and personal glimpse into the contretemps between Landais and Paul Jones is provided by Mease, the purser who spoke to Landais and was present when Landais spoke to Cottineau and De Chamillard. The latter vainly tried to impress on Landais the 'absolute necessity [of] joining in consultation with his brother officers' on an 'enterprise of some moment'. They tried to persuade him by citing 'the good of the service', and by warning him of the 'consequences of his obstinately refusing to obey the orders of his commanding officer'. De Chamillard and Cottineau clearly had a different view of their collective responsibilities to Landais, and of the Commodore's role in the task force. Landais not only disregarded their advice, he did not even listen to them politely. According to the Purser, Landais also 'spoke in terms highly disrespectful and insolent' in referring to Paul Jones. Things reached a crescendo with Landais angrily announcing in the presence of the Purser that 'he would see him [Paul Jones] on shore when they must kill one or t'other'. It was at this point that Landais sent over his written reply to the third summons to join the others: 'I shall not go on board the *Bonhomme Richard*, as I told you in my last letter: you know the reason why'.

Perhaps the real reason was that Landais was scared of being clapped in irons if he went aboard. But Paul Jones, with enough to think about in the midst of operations, decided to let things lie for the present. Back in Holland, and after more serious problems with Landais, he complained to Franklin: 'He pretends that he is authorized to act independent of my command [even though] I have been taught the contrary.' And anyway, he continues, '... supposing it to be so, his conduct has been base and unpardonable ... I have been advised by all the officers of the squadron to put Landais under arrest but as I have postponed it so long I will bear with him a little longer.' By which he means until matters could be taken up properly with Franklin.

Franklin, as we have seen, did argue matters through with Landais, though court martial proceedings were not vigorously pursued. Somewhere along the line Landais would no doubt have drawn attention to the subtle difference between the purpose stated in his orders: 'intercepting the northern trade to England'; and the version given to Paul Jones by Franklin: to 'take enemy property in those seas'. As noted earlier, Landais saw their mission as really nothing more than capturing prizes, with a view to maximizing profit – without doubt the real and only purpose of the mission as far as the financial backers were concerned. Doing this was having the effect of diverting some British naval attention in the direction of the task force, however belatedly, owing to their delay in setting sail. From this point of view, what need was there for dressing things up by conducting hazardous and profitless attacks against shore targets – apart from the mere glory of it all? In any case, as the backers would agree, as far as the next scheduled major phase of the cruise was concerned, both 'enemy property' and 'northern trade' meant one outstandingly significant thing at that time of the year: tackling one of the British Baltic Fleets.

The passage of one of these fleets was imminent; a huge escorted convoy of over seventy merchantmen, about to make its customary way out of the Baltic Sea via the Skagerrak, turning southwards of the Naze down through the North Sea via the Dogger Bank, with gradual dispersal of ships to various British ports.

Whatever was planned, the prolonged stormy weather seems to have intervened in the operations of the American task force quite decisively, and even if they had intended to pass across the North Sea to the area between the Skagerrak and the Dogger Bank, the four days of incessant gales followed by 'contrary winds' may well have prevented it. Though their prospects for some concerted and productive action had at first started to look much better when the *Alliance* appeared on the scene again north of Cape Wrath, and were boosted further when the repaired *Pallas* also caught up with them at last close to the Orkneys, the task force was still in a severely weakened condition. In fact, it could hardly be described as a task force any longer. Out of the original complement of seven ships, only three remained together: *Bonhomme Richard*; *Pallas*; and *Vengeance*, the small and lightly armed but very game companion vessel, which had so recently taken the Irish brigantine on her way back to Ireland from Scandinavia.

Bonhomme Richard and her remaining companions never attempted to cross the North Sea from the Orkneys to the vicinity of the Norwegian Naze, foregoing the chance of harrying the Baltic Fleet and pursuing the convoy from the Skagerrak all the way down through the wild expanse of the North Sea to the coast of Britain. They were in no position to do any such thing, because circumstances had so drastically changed. Paul Jones was not to know for sure what escort the convoy might have, and no longer did he have the strength of seven warships to devour the rich pickings to be had amongst the seventy merchant ships and at the same time deal with, or fend off, any escort.

In the face of such adverse weather and unknown enemy strength, Paul Jones judiciously altered his plans before eventually heading for the last rendezvous, which would be Flamborough Head, far down the English coast in Yorkshire. Landais, as events demonstrated, was aware of the significance of Flamborough Head as the final rendezvous, but Commodore Jones must have wondered as he sailed on his way southwards down the east coast of Britain from the Orkneys whether Landais would make an appearance, in accordance with the sealed instructions given to each captain at the outset of the expedition; namely, to keep company except in emergency, and to stick to the rendezvous arrangements. Landais had, they could but assume, chosen to take himself off and operate completely on his own like a privateer, despite his American commission and his obligations to a squadron operating under the new American flag. They would have to wait and see what actually transpired at Flamborough Head.

Sailing well off the east coast of Scotland, Paul Jones could not have felt much satisfaction: 'Yet I did not abandon the hopes of performing some essential service,' he noted optimistically in his report. Nothing spectacular or glorious had yet been accomplished. They took two more prizes off Dunbar, something that would go down well with the backers as well as the crews; but there was little of derring-do or honour in commerce raiding, merely easy profit at the expense of peoples' livelihoods. Paul Jones was in imminent danger of being tarred as a mere privateer, despite all his repeated denials, and the unfairness of such a stigma. He was fully aware of his status as an officer of the Government of the United States, which was at war with Britain; his squadron was flying the flag of the United States; and he had come to Europe to further the interests of the United States by bringing the realities of the war in America home to the complacent British in their home waters. These factors he would bring to the fore in the follwing action.

The two defenceless prize ships taken near Dunbar were workaday colliers outward-bound from Leith, the port of Edinburgh. From their crews he gleaned the information that 'there lay at anchor in Leith Roads an armed ship of 20 guns with two or three fine cutters'. One of the proposals for action, amongst the numerous ones that he had suggested when the plans for the expedition were being worked and reworked, was a fire-raising attack on Edinburgh. This type of attack, with several other likely targets identified in the British Isles, had been commented on and accepted in principle by Franklin as a last resort and with humane provisos. Some action against Edinburgh – echoing the captured crewmen's allegations regarding an incendiary attack on Limerick – may well have been an option locked away safely in John Paul's mind until he saw fit to disclose it. This option was now to be taken.

Unknown to the citizens of Edinburgh, John Paul Jones had chosen as a demonstration of his prowess no less prestigious a target than the capital of Scotland. He planned an aggressive descent on Edinburgh by what remained of his squadron of warships, with the threat of fire. The assault, which would have to be carried out without the assistance of the powerful *Alliance*, was conceived along similar lines to the attack on Whitehaven; altogether more ambitious in scope, but without the same potential for large-scale destruction of shipping. This time, more than four times the number of armed men would be put ashore initially, to be followed up by reinforcements. As at Whitehaven, however, there was a great reluctance on the part of both officers and men to undertake what they thought would be a hazardous and profitless endeavour. It took the Commodore several hours – in fact all night, with coffee at dawn – to persuade the captains of the *Pallas* and the *Vengeance* of the feasibility and the profitability of the operation. It was the prospect of profit more than anything else that eventually carried the argument for Paul Jones. His two colleagues only agreed to involve their ships when a large ransom (getting on for a quarter of a million pounds) was settled upon as an alternative to any destructive fire-raising.

In discussing this type of enterprise, Benjamin Franklin had been insistent on great care being taken for the inhabitants, with any destruction of property as a last resort. John Paul had first tried to persuade his colleagues into an attack for higher, political reasons, but appalling British attacks on civilian targets in America ensured they were unmoved by considerations of 'honour' and 'humanity', if they ever had been; feasibility and profit were the key considerations. Fanning says: 'At length, after many pros and cons, Jones displayed so artfully his arguments in favour of his plan that it was agreed pretty unanimously to put it in immediate execution.' Though it would be without Landais of course, and with an irresistibly huge financial inducement.

By this time the last embers of the operations of the Combined Fleet had been all but extinguished in disease and misery far to the south. In view of 'the Auld Alliance' between France and Scotland against England, the French probably would not have approved of an attack on the Scottish capital, even if things had gone better for the invasion, and certainly not as a mere diversionary ploy. The Jacobite cause was lost as the French realized, and as far as the sober citizens of Edinburgh were concerned it would have been hard to choose which was the more diabolical: Bonnie Prince Charlie or Commodore John Paul Jones. Fortunately for the sensibilities of the French, the squadron was sailing under the American flag.

It is at this point in the voyage that John Paul's conception of the higher interests of the United States of America appears to sideline French interests completely, whether political, martial, or commercial. The evidence is the apparent change of plan, and the prolonged and contentious discussions between Paul Jones and his captains. Landais, of course, would have been appalled at the proposal and would never have been persuaded into the attempt. Cottineau of the *Pallas* and Ricot of the *Vengeance* clearly had no idea what Paul Jones had in mind before the proposal was put to them, and though they objected very strongly to an enterprise which was suddenly sprung on them, they were in the end won over. Landais, as we have seen, touched a nerve in Paul Jones by asserting that he was the only American officer – and with an American ship – in the task force. In contrast to Landais, Cottineau and Ricot were French naval officers who had been granted United States commands by Benjamin Franklin for the sake of the present enterprise, which was financed by the French, who owned the ships, except *Alliance*. As far as Paul Jones was concerned, however, he had been put in command of an American expedition, flying the Stars and Stripes, and directed against the British. England and Scotland were firmly united by then in the political entity called Great Britain (the Act of Union now seventy years old), inhabited not by the Scots or the English but by the British, ruled over by King George, the scourge of the new republic across the Atlantic.

British depredations in America had been most recently exemplified in a purely punitive action against civilian targets by a sea-borne expedition along the coast of Connecticut. Troops were landed at various points to attack and burn out towns and villages and generally terrorise the population. This was probably partly intended to be seen as a reprisal by the British for the alarming attack on Whitehaven that had taken place about a year before, and as a salutary deterrent. On a grand scale, the British showed once more that they were terrifyingly more efficient at causing this sort of havoc than their colonials. The American Congress was outraged, and considered instructing Benjamin Franklin to employ fire raisers to set London ablaze in retaliation, with the Royal Palace and the Houses of Parliament heading the list of targets. They stopped short of actually ordering this fiery reprisal. In his contemplated action against Edinburgh, perhaps this Congressional anger, which had been building to boiling point for some time, put a fire in the belly of Paul Jones.

Someone else had already toyed dangerously with the idea of fire to be deployed devastatingly against the Royal Navy, through the destruction of its support structure by secret incendiary attack against five targets: the major royal dockyards at Portsmouth, Plymouth, Deptford, Chatham and Woolwich. The would-be perpetrator, who was attracted ideologically to the American cause, proposed his services in 1776 to Silas Deane, the sole representative of Congress in Paris at the time, and rather out of his depth. James Aitken had a criminal record and adopted several aliases. He came to be known as John the Painter, from his occupation as a house painter. He was a young and intelligent Scotsman from a notably deprived background in Edinburgh. Deane put him in touch with Dr. Edward Bancroft, living at 4 Downing Street of all places. Bancroft, as noted earlier, was ostensibly an American agent, but was in fact working principally for the British. Dr. Bancroft was landed in an alarming predicament and wanted to see as little of Aitken as possible, after Aitken told him what he had already done and disclosed all of his future plans, which Bancroft could not pass on to the British without ruining himself: the classic dilemma for the double agent. Dr. Bancroft was just over thirty, very intelligent and certainly without scruples, so the dilemma did not completely floor him.

Aitken had methodically surveyed all the Dockyards on his list, and on 9 December 1776, after gaining access to the yard, he set fire to the huge and inflammable rope works at Portsmouth, with great hopes of burning out the whole dockyard; though he only succeeded in completely gutting the rope works. Aitken's next target was the Dockyard at Plymouth, though he contemplated setting fire to Bristol on his way there, attracted by the close-packed wooden buildings of the old city and port. He passed over Bristol for the time being and continued on to Plymouth, where he found the Dockyard to be in a high state of alert. However, not put off by this, he gained access on more than one occasion; but was deterred from carrying out his out plans by the disturbing number of people around, including sentries. He returned to Bristol where, on a number of occasions, he made determined attempts at night to set fire to buildings and shipping, finally succeeding with a fire which destroyed several warehouses and nearby dwellings. There were several similar incidents in England before people began to put two and two together and came to suspect the Americans of the copycat fires. Aitken was eventually identified and arrested on 27 January 1777. He was sentenced to death. Anxious that his mother should not discover his fate, he was hanged on 10 March 1777, only some seven months before Paul Jones embarked in the *Ranger* from Portsmouth, New England, on 1 November 1777, for his spectacular entry onto the world stage. The *Cumberland Pacquet*, on the day of the American fire-raising attack on Whitehaven in 1778, suggested that the 'infernal plan' that day was 'unprecedented, except in the annals of John the Painter'. And certainly, Paul Jones had fire in mind when he turned his attention towards Edinburgh as his next objective.

Leith, the seaport of Edinburgh, is only a stone's throw from Edinburgh Castle itself. The American squadron would carry out the dire threat if they were not bought off, and the heart of the capital could not expect exemption. Paul Jones himself had definitely wanted to carry any attack into Edinburgh itself if possible. It was a dreadful prospect, one that would have to be considered virtually on the instant by the Provost of Leith: half the ransom money was to be delivered within half an hour, with hostages taken to guarantee the rest. One London newspaper went so far as to praise Paul Jones and the American government for moderation and forbearance in suggesting ransom as an alternative to destruction. Though the final plan adopted may have owed something to the captains of *Pallas* and *Vengeance*, the newspaper was sure that Paul Jones, unlike British troops in America, 'has no order to ravage and lay waste the dwellings of the innocent'. The newspaper declaimed: 'What fools and madmen are those who venture to destroy the towns of the Americans in so lawless a manner. Their horrid example brings desolation on this country'. Well, John Paul Jones had not in fact brought desolation to Whitehaven, but it was not for want of trying very hard to do so, and there had been no thought of a ransom there, or of saving the town. As Freeman, who quietly sloped off at Whitehaven, reported to those assembled in Haile's Coffee Room, Paul Jones had anticipated that the flames gushing out like wildfire from amongst the vulnerable shipping would soon leap in amongst the houses and other buildings of the town. Benjamin Franklin had on consideration counselled – indeed commanded – restraint in connection with land attacks; but how would events develop in Edinburgh?

There was a precedent; a sudden attack on Leith and Edinburgh had been perpetrated by Henry VIII. Some two hundred years before John Paul was born, Henry had been furious when the Scots reverted to an alliance with the French. He instigated a 'rough wooing' of the Scots by bringing devastation to their borderlands and by combined sea and land operations against the Scottish capital and its port. The fast-moving land attack developed out of Northumberland, in support of an amphibious attack by troops carried to the Firth of Forth by a fleet of ships assembled in the Tyne, drawn from London and the main English east coast ports. The instructions were ruthless. There was to be a time limit, but fire and sword were quite literally the order of the day; Leith and Edinburgh were to be sacked. Leith was laid low without a fight, and Edinburgh was sacked and devastated by fire as thoroughly as possible in the time available. The attackers eventually left the blazing city and went back to their ships; there was no question then of any humanitarian offer of a ransom, however enormous.

Henry's attack was sudden, and on a large scale: there were around 4,000 border horsemen in the land attack alone. The proposed strike by Paul Jones was on an infinitesimally smaller scale, with complete reliance on the element of surprise, as usual. However, that well-favoured and exploited advantage was lost in the Firth of Forth. His squadron was spotted and correctly interpreted as hostile by telescope some miles off Dunbar, before it even entered the Firth. Furthermore, adverse weather conditions gave rise to protracted ship manoeuvres actually within the confines of the Firth, with the result that the towns and villages on both sides of the water knew something was afoot and were in an apprehensive uproar. The only question was: where would the villain, whoever he was, strike?

He was soon to answer. Jones had taken a prize vessel in the Firth, the *Friendship* out of Kirkaldy, and was using the captain, who foolishly expanded on the lack of effective defences at Leith and Edinburgh, as his pilot. The consternation on shore could be appreciated on board the *Bonhomme Richard* when she was mistakenly hailed as a British ship by the yacht *Royal Charlotte*, requesting powder and shot for the defence of a mansion ashore from the dreaded Paul Jones. To the amusement of the crew, Jones, going along with the misconception, obligingly supplied a hundredweight keg of gunpowder, and actually apologised for having no shot of the right calibre! However, he detained the master – in the name of the British government of course – for his local piloting skills. Chatting with the hapless man and asking for the latest news ashore, he was told in no uncertain terms that the 'rebel and pirate Paul Jones is off the coast, and he ought to be hanged'. John Paul just could not help dramatically revealing his identity. The dragooned pilot was dumbfounded and full of grovelling apology. John Paul was wryly amused: 'Get up man! I won't hurt a hair on your head', adding as an afterthought; 'but you are my prisoner'. Paul Jones was not going to let him blow his cover, which had been artfully arranged, with false ship names and fake uniforms according to Fanning, as well as false flags flying aloft.

Contrary winds still impeded the progress of the squadron on its final attacking run up the Firth. Eventually his ships approached Leith, with Edinburgh Castle only a mile away on its great rock – its terrifying ranks of powerful twenty-four- and forty-eight-pound cannon a forbidding presence, besides which the guns of the warships seemed suddenly puny. Fortunately for the task force, as John Paul knew already, the guns of the fortress could not reach them; and Leith had no gun batteries, being protected only by the relatively weak twenty-gun vessel, which they already knew about (and which sheared off at the approach of the squadron), some even smaller vessels, and a few soldiers. After the raid, a strong fort would be built at Leith, and a large garrison installed in the town;

but in 1779 the door to the Scottish capital was wide open. On 16 September, at about half past four in the afternoon, the steady – but as-yet distant – approach of the task force was spied by telescope from the high ramparts of the Castle.

The seaport of Leith was in ferment as the squadron drew closer, the quayside observed closely for evidence of organised opposition by John Paul. There seemed to be none to speak of. The French officer in charge of the squadron's marine landing force had received his instructions. He was to demand the huge indemnity and to allow only the agreed thirty minutes for acceptance or rejection of the terms. Nathaniel Fanning, on board the *Bonhomme Richard*, says in his memoirs that after thirty minutes the plan was for Leith 'to be set on fire by the squadron with red hot shot' – which he says was at the ready. First though, a letter from the Commodore was to be handed to the Provost of Leith. In it the accompanying marines are referred to ominously as a vanguard, the implication being that there were many more armed men to follow. The deplorable conduct of the British in America is highlighted, but in respect of Leith, John Paul says, 'I do not wish to distress the poor inhabit-ants'. He continues; 'Leith and its port lie now at our mercy, and did not the hand of humanity stay the hand of just retaliation, I should, without advertisement, lay it in ashes'; as he had tried to do secretly by night at Whitehaven. 'Before I proceed to that stern duty as an officer, my duty as a man induces me to propose to you, by the means of a reasonable ransom, to prevent such a scene of horror and distress.' In other words, pay up, or else. But the provost would never be handed the letter.

Though any element of surprise had long been lost due to the adverse winds in the Firth, there was still no sign of serious resist-ance when the boats carrying the marines were lowered away and the ships began towing them astern. *Bonhomme Richard*, *Pallas* and *Vengeance* were closing rapidly to within cannon shot of Leith. Expectantly embarked, the landing force of over a hundred and twenty marines, together with the officer in charge, were soon ready to cast off their towropes and storm ashore.

It seemed at this final moment that nothing could go wrong, but it did. John Paul Jones was thwarted yet again by the weather. A sudden squall hit the ships, turning rapidly into a severe gale. The suddenly terrified soldiers were got back on board only with difficulty. The gale was so severe that one of the prizes sank and her crew had to be rescued. The other prize had to be abandoned and allowed to make off. The squadron was now in an impossible position, with the gale continuing unabated for some time. Another attempt on Leith was out of the question. According to an anecdote recounted by a later traveller, a Mr Henderson, quoted by J. H. Sherburne:

> There was an old Presbyterian minister in the place [Kircaldy on the Firth of Forth] a very pious and good old man, but of a most singular and eccentric turn, especially in addressing the Deity, to whom he would speak with as much familiarity as he would to an old farmer, and seemingly without respect ...

Only a short time before the storm this redoubtable minister of the Kirk was 'seen making his way through the people [clustered by the shore] with an old black oak armchair, which he lugged down to low water mark [the tide then flowing] and sat down in it'. Thus comfortably settled by the sea and glaring out over the waters of the Firth of Forth towards the squadron, he called the Lord to account and cajoled His Divine assistance in very homely terms. He began his singular address accusingly:

> Now deer Lord, dinna ye think it a shame for Ye to send this vile piret to rob our folk o' Kirkaldy; for ye ken they're puir enow already, and hae naething to spaire ... I hae been lang a faithfu' servant to ye, Laird; but gin ye dinna turn the ween [wind] about, and blaw the scoundrel out of our gate, I'll nae staur a fit, but will just sit here till the tide comes. Sae tak yere wull o't.

His self-sacrificing straight-talking to the Almighty had the desired effect, because the wind did exactly what he asked for, it changed direction and blew the scoundrel clean out of the Firth of Forth, never to return. Although he could not be sure who exactly the dissembling scoundrel was, like others, he might have guessed.

Through correspondence in the *Edinburgh Advertiser*, the citizens of the Scottish capital were pretty well informed about machinations involving the Combined Fleet, and the *Edinburgh Evening*

Courant also covered some of Paul Jones's manoeuvres off the Irish coast. However, neither newspaper realised who was causing such alarms on their own doorstep in the Firth of Forth. Paul Jones told no-one (at least no-one who could readily pass on the information) who he was, though it would have soon become plain if the weather had smiled on his endeavours. Whoever the marauder was, and the flags he flew revealed nothing of the truth, the jittery banks were ready to spirit their money out of the city on the instant.

On 18 September the *Courant* carried a long report of the strange events off Leith, The ships seen 'were assumed to be French', close to the truth. The paper reports that:

A swift sailing cutter was sent out to reconnoitre. The cutter fell in with them, and found herself within pistol shot of a French 50 gun ship. She immediately racked [broke away] and fell in with a prize they had taken in the mouth of the Frith [Firth], which she retook, but was obliged to abandon her, for a French 24 gun frigate immediately made up to her. A boy, however, very spiritedly jumped from the prize on board the cutter, which immediately brought him to Leith.

The boy recounted conversations with sailors who spoke English and reported something of what he saw. The sailors said they had intended to come into Leith 'but the violent wind drove them away'. He reported: 'The commander of the 50 gun ship is said to be a Scotsman and to know the coast'. The penny still did not drop however, and the *Courant*, had the following to say in the next issue, on 20 September:

It is presumed that the squadron of French ships who lately visited our Frith, has now left it, as they have not been seen from Leith since Friday evening ... Although this squadron has been on our coasts near eight days, it is yet matter of doubt whether they are French or Americans: however, as they were certainly enemies ships, we are no ways concerned at their departure.

Five days later, on 25 September, the *Courant* still saw no connection with Paul Jones, though they printed a letter from Newcastle-upon-

Tyne which described him as 'hovering about' beyond the bar in the vicinity of Tynemouth. 'It is now the general opinion', says the Courant, 'that the gentry who recently appeared in our Frith, and struck such terror along the coast, were no more than Flushing cutters with prohibited goods'. The newspaper then provides the observation, garnered from who knows where, that 'the largest ship which seemed to carry 50 guns, was a mere deception, three fourths of them being timber'. Showing at least some limit to its credulity, the paper does say that it is not sure whether there is any truth in the conjecture or not. One wonders whether Paul Jones had perhaps been ladling out misinformation; as he had already done in respect of the request for powder; to the great amusement of his crew. By Monday 27 September, nearly ten days later and three days after the epic battle off Flamborough Head, the penny had finally dropped at the Courant, and the connection was at last made between the 'French' ships in the Firth and Paul Jones.

Leith, and the whole of Edinburgh too, breathed a huge sigh of relief when the prolonged threat in the Firth of Forth evaporated. Paul Jones, seriously discomfited by events, must have been in a desperate state of mind at another failure, reminiscent of the outcome at Whitehaven, no matter that it was caused by a trick of the weather and was beyond his control. He would not have forgotten that one of his officers had thought the attack on Leith a reckless undertaking anyway, which in hindsight looked to be a fair call. Had the attack taken place and been successful of course, the words would have been audacious and intrepid, rather than reckless, in America anyway and possibly France. Had Leith and possibly parts of the Scottish capital been reduced to ashes as threatened, because a peremptory and perhaps unrealistic ransom demand had not been met, or could not be met, other words would have sprung to British (and again, possibly French) minds, and the British newspapers would have been singing a different tune.

Leith today is physically part of Edinburgh, but in the 1770s it was a small port, quite distinct from the nearby Scottish capital. Visiting Leith one can appreciate just how vulnerable it was, and how susceptible to the attack which Paul Jones had planned. The old harbour, swamped by later development, is now a heritage site. The curve of the harbour wall seems much as it was, with an old stone signal tower dominating the stretch of buildings and old

1 & 2 The heroic, extravagant marble and bronze sarcophagus entombing the body of John Paul Jones, in the crypt of the Naval Academy Chapel at Annapolis, fittingly surmounted by oak foliage, also in bronze. (Courtesy of the U.S. Naval Academy Museum, Annapolis)

The DELEGATES of the UNITED STATES of *New Hampfhire, Maffachufetts Bay, Rhode-Ifland, Conne&icut, New-York, New-Jerfey, Pennfylvania, Delaware, Maryland, Virginia, North-Carolina, South-Carolina,* and *Georgia, TO*

John Paul Jones, Efquire,

WE, repofing efpecial Truft and Confidence in your Patriotifm, Valour, Conduct, and Fidelity, DO, by thefe Prefents, conftitute and appoint you to be *Captain* ~~of the armed~~ ~~called the~~ ———————— in the Navy Service of the United States of North-America, fitted out for the Defence of American Liberty, and for repelling every hoftile Invafion thereof. You are therefore carefully and diligently to difcharge the Duty of *Captain* by doing and performing all manner of Things thereunto belonging. And we do ftrictly charge and require all Officers, Marines and Seamen under your Command, to be obedient to your Orders as *Captain* And you are to obferve and follow fuch Orders and Directions from Time to Time as you fhall receive from this or a future Congrefs of the United States, or Committee of Congrefs for that Purpofe appointed, or Commander in Chief for the Time being of the Navy of the United States, or any other your fuperior Officer, according to the Rules and Difcipline of War, the Ufage of the Sea, and the Inftructions herewith given you, in Purfuance of the Truft repofed in you. This Commiffion to continue in Force until revoked by this or a future Congrefs.

DATED at *Philadelphia October 10th 1776.*

By Order of the CONGRESS,

John Hancock PRESIDENT.

ATTEST. *Cha Thomson fecy*

From the Original in possession of Col. John H. Sherburne, Author of "The Life and Character of John Paul Jones".

3 *The captain's commission granted to John Paul Jones by Congress in 1776. After his death this document came into the possession of Colonel J. H. Sherburne. Sherburne used it as the sole illustration in his substantial biographical work (see bibliography). This illustration is taken from Sherburne's edition of 1851. The original commission, with some later blemishes, is now in the possession of the U.S. Naval Academy Museum at Annapolis, whose representatives kindly approved reproduction here.*

4 *Jones's brother William's house in Fredericksburg, Virginia. John Paul Jones would spend twenty months in America, more or less in obscurity, most of the time at Fredericksburg. 'America,' Jones declared many years later, 'has been my favourite country since the age of 13, when I first saw it.' (LOC)*

Left and above: *5 & 6 Engraved goblet marking the launch of the Whitehaven slaver* King George. *It was aboard the* King George *that Paul Jones, urgently seeking work when his apprenticeship collapsed, eventually sailed as third mate (see page 17). One side of the goblet displays the only image of the ship herself, the other the Royal Arms. Engraved above the ship is the motto: 'Success to Whitehaven's African Trade' – meaning the slave trade of course. However 'successful' the* King George's *maiden voyage to West Africa might have been (and slaving was lucrative), the 'middle passage' across the Atlantic from Africa, most probably from the Windward Coast, to the Americas, would have been a harrowing experience for the 17-year-old John Paul. But he was not put off further trips. (Courtesy of Copeland Borough Council and The Beacon, Whitehaven)*

9 A hand-coloured
lithograph of the great
scientist and statesman
from the New York
firm of Currier and
Ives, produced in
1847. Franklin was so
popular in France that
it became the custom
for wealthy French
families to hang a
portrait of him in the
drawing room! (LOC)

Opposite above: 7 Liberia, the first African Republic, is situated on the old Windward Coast favoured by Whitehaven slavers. Benjamin Franklin was one of the main architects of American Independence, as well as being the American diplomat in France to whom Paul Jones was principally accountable. Franklin, a keen abolitionist, was on the point of securing the abolition of slavery by Congress soon after Independence, when a last-minute spoiling amendment by slaving interests thwarted the move. The initiative that eventually created Liberia as a haven for freed slaves was American, with Franklin a contributor. The American connection carried on after Liberia declared itself a republican state in 1847, the government institutions of Liberia being modelled on those of the U.S.A. This 1976 Liberian stamp marked the bi-centenary of the American Declaration of Independence. (Courtesy the Liberian Embassy, London)

Opposite below: 8 The Reception of Benjamin Franklin in France by C. Brothers, c1882, New York. The utterly stylised, romantic scene indicates what a strong hold the story of Ambassador Franklin in Europe had on the American imagination. (LOC)

1. *General Washington.* 2. *General Gates.*
3. Dr *Franklin.* 4. Prəʃid *Laurens.* 5. *Paul Jones.*

10 Heroes of the American Revolution. This engraving by Daniel Berger of 1784 shows George Washington and Horatio Gates in right profile, Franklin bottom right, and Henry Laurens bottom left. John Paul Jones, as so often, is centre stage. (LOC)

Opposite above: *11   A section from a long panoramic engraving of Whitehaven Harbour by W Westall, published in 1834. The huge coal staithe building is to the left of the white lighthouse, looming up behind the clustered ships. There were changes to the harbour by 1834, but the Staithe was still there. (Courtesy Cumbria Library Service, Carlisle)*

Opposite below: *12   Whitehaven Harbour 1780 (Artist unknown). Painted only two years after the American raid, details of the lighthouse and harbour building are clearly depicted. (Courtesy Tullie House Museum and Art Gallery, Carlisle)*

Left and below: *13 & 14 The Old Quay today. The lighthouse, with its sundial, is much as it has always been; but the harbour building is substantially changed, having been added onto during the course of the nineteenth century. Both the lighthouse and the adjacent building have been more or less neglected for many decades. A sad fate for two of Whitehaven's oldest and most prominent historical features.*

Above: 15 *Said to be the only gun surviving from the day of the attack on the Old Fort, barrel buried deep, used as a bollard on the quayside. The gun was dug out quite recently for conservation prior to more appropriate display.*

Below: 16 *Known as 'Long Tom', a Half-Moon Battery gun long lost, but rescued from the beach near Tom Hurd's Rock after being exposed by the action of the sea in 1963. It is a 32-pounder, now situated not far from the site where the buried Half-Moon Battery once stood. The view straight from the barrel is towards the barely revealed Tom Hurd's Rock.*

Above and opposite: *17, 18, & 19 A very professional-looking Jones as now portrayed on the signboard of the 'John Paul Jones' public house (above). It replaces the villainously piratical looking image (below right) that once featured there; before Jones was formally 'pardoned' by Whitehaven in 1999, with the U.S. Navy in attendance. Affixed alongside the pub door, these oval likenesses (the one at the top replaced the one at the bottom) epitomise the favourable transformation of John Paul's reputation in Whitehaven: though not everyone approves! Contrasting though they are, both these depictions, judging by the eyes, seem modelled on the portrait of Jones by the celebrated 18th-century French artist Moreau (see plate 36). Artists' portrayals of Paul Jones, even those taken from life by contemporaries, are startlingly varied, as though representing quite different people.*

John Paul Jones

20   *A French view of Jones (left); engraving by Carl Guttenberg after a painting by C. J. Notté, completed some time in the 1780s. Jones reaches for one of his pistols. A lengthy note accompanied the print, describing the action off Flamborough Head. (LOC)*

21   *A less aggressive portrait of Jones, with telescope and and anchor, mezzotint published in 1779, artist unknown. (LOC)*

22 *The idiosyncratic and ornate Achievement of Arms conceived by Paul Jones around 1777 in New England, just before he took command of the* Ranger. *(Provided by the National Heritage Museum, Lexington, Massachusetts, with kind permission of the Grand Lodge of Masons in Massachusetts, Boston)*

Left: 23 *A lesson in how to spike a gun. Bronze life-size figure, part of a tableau of three cannon situated close to the site of the Old Fort, where the Americans boldly scaled the wall, Paul Jones in the lead, and hammered the spikes home, though presumably with a muffle of some sort for the hammers. (Author's photograph, by kind permission of W3M Charitable Trust, Whitehaven)*

Below: 24 *The Earl of Selkirk's House, as it was in the eighteenth century; in peaceful seclusion on St. Mary's Isle. (Courtesy the Stewartry Museum, Kirkcudbright)*

Right: 25 *Portrait of the Countess of Selkirk who, heavily pregnant with her twelfth child, dealt so coolly with the crew of the Ranger when the tranquility of the Isle was so rudely disturbed by the 'press gang'. (Courtesy the Stewartry Museum, Kirkcudbright)*

Below: 26 *Almost omitted from the loot in the flurry of events at the house, this silver teapot, still containing wet tea leaves from breakfast, was thrust into a bag along with the rest of the silver tableware; all to be returned later to the Countess, as promised by Paul Jones, at his own expense. (Provided by the Stewartry Museum, Kirkcudbright, courtesy of Sir David Hope-Dunbar, who eventually inherited this souvenir of the raid on St. Mary's Isle)*

Above and below: *27 & 28 Carrickfergus Castle, commanding the small harbour at Carrickfergus and overseeing Belfast Lough, where the* Drake *was lying at anchor until alerted and drawn out to sea by Paul Jones. (UK postage stamp image courtesy of Royal Mail)*

CARRICKFERGUS CASTLE

29 *View near the promontory of rock and sand dunes stretching northwards from Durness in the north of Scotland, showing Loch Eriboll, from whence Bonnie Prince Charlie was spirited back to France after the failure of the 1745 Jacobite rebellion. This place would have been one of ill omen for the British, as they grimly outfaced, yet again, the threat posed by a powerful Armada (Franco-Spanish this time), far off on the south coast of Britain. Before 1745 there had been five attempts to restore the Stuarts. At least three of these, especially that in 1715, had serious potential, involving foreign assistance and action in the south of Britain as well as in the north – a distraction ploy similar in principle to that of 1779. There was to be no comeback for the Stuarts; though the ill and ageing 'Bonnie Prince' could have been dragged out of his cups if there was a chance!*

30 *Leith: target for a ransom demand, with dire menaces! A public information plaque on the quayside, showing a fine 18th century view of Leith harbour. Leith's vulnerability to attack was luckily untested by Paul Jones, because of a sudden and dramatic change in the weather.*

31 Portrait of Captain Richard Pearson, Commodore in command of the British at the Battle off Flamborough Head. Though he struck to Paul Jones (after the longest ship-to-ship fight in British naval history), Pearson fulfilled his prime responsibility of preserving intact the Baltic fleet of merchant ships under escort by himself in the Serapis and Captain Piercy in the Countess of Scarborough. Pearson was knighted after the battle, and eventually ended his days in charge of the Royal Naval Hospital at Greenwich. One of Captain Pearson's sons, another Richard, attained the rank of Vice-Admiral. (© National Maritime Museum, London)

32 *The cliffs at Flamborough, where crowded sightseers thronging the cliff tops stared out towards the lurid night battle scene, as Paul Jones and his squadron engaged the British warships. The battle took place in rapidly gathering misty darkness towards the end of September, between about 7.00 and 10.30 pm.*

33 *The theatrical atmosphere of the battle scene off Flamborough Head, captured vividly in an oil painting by James Hamilton in 1854, entitled 'Capture of the* Serapis *by John Paul Jones'. It depicts the terrible scene as it would have been viewed by the thrilled and appalled spectators lining the cliffs. It conjures the seasonal darkness and obscurity, with the glare of fire, and the mingling of clouds, mist and drifting gunsmoke, the moon shining only fitfully overhead. The main combatants, soon grappled inextricably together, are indistinguishable. The three other ships present can barely be made out in the surrounding gloom. (Courtesy Yale University Art Gallery, Mabel Brady Garvan Collection)*

Above: *34 'Combat Memorable entre Le Pearson et Paul Jones', a hand-coloured engraving by Balthasar Leizelt after the painting by Richard Paton, reversed (page 184). Here, the battle looks to have been fought in broad daylight. Even the resourceful ladies of Portsmouth, New England, could not have provided such sails. (LOC)*

Left: *35 This 1780 London mezzotint shows Jones theatening to shoot a sailor who had attempted to strike his colours at Flamborough Head; an exaggeration of the original story that Jones hurled his pistol at the chief gunner for the offence, dropping him to the deck. The original is housed at Annapolis. (LOC)*

36 *This well-known portrait of John Paul Jones by J.M. Moreau Le Jeune was engraved in Paris, in the heady atmosphere of adulation which followed Paul Jones's dramatic victory over the* Serapis, *and a year after his attack on Whitehaven and the capture of the* Drake. *(Courtesy collection of the New-York Historical Society, New York)*

37 & 38 The unique, belated Gold Medal awarded to John Paul Jones by unanimous vote of Congress in 1787, with his portrait on the obverse and the battle scene off Flamborough Head on the reverse; the location of the battle mistakenly given in the superscription as off the Scottish coast; which Jones must have found irritating! (Courtesy the United States Naval Academy Museum, Annapolis)

39 *The famous portrait bust of Paul Jones by Houdon, a fellow Mason in the Nine Sisters Lodge. Commissioned by the Lodge, several castings were made. It was sculpted and cast in the heady aftermath of the Battle off Flamborough Head, and highlights his new status as a Chevalier by featuring the eight pointed star of the 'Ordre du Mérite Militaire', awarded by the King of France, suspended by a ribbon on his breast (seen more clearly in plate 51). The bust above is now at the U.S. Naval Academy. (Courtesy the United States Naval Academy Museum, Annapolis)*

I have not yet begun to fight

John Paul Jones
US Bicentennial 15c

40 *The portrait of John Paul Jones by Charles Willson Peale (1781), reproduced on a bicentenary stamp of 1976 (see plate 51). The image perhaps goes some way to explaining John Paul Jones's undoubted success with women. Readers outside the US will by now appreciate why the words quoted above the portrait have such ringing significance for Americans today. The original portrait is located in Independence Hall, Philadelphia.*

41 'The Russian bear and her invincible rider encountering the British Legion.' The cartoon, published in London by W. Holland in 1791, shows Potemkin in Hussar's uniform riding Catherine the Great dressed as a black bear. They approach George III and his ministers, William Pitt, Salisbury and Edward Thurlow, who are carrying spears, three of which have their points broken off. Even as early as the end of the 18th century, the 'Great Game' was afoot and a major war between Britain and Russia over control of Asia, as the old Islamic orders decayed, seemed inevitable, once the threat from France to both nations faded. More immediately, the British were exercised by Catherine's territorial ambitions around the Black Sea, in the Balkans and Greece. She wanted Constantinople in order to place her grandson — Alexander — on the throne of a new Greek Empire. The cartoon is of course riddled with doubles entendres. (LOC)

Above: 42 *This lampoon of 1780 features both Catherine the Great and John Paul Jones. Catherine, with caduceus and sword, attacks the dog, England, along with members of the Armed Neutrality League. In the background, the 'Queen of the Sea' hangs by her wrists from the gallows and is flogged by Jones. The figure on the far right with a feather in his hat is an American. The title of the cartoon, 'Loon na Werk', translates as 'A Due Reward'. (LOC)*

Below: 43 *The humble cottage birthplace of John Paul Jones at Kirkbean, the grey sky merging in the distance with the waters of the Solway Firth.*

44 & 45 *Captain Richard Pearson's birthplace was shown to me near Appleby in the Vale of Eden, in the English county of Cumbria. But this more modest stone-built house, in exactly the right place, at Langton, is much the more likely candidate. It has a dated lintel (1697) displaying the initials R and I, surname P. The house was pinpointed in a welcome response to a letter of mine in the* Cumberland and Westmorland Herald *requesting information. Evidence is not yet conclusive. Captain Pearson's father, and very likely his grandfather, were also named Richard. His mother's name was Hanna. The date is about right for his grandfather's marriage to a miss 'I' (or 'J'). Pearson was the eldest child in a very large family, and attended the local grammar school in nearby Appleby.*

46 & 47 Picturesque Caerlaverock Castle, once the centre of power of the notorious Maxwell clan, or 'name', to use the local idiom, is situated not far from the birthplace of John Paul Jones at Kirkbean, across the wide estuarial waters of the River Nith. How much influence did the lurid folklore and wonderful border ballads based upon the bloodcurdling deeds of such men, have on the young John Paul Jones, and on his later actions?

48 & 49 *Freemasonry was always part of John Paul Jones's adult life. The compass and square, here on the Masonic Arms in Kirkcudbright, featured in his fake Achievement of Arms. Dated 1790, the Masonic Arms was once the hall of the St. Cuthbert's Lodge, built when the general area was redeveloped just before John Paul's death in Paris. The St. Bernard's Lodge, where he gained early acceptance into the Masonic brotherhood, was closed in 1816, though the minutes recording him are still extant. Jones's burial was attended by brethren from the Nine Sisters Lodge.*

Above: *51 Portrait of Chevalier John Paul Jones, by Charles Willson Peale (1781). Jones is wearing on his breast the cross of the 'Ordre du Mérite Militaire'. This painting in oil is perhaps the most sensitive portrayal of Paul Jones by a contemporary artist, concerned rather with his personality than his heroic status. Ivak the Cossack boatman said he had never before met a man like Jones: 'As sweet as wine when he wanted to be, but when necessary, as hard as a rock.' Richard Dale, who served under Jones on the* Bonhomme Richard *and knew him well as a friend, considered Peale's portrait to be an 'excellent likeness'. Is there any trace here of Helmy? (Courtesy Independence National Historical Park, Philadelphia)*

Opposite: *50 The haunting image of Baroness Helmy Weissereich, who turned up in 1926 at the American consulate in Riga, claiming descent from Paul Jones and Anna Kourakina, a Russian Princess and maid of honour at the Court of Catherine the Great. This photograph appeared in the* New York Times Magazine *on the 23rd of September 1934. (*The New York Times *is part of the American Newspaper Repository Collection, image courtesy the Rare Books, Manuscripts and Special Collections Library, Duke University, Durham, NC, U.S.A.)*

JOHN PAUL JONES said:

'I have not yet begun to fight'

Fight with War Stamps & Bonds

52 *Just as Theodore Roosevelt had exploited the John Paul Jones legend in his attempts to build US naval power prior to the First World War, so in the Second, Jones was called to the colors to sell war bonds in 1942. The artist was James H. Daugherty, who opted for a circle of stars in the flag. (Courtesy University of North Texas Libraries, Denton)*

pubs alongside. The Signal Tower was originally a large windmill, and would have drawn Paul Jones' eye as he surveyed the reassuringly quiet scene on the waterfront from outside the harbour. The battlements now surmounting the tower were added during the Napoleonic Wars, when the old windmill did in fact become a signal tower. How many of the inhabitants of Leith, one wonders, were aware that the Paul family hailed from Fife, and that John Paul Jones's paternal grandfather kept a roadside inn just outside Leith?

Paul Jones had been defeated by the weather at the last instant, but resilient as always, he did not despair for long. As his depleted squadron progressed through British coastal waters southwards from the Firth of Forth, a sense of consternation was rippling down from Scotland to the people on the English seaboard. In some places the local militia was mustered and everywhere the cruise was in the news, whether through the papers or more often by alarmist word of mouth. Having diverged pretty fundamentally from the terms of the orders regulating the voyage, or at least their ostensible meaning, and with no success ashore at Leith to compensate, Paul Jones turned his attention more towards the substance of his mission as perceived by the French (if not by Franklin).

He continued and intensified the plunder of shipping, but also posed a threat of land attack along the coastline from Scotland through Northumberland and soon down into Yorkshire, especially in the vicinity of the Humber, galvanizing the citizens of Hull and causing panic at other coastal locations and around Flamborough Head. The foundation of the John Paul Jones historical legacy was set down as he sailed ever southwards from Scotland, taking prizes and provoking panic on shore. The following local anecdotes are an exemplar of how such legends come about.

According to Admiral Morison, as the *Bonhomme Richard* passed from Scotland down the coast of Northumbria, Paul Jones found time – no doubt to the amusement of the crew who would most probably have placed bets on it – to loose off a distant sporting shot at Bamborough Castle, something of a ruin by that time and not thoroughly renovated until the nineteenth century. Morison says that the iron ball missed the old fortress glowering down from its rocky prominence above the sand dunes lining the windswept beaches of Northumberland, and instead became an extraordinary souvenir of the American corsair when it landed with a crash in the garden of a nearby house. There, writes Morison in 1959, it 'is treasured by the owner's descendants to this day'. When I visited Bamborough recently to have a look at this curious memento, I could not find it; nor could I find anyone who knew anything about it, despite enquiring around the village itself, at the Castle, and in the county reference library and archives. There was not a trace, and no local recollection of such an event. I did, however, find that the story is told in pretty much the same way about Alnmouth, about fifteen miles further down the coast towards Tynemouth. It is recounted in Tomlinson's 1897 *Guide to the Northumberland Coast*:

> On September 23ʳᵈ 1779, Paul Jones, who had been cruising about the coast of Northumberland the whole day, appeared off Alnmouth at six o'clock, and at eight took a brig. He then continued his way south, after firing a cannon shot at the old church.

Situated on a hill then connected to Alnmouth by a substantial sandy isthmus, this imposing, but by then ruinous, Norman church might well have been mistaken for Bamborough Castle as the *Bonhomme Richard* hovered near the small port in the rapidly fading light of day.

> The ball missed, but grazing the surface of a small field east of Wooden Hall, struck the ground and rebounding three times, rent the east end of this farmstead from bottom to top. It weighs 68 pounds and is in the possession of Roger Buston Esq., of Buston, a country house about a mile and a half south-west of Alnmouth.

This ball, which I saw, is at the time of writing in the possession of Gordon Farr of Wooden Farm, as is a smaller ball 'about a third of the size' according to Mr. Farr, and much more like a ball from one of the *Bonhomme Richard*'s eighteen-pounders. He could not lay his hands on this very well preserved second ball, which he found whilst ploughing close to the farmstead some years ago, lying in the right location for a shot but having no acknowledged connection with Paul Jones. The sixty-eight pound ball, which Mr.

Farr says has always had the long-established connection – he is adamant on this point – now weighs about sixty-four pounds, having been drilled to take a hollow spike and been much corroded by long exposure to the weather; placed as it was atop the gable end of a building.

At least one other account alleges that Paul Jones fired several shots at Alnmouth itself, in addition to the shot which missed the old church; and that after the battle off Flamborough Head, he also fired shots at the small coastal settlement of Skinningrove, further to the south on the coast of Cleveland. This was the type of minor, but alarming – and perhaps apocryphal – activity that caused the panicky mustering of troops in anxious anticipation of another landing attempt, and generated a disproportionate state of alarm down the length of the eastern seaboard. During the eighteenth century a number of naval encounters involving French warships and privateers occurred off Alnmouth, and elsewhere up and down the coast (off Tynemouth for example), but none were linked to landing attempts enough to really panic the inhabitants, unlike the events in Whitehaven the previous year and Paul Jones's designs on Limerick and Leith. There was much potential for confusion between hostile actions by Paul Jones and by the French and Spanish, who were both now at war with Britain again. The sixty-eight pound ball is the one linked to Paul Jones, but did he fire the shot in the evening of 23 September? According to Paul Jones himself, as he reported officially to Benjamin Franklin, he was on that evening engaged in mortal battle with the British from around 7.00 p.m. until about 10.30 p.m. In his study, 'John Paul Jones and the Battle off Flamborough Head' (American University Studies, Series Nine, History, Vol. 82) Thomas J. Schaeper puts forward a powerful case for changing the date of this battle from 23 to 24 September. The log of the *Bonhomme Richard* also places this battle in the evening of 24 September. Paul Jones, the lead player in all this and naturally followed by most others, misrecords dates on more than one occasion (for example off Cape Wrath as mentioned earlier), pointing to some confusion between the calendar date (running from midnight to midnight) and the log date (running from midday to midday). The date would make little real difference as far as action at Alnmouth was concerned, because at the relevant time Paul Jones seems to have been stirring things up quite far away, amongst the shipping around the Humber and Flamborough Head. Could another vessel in Paul Jones's squadron have loosed off the ball that was attributed to the bogeyman himself? The *Alliance* would seem to be the most likely candidate. Missing from the squadron since the storm off the Orkneys, she had been doing her own thing for more than two weeks, until she eventually rejoined the others, in company with *Pallas* whom she had not long encountered. Both were not recognized, though they were spotted during the night, until very early in the morning of either the 23rd, as Jones says, or according to Schaeper, the 24th. A brig was taken off Alnmouth, and afterwards Landais could have fired a parting shot or two at the old church on its prominent sandy isthmus, mistaking it for Bamborough Castle. It would have been an uncharacteristic action perhaps, but maybe the crew wanted that bet!

We come to the difficulty that the discerning reader will have already pinpointed, the massive size of the cannon ball. At sixty-eight pounds, it is nearly four times the weight of one of Jones's eighteen-pounders, his largest ordnance. The *Alliance* did not even have 18-pound shot on board, and no ship in the squadron is recorded as having a sixty-eight pound carronade, or 'smasher', as this large, short-range gun was familiarly called. A 'smasher' was useful for landing a devastating ball on a nearby quarterdeck, but although lying in exactly the right direction to receive a chance cannon ball misfired at the elevated old church, Wooden Hall would have been over a mile from any ship reasonably placed to fire off a ball. Mr. Farr had a marvellous stroke of luck in finding the smaller cannon ball, which lay not only in the right place for a stray shot but in a spot quite likely to have been part of the garden of Wooden Hall, which was demolished in the nineteenth century to make way for Wooden Farm on much the same site. Could the ball have been lost in the overgrown garden, and found again by the plough? Mr. Farr has a wonderful talking point in his two cannon balls; but the larger of the two could not have been an extravagant *carte de visite* from John Paul Jones.

Of course, Paul Jones – with weightier things even than the ball of a smasher on his mind – was unaware of the rich trail of half-truths he was leaving around the British Isles; unshakeably linked with his name. Thwarted by Nature in the guise of a sudden squall at Leith, and no doubt in a desperately determined state of mind, he hovered menacingly in the vicinity of the wide estuary of the Tyne. His actions in the neighbourhood were reported in the *Newcastle Courant* on 25 September 1779, including information in letters sent to the newspaper by various informed correspondents. There were letters from Edinburgh and Leith, dated 19 September, regarding 'French ships in the Firth, which they supposed to be the noted Paul Jones'. The *Newcastle Courant* reports: 'On Sunday morning they appeared off Tynemouth bar', and took the *Speedwell*, a sloop carrying timber from Hull to the Tyne, 'about four leagues off Tynemouth bar'. The *Speedwell*'s Master, John Watson, gave an interesting account of what he saw and heard before he got back to Newcastle. He says that Paul Jones's ship was present, though he did not know her name and mistakenly thought that she was armed with forty-four eighteen-pounders. He says that *Pallas* was the vessel mainly concerned in capturing his ship, as well as another, the *Union*, which he described as being 'a Chatham brig'. He reports that Paul Jones and Cottineau disagreed about these two ships. Paul Jones wanted to turn the brig into a fireship and 'send her into Shields harbour', but Cottineau vetoed the scheme. For his part, says Watson, Cottineau wanted to ransom his sloop the *Speedwell*, 'as she had a woman on board big with child'. Paul Jones would not agree, 'saying his orders were to ransom none, but to burn, sink or destroy all'. However, on the next day, 'about 12 leagues off the land between Scarboro and Filey Bay', Cottineau did ransom Watson's sloop, for three hundred pounds (keeping the mate hostage for the money), and sank the brig.

Watson considers that, had the heavily pregnant woman not been aboard, Cottineau would also have sunk the *Speedwell*. He seems a sound, independent eyewitness to these matters, which both Paul Jones and Cottineau refer to in their differing accounts of the cruise, as we shall see. Watson says, in passing, that Jones '… had one or two, and the *Pallas* four or five English masters on board whose ships they had taken and destroyed'. Interestingly, Watson also states that Cottineau described himself in his ransom document as 'Captain of a man of war in the service of the United States of America, and commander of the American frigate the *Pallas*'. At this point, Watson noted: 'They hoisted and fought under English colours,' though he says that they also had 'both American and Swedish colours.'

In the same issue of the *Newcastle Courant* there is another report of an encounter with Paul Jones's squadron roving off Tynemouth. The *Prospect*, an eighteen-gun 'light collier' of Newcastle, commanded by Captain Cram and on her first voyage from London, found herself 'becalmed near Jones's ship for some time'; an uneasy predicament for the crew, and no doubt an agonising temptation to Paul Jones! Cram 'made preparations to engage if attacked' and asked the crew if they would stand by him, upon which they all affirmed, 'to the last!' One of them declared that 'he would rather have a 36-pounder in his guts than go into a French prison'. The loyal vow would not be tested nor the ball in the guts suffered because the *Prospect* escaped Paul Jones's clutches when a fresh breeze sprang up, and the crew got her safely into port.

The *Courant* received another letter, dated 21 September, from Sunderland this time, then just a little way south of the Tyne estuary; though now, like Newcastle, part of the wider Tyneside conurbation. Observers were 'persuaded' that ships they saw were Paul Jones's squadron 'from the description of his ships and the numbers of men we discovered by glasses to be aboard them'. They noted that 'the largest ship' – the *Bonhomme Richard* of course – had 'his main top struck for a decoy, as if carried away'. The top-mast was not in place, right enough, but was not removed for decoy purposes; having been taken down to carry out essential repairs, says Paul Jones in his report to Franklin; repairs which caused the *Bonhomme Richard* to leave the vicinity of the Tyne later than the rest. According to the watchers, Jones at one point signalled his other ships 'to chase some loaded colliers which had sailed from Shields that morning'. Luckily, says the newspaper's correspondent, 'being a good way ahead, and having a favourable wind, they got safe away'.

The watchers were right in their surmise about the identity of the squadron, and were able to warn the captain of the *Ferret*, a very eager, but small, government cutter, that his ship was about to take on a number of warships by herself, and not the small one he was aiming for (probably the *Vengeace*) The Captain of the *Ferret* mistook the larger ships for friendly 'government armed ships', which would have been a fatal error had he not got the watchers' scribbled message delivered by a cobble, and sheared away from the scene in the nick of time.

Reading newspaper reports from places along the east coast of Britain and elsewhere, it soon becomes clear what a scourge the depredations of privateers – and pirates for that matter – constituted on the seas between Britain and the Continent of Europe in the eighteenth century. Confusion as to exactly who was who was bound to arise at times; Paul Jones was different from the rest but lumped in with them anyway. He was different because he was interested in carrying out armed landings, his purpose being the prosecution of naval warfare with Britain. The British, especially the establishment, tended to see him as no more than a renegade British subject, fighting his own people. Privateers operated against only enemy vessels, in accordance with 'letters of marque' drawn up by their own governments. Pirates were criminals with no authority to operate and who did not distinguish according to nationality between friend and foe. Paul Jones was always struggling to assert his legitimacy in these murky waters, which brings us to the subject of his planned attack on Newcastle.

Paul Jones says in his report to Franklin that he contemplated mounting an operation against the city, repeating in principle his attack on Whitehaven, though he realised that Newcastle would be a more difficult proposition in its own right, and – as he anticipated when mulling over possibilities in France – because of the heightened state of alert and preparedness he might encounter on a second expedition. Though there had not been much evidence of this at Leith.

Paul Jones wanted to follow a possibility mooted at the planning stage in France: the disruption of the winter coal supply for London. Apart from any economic impact, which could not be permanent, it would constitute a notable propaganda coup. As he could not pen the shipping up for long enough to have an effect, or easily get at them or their coal supplies at sea, any plan would entail a landing by the French marines under Chamillard (some one hundred and thirty of them), as well as by his own men.

From beyond the bar they could see ships lying in the river Tyne, and the guns of the Spanish Battery, prominent on its headland above the river mouth. They might even have seen from afar the guns of Clifford's Fort situated alongside the narrows at North Shields; its battery of some forty heavy guns trained forbiddingly along the navigable channel through the treacherous waters of the

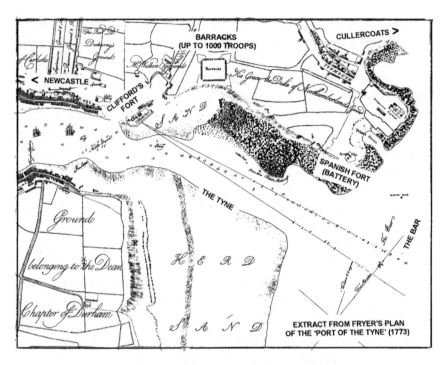

Fryer's 1773 map of the treacherous River Tyne, showing the Spanish Fort/Battery, Clifford's Fort, with its field of fire on the seaward side, and the barracks (for accommodating up to a thousand regular troops and/or militia) situated between these two strongpoints. (Courtesy North Tyneside Council Central Library, North Shields)

Tyne. The object of the gunners at this fortification would have been to wreck the masts and rigging of any hostile vessels immediately in front of them downriver, or across the narrows. Their guns ranged down the estuary beyond the sand bar, and would have been point blank across the narrows in front of them. The gunners would have wanted the ships drifting till they beached or went aground, rather than sunken and blocking the channel to commerce. Paul Jones does not say how he intended to carry out the operation at Newcastle, though it would most likely have been along the lines of the landing at Whitehaven and the attempted landing at Leith. This time however, it would have had an economic target, in the manner of another contemplated attack on Whitehaven directed at the huge wooden Staithe building and the lucrative coal trade with Ireland, and an earlier coastal attack on the fishing industry in Nova Scotia when in command of the *Alfred*. On this occasion he had sent boats in to burn a laden transport vessel lying inshore and oil storage warehousing which serviced the fisheries there, as well as capturing – in a fog – four merchant ships escorted by the British frigate *Flora*.

With oars muffled, as the oars of his own boats already were, he probably intended to land the considerable body of marines, as well as his own crewmen, in several parties, and mount covert overland attacks by night. He was no doubt aware that the militia might by then be mustered and on the alert, but probably banked on the superiority of his professional soldiery in unexpected hit-and-run raids to achieve results, fending off any militia that might be deployed against the confusion of targets which he would present after dark. The intruders would hopefully be gone by the time the militia and any regular soldiers, if there were any present, could mount an effective counter-attack. Although such tactics were never tested, the scenario had been foreseen on Tyneside. The written evidence, a short newspaper statement in the *Newcastle Courant* of 25 September, actually relates to nearby Sunderland: ' The regulars and militia in quarters here were under arms all night, and were divided into parties along the shore, to be ready in case they should return and attempt to land.' The lessons of Whitehaven and Leith had not been discounted on the Tyne.

The response capability of the local militia was partly revealed following the raid on Whitehaven by the *Ranger* on 23 April in the previous year. An 'express' was transmitted from Whitehaven to the government on that day. A week later, at two o'clock in the morning on 1 May (as recorded in the *Historical Register of Remarkable Events* in the Library at North Shields), an 'express' from the 'Secretary at War' in London was handed to Lord Percy, 'ordering the Northumberland militia to march to Newcastle and Tynemouth barracks'. They marched off promptly 'early on the morning', only a very few hours after Percy received the 'express'. On the march, Percy 'generously ordered them refreshment'. They arrived in Newcastle on 2 May, 'where they were received with the greatest joy by the inhabitants, who expressed a heart-felt pleasure in seeing a Percy [remembering Shakespeare's Hotspur] heading Northumbria's martial sons'. The Northumbrians had been inured to warfare by constant past conflict with the Scots and countless raids and counter raids across the border. But the border was now

quiet and the militia were not professionals in the mould of Paul
Jones's French marines. However, given the general commotion
caused by Paul Jones's marauding progress around the coast and his
recent thwarted attack on Leith, they would certainly have been on
the alert and already mustered in anticipation, most likely in their
large barracks situated on the north side of the Tyne, between the
Spanish Battery and Clifford's Fort. The garrison could hold a thousand troops, whether regulars, or militia, or both. There were in fact
regulars as well as militia at Sunderland, as reported in the *Courant*.
But we cannot know if the troops at the barracks would have been
deployed in well armed, well-organized reception parties.

The coal industry on Tyneside then consisted of a large number
of small pits situated inland along the edges of the Tyne estuary
and the adjacent coast. The pits had their own wooden tramways
to shift the coal from the pit to the shoreline (mostly to a jetty)
where the coal was loaded onto barges for transport to ships off-
shore. It was a very labour-intensive, small-scale affair. On the face
of it, such a set-up would be very difficult to damage; it was not

*Eighteenth-century view over the Tyne towards the Port and Clifford's Fort. From John
Brand's* History and Antiquities of the Town and County of Newcastle-upon-Tyne,
Vol. 2, 1789. *(Courtesy North Tyneside Council Central Library, North Shields)*

beyond serious disruption, but only given time, which Paul Jones did not have. The pits could be accessed at night time by following their tramways; but what then? Would they cripple the pits by casting the winding gear down the mineshafts? Paul Jones, after his triumphant return to France in the *Ranger* the previous year, suggested to his masters, amongst other enterprises, 'destroying the coal shipping of Newcastle'. Ships could certainly be burnt and barges destroyed, but it would all be pretty arduous, and without a central focus would take time. At Whitehaven the year before, there existed a huge and very forward-looking centralized system of coal shipping and storage, with overhead chutes to load up to five vessels at any one time, moored at the wharf alongside. The fire aboard the *Thompson* could have caused severe economic disruption at Whitehaven had it spread as planned, perhaps even involving the coal 'hurries'. There was no such objective to disable on Tyneside at that time. However, on the plus side for the attackers, it seems unlikely that the militia would have been expecting an attack on the coal trade. They would have been more prepared for thwarting attempts to burn shipping, to which Paul Jones specifically referred during his planning.

The defences of Newcastle were kept under pretty continuous review, and only the previous spring a subscription was collected in response to the attack on Whitehaven, on 16 May according to an entry in the *Historical Register*. This was only three weeks after the Whitehaven attack, and intended 'for the defence of that town [Newcastle[, its port and neighbourhood'. The sum collected amounted to close on £2,000, with the town's Corporation contributing over half. Both the Spanish Battery and Clifford's Fort, which was the main defence of the Tyne, were eventually superseded; but built in 1672 and only recently modernized yet again around 1757, Clifford's Fort, linked with the Spanish Battery, was something to be avoided at almost all costs by any hostile warship at the time Paul Jones was in the vicinity. At any rate one would think so, were it not for an entry in the *Historical Register* that pointed up a problem. Dated 23 May 1779 – only a few months before Paul Jones put in an appearance – it refers to a small French squadron playing havoc near Tynemouth with a large fleet of laden colliers and other vessels. 'A shameful neglect appeared on this occasion in the want of ammunition at the Spanish Battery, at the mouth of the river.' Nevertheless, there is no mention of any problem with the guns themselves, nor of any unreadiness at Clifford's Fort, which would have been less involved anyway in an action over the wider estuarial waters.

In view of the obvious hazards, it is fairly certain that at Newcastle Paul Jones would not have attempted to enter the restricted waters of the Tyne with his warships. The point from which he would have staged any overland attack, or attacks, can only be surmised. There are several options, involving only short and fairly easy marches, but they would be difficult to organize and synchronise, especially without local knowledge.

Such practical considerations were rendered academic, because both the captain of the *Pallas* and of the *Vengeance* were of one mind on the Commodore's proposal to stage an attack on Tyneside, and could not be budged. They would just not entertain it. They considered that, apart from being dangerous, it would be totally profitless, meaning without prizes rather than militarily ineffective; and they would be foolish to stay in the area any longer in the face of the British naval power that was certainly gathering. They threatened to desert Paul Jones if he did not turn south with them. Reluctantly, he acquiesced, though his own crew was surprisingly supportive of the enterprise, and as noted above, already had the oars of their boats muffled in readiness for a surprise night attack, which Jones for one moment of madness contemplated mounting with the *Bonhomme Richard* alone! Perhaps he intended an attack on the coal pit inland from the secluded cove at Cullercoats, near to the Tyne, but a spot not overlooked by guns. However, no attempt on this target, along its tramway from Cullercoats, was made. To judge how seriously Paul Jones was considering the whole enterprise we would need to know how he intended to use the ships, crewmen and marines at his disposal, which we do not. We only know that his ship was ready and his crew willing, and that Cottinineau and Ricot saw only peril in Jones's proposal; and no profit.

At Liverpool, Whitehaven, Leith and other ports around the British coastline, the presence of Paul Jones stimulated the improvement of often long-neglected defences against attack from the sea. Hull, where Paul Jones was soon to put in an appearance, is a case in point and well documented in a long letter from the Marquis of Rockingham to the government, dated 28 September 1779. He says

Hull was 'entirely without defence' against attack from the sea. The guns in the fort there – the only ones protecting the port – were unserviceable because of 'the carriages being entirely rotten' and the heavier guns 'honeycombed [with corrosion] and dangerous to use'. With Paul Jones in the vicinity, the Marquis took it upon himself at a town meeting one Friday evening to commandeer on behalf of the Government twenty eighteen-pound cannon in transit on board a ship lying in the port. It was thought that it would take seven to ten days to make carriages for them, but amazingly two contractors who appeared at the meeting undertook to have them made and delivered by nine o'clock in the evening of the next day. The Marquis actually saw several of them in place and ready for use by midday Saturday and expected the rest to be delivered as contracted.

Paul Jones was aware, especially following the cruise of the *Ranger*, that he did not necessarily have to do very much to achieve results, especially if politically sensitive targets like Edinburgh were chosen. An attempt on the London/Newcastle coal connection would have brought rich publicity rewards for the Americans, whether or not it had any material effect. The uproar in the British Isles as John Paul Jones progressed, practically with fanfares, down the east coast of Britain was in fact out of all proportion to his actual destructive impact, and the shiver of fear it inspired engaged the newspapers and local people mightily.

An image of the Bonhomme Richard *from the US National Archives. Whoever the artist was, he was of course guessing to some extent, but if his attempt at marine archaeology is accurate (and there is no reason to believe it is not), she was an imposing vessel.*

8

A Bloody Punch To The Lion's Snout:
The Battle off Flamborough Head

After carrying out some necessary repairs to the main topmast, the *Bonhomme Richard* sailed off southwards, in the wake of *Pallas* and *Vengeance*, from the Tyne towards the Humber and Hull, shaping up for the final fixed rendezvous off Flamborough Head. After that they would make for the Texel, Amsterdam's deep-water harbour and a safe haven, to conclude the expedition. The task force was due at the Texel on 1 October 1779, just over a week away. Soon they would be taking more easy prizes off the Yorkshire coast, with the neighbouring countryside again in turmoil, fearful of the rapine of the devilish American! However, a letter from Hull to the *Courant* was optimistic: 'We are in the most sanguine expectation of hearing an account of this vile fellow Jones and his squadron being taken.' The atmosphere on the Yorkshire coast in the run-up to the fateful naval engagement of Flamborough Head is captured in the following disparate but newsworthy events, which would have challenged the self-declared sanguinity of the author of the letter.

Towards the end of September whilst operating lucratively (two prizes taken), as well as destructively (several colliers sunk), near the prosperous port of Whitby, with the losses reported by the town in a letter to the government, the tables were nearly turned. Paul Jones, a mite too close to shore, was fired upon by the Haggerlythe Battery, sited on a cliff above the beach at Whitby. Unfortunately for the shore battery, there was an explosion amongst the guns as they were fired, and two of the soldiers manning them were flung from the gun emplacement and killed when they hurtled down onto the rocks below. As before, Lady Luck did not desert Paul Jones.

Reporting this providential escape, a letter from a Bridlington correspondent to the *Newcastle Courant* describes how the squadron appeared off Bridlington Quay and threatened both the town and ships, '… which had sheltered themselves in the harbour, amounting to near 40 sail of colliers'. However, Jones evidently thought discretion was the better part of valour that day and the danger passed, despite the ships' masters being reluctant to put ashore guns to form a defensive battery for themselves; only one of them did so.

One attack by Paul Jones was reported at the small coastal village of Skinningrove, which then – though always an attractive geographical location – comprised but a dozen hovels and two 'mansions', one dating back to the sixteenth and the other to the fourteenth century. John Paul Jones, or one of his vessels, is said to have put ashore a raiding party, which fired shots into the village. The raiders did not destructively sack the mansions, now the pub and post office, so Paul Jones's jealously guarded image as an officer and a gentleman was preserved. All that the raiders did at Skinningrove was to plunder the larders and cellars of the locals, no doubt concentrating on the 'mansions'. No one was killed or injured. Paul Jones does not mention such an attack, and one can only assume that the 'locals' identified him as the perpetrator because they wanted it to be him, or through a word or two with members of the raiding party, who might have been joking with them as to their identity, and not averse to giving Paul Jones a bad name! Any one of Jones's crews might have been short of food and water, or liquor perhaps. Midshipman Fanning mentions the capture of a couple of fifteen-ton pilot boats in the general vicinity, one of which, he says, '… we converted into a small tender; she served us for a decoy, and likewise for to land in, when we had occasion for fresh water and fresh provisions etc'.

A number of tales told about Paul Jones around the British Isles are certainly inaccurate or simply false, including provisioning forays like the one in Ireland where cash payment was supposed to have been made. Dates were sometimes unlikely or even impossible, although in fairness people in general were not particularly conscious of the date and there were not many newspapers around to remind them, even for those that could read. Word of mouth left plenty of scope for error and embellishment in transmission.

Setting aside the mayhem either caused by, or merely ascribed to, Paul Jones and his squadron whilst marauding around the British Isles, it would seem that now, as far as Paul Jones himself was concerned (though he appreciated the publicity value of the alarms) there was a very important, genuine blow to be struck before the cruise ended: against the Baltic fleet.

When the expedition left France, John Paul Jones possessed a good awareness of certain British shipping movements. For example, well before their arrival he seems to have known details about the fleet of West Indiamen due to arrive in the Shannon, bound for Limerick. That fleet was delayed by the weather, and in the trying circumstances (partly through taking notice of Landais), he had missed them; the larger consequence being that he had not burned Limerick, as his captured boat crews alleged he was going to do. However, dwarfing this Jamaica Fleet, far away in the wild expanse of the North Sea, one of the very large Baltic fleets, so important to the British naval effort, and indeed the British economy, was by now steadily making its way towards the British Isles. The convoy of over seventy ships was expected imminently. As a seafarer, and even without any special secret intelligence – which the French (and Franklin) did have of course – Paul Jones would have known a great deal about these regular major shipments of valuable merchandise by equally valuable vessels. He may well have known about a second fleet from the Baltic which, according to the Marquis of Rockingham's letter, was due to set sail six days after the first, and which the Marquis said was 'of even larger value' than the first. Paul Jones had talked about attacking a Baltic fleet when plans had been laid for the expedition. He and the financial backers of the task force must have had it on their minds from the outset. With a reduced squadron and prolonged gales, maybe he was better attacking late than never.

The final operational orders from the French Minister of Marine must be borne in mind, countersigned by Benjamin Franklin and delivered to John Paul Jones, followed by a letter incorporating Franklin's version in translation. The force was to make its way to the west coast of Ireland, then proceed northwards towards the Orkney Islands, sailing into the North Sea and making for the Naze (if Admiral Morison is right) at the southern tip of Norway. From that general vicinity, the squadron was to make for the Dogger

Bank in the midst of the North Sea, with the main purpose of surprising, harassing and preying upon one of the fleets of merchantmen as it left the Skagerrak and made its way southwards towards the British Isles, with no nearby haven to run to. The convoy of ships would be under armed escort of course, but just what this amounted to would have to be assessed on the spot. With the two formidably armed privateers and the *Cerf* gone, and the powerful *Alliance* vanished, the original squadron of seven had been reduced to three, and one of these, *Vengeance*, could be discounted for any really serious work. Realistically, in these circumstances, a set piece attack in the middle of the North Sea on the Baltic Fleet with its naval escort would have been worse than foolhardy.

It is impossible to read Paul Jones's mind here; as he said himself, he made a point of playing his cards very close to his chest. Writing his *Memorial* with the full knowledge and benefit of the accounts of pretty well everyone else, Landais says that Jones 'intended to land at Shetland and other places, did never cruise, and met only accidentally the Baltic Fleet off Flamborough Head'. In contrast, Landais did cruise, and very fruitfully, the *Alliance* taking most of the prize vessels on her own, and thus in his own estimation 'doing far more harm to the English trade than all the ships with Capt. Jones together'. An encounter with the Baltic Fleet would fit Landais's perception of his orders perfectly, but he could not do it in isolation. With regard to coming events at Flamborough Head, he later criticized Paul Jones for not going for the merchant ships rather than the Royal Navy escort. In his *Memorial*, Landais presents a 'piece' from Cottineau to Chaumont, which was shown to Sartine and Franklin (in translation):

> The said Mr. Cottineau disapproved Capt. Jones's conduct, for remaining three weeks off Scotland, to burn colliers vessels, rather than go off Cape Muis, where he was ordered to cruise, warning him, that when one don't follow the orders he has, nothing but a complete success can justify him.

This sounds like another reference to the Norwegian Naze, which Paul Jones never went near, though it looks very much like he should have done. Unfortunately 'Muis' is as obscure as 'Dirneus' (or 'Cap d'Erneus' as Cottineau equally obscurely renders it). The suspicion is of a deliberate effort to confound the British through disinformation so effective that it is still baffling today! In the main, we have only John Paul Jones's actions by which to judge him. He did not put much significant operational thinking into words, and even after the event pretty well kept his thoughts to himself. Though there are numerous indications that Franklin knew what he had in mind. It is frustrating that in his report to Franklin he seldom properly identifies his rendezvous locations by name, circumspectly referring to them only by number.

Feeling bruised by Jones's comments about him, Cottineau was later to say sarcastically – but unjustly – that during the engagement off Flamborough Head, Jones 'forgot that his ship had a rudder and sails'. Despite his detractors, Paul Jones must have got it pretty well right; as afterwards he was praised to the skies rather than pilloried, exemplifying the escape clause in the words, 'when one don't follow the orders he has, nothing but a complete success can justify him'.

Nathaniel Fanning's eyewitness account of the cruise of the *Bonhomme Richard* is important at Flamborough Head. Fanning, a young American from Connecticut, was taken on as a midshipman in France following the personal and somewhat deceptive persuasion of no less than Paul Jones himself. Fanning (soon acting as Jones's shipboard secretary) reports that, as he had valuable experience at sea, during the battle he was put in charge of the main top, the highest fighting platform on the mainmast, with immediate responsibility for fifteen marines and four sailors armed with a range of small arms – and with plenty of grog on hand, he says! Lieutenant Stack, also stationed in the main top, seems to have been in overall command aloft. Fanning states in passing that neither of the other midshipmen, or 'captains of the fore and mizzen tops' as he calls them, was over the age of seventeen. Fanning's states that as soon as Paul Jones identified the Baltic fleet approaching them off Flamborough Head using his 'spy-glass', he said to the officers clustering around him on the quarter deck; 'That is the very fleet which I have been so long cruising for.' No doubt there was some luck involved in the encounter, but it was almost certainly not the pure accident that Landais so dismissively claimed it was.

Whilst well out at sea with no sign of the *Alliance* to reinforce the task force, Paul Jones seems to have reached a decisive moment after the remaining ships of the squadron left the Orkneys region. He made an abrupt change of course at 7.00 p.m. on 6 September, from a westward one, straight towards the Naze, to the south. On 10 September, the course of the *Bonhomme Richard* changed substantially again, this time heading directly for the Scottish coast and the Firth of Forth, finally foregoing a direct approach to the Dogger Bank, as Franklin had apparently envisaged in his letter of instruction governing the parameters of the cruise, and as Landais had understood the instructions to be.

From then on a huge blaze of publicity had attended the progress of John Paul Jones down the eastern seaboard of Britain, cruising close to the coast and causing maximum tumult in a location which was clearly outside the written scope of his orders. An attack on a British Baltic fleet would obviously have fitted well with – indeed could have been tacitly central to – the Minister's orders for the cruise. As Landais pointed out, land operations in the Shannon and in the Shetlands could not have so fitted, and the high-profile attack on Leith and the proposed assault on Newcastle certainly could not be seen as within the written orders that they were given, 'to take enemy property'. Once ransom money was suggested his two subordinate captains had, after prolonged deliberation, gone along with the Leith proposal. However, the Newcastle project would have been totally and deliberately profitless, and they rejected it out of hand, even though the officers and crew of the *Bonhomme Richard* were dutifully willing and fully prepared for an attack. Paul Jones seems to have been deadly serious about Newcastle, but his entreaties and attempt to lead by example were in vain.

At this moment the unsuspecting Baltic fleet was well on its way across the North Sea from the Skagerrak. Merchant ships destined for Scotland had already hived off from the main body of the convoy, as did others in due course.

Sailing past Scarborough, John Paul Jones was now so intent on flushing out ships and taking prizes that any memories of the other Scarborough, the familiar port in Tobago where the 'ringleader' met his unfortunate end, were probably far from his mind. Cruising, no doubt anxiously by this time, off Flamborough Head, which the three ships had reached by 21 September, their depleted ranks were augmented by the appearance of Pierre Landais in the *Alliance*, which had already been cruising off the coast. Prior to rejoining the squadron, the *Alliance* had hauled in some worthwhile prizes, including the *Charming Polly*, which, like others, had been sent to Bergen in Norway, but was lost when returned by the Norwegians to the British two weeks after its arrival. When Landais's contrary frigate, having not long met up with *Pallas*, was identified early in the morning of the fateful 24 September (Schaeper's revision from the 23rd), John Paul must have experienced feelings of relief mixed with fury.

The Commodore did not have time at that moment to vent his feelings, however. He had been active in taking more valuable prizes, and had tried to tempt ships out of the Humber to battle, without success. Paul Jones was reluctant to enter the Humber estuary, as it was extremely treacherous to navigate. Off the Spurn (a long spit of shifting sand), and 'with English colours flying' as observers noted, he signalled for pilots. Two boats 'immediately put off, expecting a good job'. One pilot went on board the *Bonhomme Richard*, the other onto a light collier from Sunderland, not long captured and marked down to be plundered and sunk the next day. However, the latter pilot, clearly a man of some initiative, along with some followers, got the prize crew blind drunk, put them ashore, sailed the vessel into the Humber and docked her at Hull. The other pilot was badly injured during the forthcoming battle; he would lose an arm, but be very generously treated by Paul Jones.

As already noted, Jones had made no secret of his presence off the eastern seaboard of England – in fact he had flaunted it – and the newspapers relished and sensationalised the saga of plunder and mayhem, and the dire menace to the coastal towns posed by the renegade, which was so swiftly reacted to at Hull. In the wake of the heartfelt popular relief that followed upon the dissipation of the threat posed by the Franco-Spanish Armada off the south coast, the British Government was discomfited, extremely angry and seemingly impotent in the face of this provocation by their traitorous colonials, abetted by the unspeakable French and personified in Paul Jones!

Now in the shadow of Flamborough Head, *Bonhomme Richard* was beginning to pick up more precise news about the Baltic Fleet from captured mariners, including the couple of pilots taken by ruse de guerre. The convoy, delayed somewhat by the weather in exiting the Baltic, was now making steady progress southwards and the task force had not missed it. In fact, it was expected by the hour. In the early afternoon of 24 September, spectators crowding on top of the huge bulk of Flamborough Head could clearly see the Baltic Fleet, still comprising over forty merchant ships, approaching from the north towards this magnificent headland. Turning their gaze they could also see the American task force patrolling to the south of it, out of view of the approaching ships; still taking prizes, though ever watchful for the rich fleet of merchantmen, which they intended to take by surprise, if at all possible, as the ships rounded the Head. At about thee o'clock in the afternoon, the Baltic Fleet at last hove into view of the *Bonhomme Richard*. Fanning says that Paul Jones:

> ... immediately ordered a signal to be made for the squadron to abandon the small fleet, which we were then almost in the possession of, consisting of thirteen sail of vessels, some of which were said to be very valuable.

One of the captured pilot boats was under the command of one of Jones's best officers, Henry Lunt, the brother of Cutting Lunt (captured earlier on the Irish coast). He had a crew from the *Bonhomme Richard* aboard, and was involved at that time in engaging with a brig. In the flurry of activity Lunt's vessel was left on the fringe of the action in company with the *Vengeance*. Lunt and his men were soon to be sorely missed from the imminent battle.

It was soon clear that the infinitely more valuable Baltic convoy was being escorted by two British warships. One was the *Serapis*, a fifty-gun frigate under the command of Captain Richard Pearson, the other the *Countess of Scarborough*, a twenty-gun sloop commanded by Captain Thomas Piercy, whom Paul Jones in a throwaway line elsewhere identifies as 'an illegitimate son of the Duke of Northumberland'. The lookout in the crow's nest of the *Serapis* had spotted the task force.

Captain Pearson had been in any case well aware of the presence of an American squadron in the vicinity. The customary red warning flag could be seen hoisted high at Scarborough Castle, and a boat had also been sent out urgently to give him the most recent intelligence. Pearson ordered the fleet of ships to close with the shore as far as possible, but because of a reluctance to put their ships at hazard until dire necessity drove them to it, the order was only carried out when the American ships were actually sighted. The fleet then crammed on sail, firing alarm shots, and smartly turned tail, heading northwards helter-skelter towards the protection of gathering fog and the powerful guns at Scarborough Castle. Such a move towards safety would not have been possible of course out by the Dogger Bank, where the merchantmen would have been in the midst of the open sea, exposed and vulnerable. Breaking up a convoy totalling over seventy merchant ships in open water by attacking with his original squadron of seven warships might have confounded its two-warship escort and yielded success; in fact, it almost certainly would have. If Paul Jones had been more loyally served by *Alliance*, it might have been possible even without the two departed privateers and *Cerf*. Such an attack was a much more daunting task in the restricted and treacherous environment of British inshore waters, even though John Paul now commanded four warships, including *Alliance*.

In the vicinity of Flamborough Head there were sandbanks, reefs and hazardous currents centred on the Head itself. For threatened merchant ships there was also the welcome security of nearby land-based gun batteries. The guns at Scarborough would have the advantage of firing very heavy shot from a fixed platform below the castle, and would unquestionably command the seas before and below them, providing a safe haven.

The *Countess of Scarborough* had been sailing ahead of the convoy, and stayed in position, facing the oncoming squadron of American vessels. *Serapis* had been sailing protectively on the seaward flank of the convoy. She now turned shoreward to maintain this protection by also getting in between the convoy and the American squadron. Pearson signalled the *Countess* to join him. He was resolutely about to face up to what looked like a greatly superior enemy. John Paul Jones could see that he would have to engage the two British warships before he could get at the convoy; and that it would be suicide to approach it once in the vicinity of Scarborough, within range of the heavy guns there. In view of his overt activites by the Humber, Paul Jones must have been expecting this scenario.

The experienced and dutiful Pearson did not know that his opponent was afflicted with the loose cannon, Pierre Landais, though he sensed that the American squadron of four ships was approaching somewhat raggedly, and was encouraged by this. In fact, unknown to Pearson, the squadron was in disarray not because of the quality of its seamanship, but because of reluctance to follow orders, even if these were adequately signalled and fully understood.

The *Serapis* was a brand new, purpose-built warship, sailing on her first commission. She carried fifty guns in total, comprising a main battery of twenty eighteen-pounders on a lower gun deck, a battery of twenty nine-pounders on a covered upper gun deck, and ten six-pounders on the quarterdeck. In comparison, *Bonhomme Richard* carried forty guns. She was definitely inferior in firepower to the *Serapis*, mainly because of the twenty eighteen-pounders carried by the British frigate as her main armament; *Bonhomme Richard* carried only six of these, awkwardly placed towards the rear of the main gun-deck during the conversion of the East-Indiaman for war. They were dispensed with very quickly anyway, as they proved extremely dangerous in use. The advantage which these heavy guns gave to Captain Pearson was not cancelled by the fact that the *Bonhomme Richard* carried twenty-eight twelve-pounders compared with the twenty nine-pounders carried by *Serapis*. But crucially for Paul Jones, his ship carried six nine-pounders on the quarterdeck, compared with Pearson's ten six-pounders.

There were other important differences between the two ships. The *Bonhomme Richard* was a much older vessel, and unlike the *Serapis* was not specifically built for use in sea battles. She had made several long and debilitating round trips to the East Indies before being converted for use by the task force, originally with the attack by troops on Liverpool in mind, hence the roundhouse on deck. There was rot and worm in her timbers, making her more vulnerable to damage by heavy iron shot discharged at point-blank range. The situation for Paul Jones in the *Bonhomme Richard*, about to face up to a pristine British warship off Flamborough Head was, in fact, a complete reversal of his situation on board the *Ranger* in Belfast Lough in the previous year. Then the *Ranger* had been the brand new, purpose-built warship, and the *Drake* an older, converted tobacco freighter. The *Ranger* had also been superior in firepower to her enemy, as now the British ship Paul Jones faced was to the *Bonhomme Richard*.

One difference that weighed very much in favour of Paul Jones during the coming engagement were the unusually large fighting tops attached to the masts of the *Bonhomme Richard*. These amounted to a significant innovation in naval warfare; a tactical development that placed much stronger emphasis on small arms and other weaponry in clearing enemy decks, causing serious damage from above, and facilitating boarding. Paul Jones was at the forefront of the development, which soon proliferated. At the Battle of Trafalgar for example, the talented Captain of the French ship *Redoubtable*, initially firing broadsides, went so far when close combat developed with Nelson's flagship *Victory* as to fight with most of his gun ports deliberately closed up, in favour of concentrating the whole effort of his crew on deck, aloft in the rigging, and manning the fighting tops. One of his sharpshooters aloft was the man who fatally shot Nelson as he paced the quarterdeck; but as far as the *Redoubtable* – and the French fleet as a whole – was concerned, the killing of Nelson that day changed nothing, together with the tactic of concentrating on the destruction of rigging and sails and the use of small arms, which failed utterly in the face of the far superior rate of fire of the British ships.

Nathaniel Fanning, in charge of the formidable fighting top on the main mast, was called down to the quarterdeck, together with the midshipmen in charge of the fore and mizzen fighting tops, for final orders from Paul Jones 'on how to proceed during the action'. He wanted nothing to reduce the effectiveness of the tactical emphasis on the fighting tops. At the outset, the fighting tops were instructed to direct their entire efforts with all weapons against the nearest top in the enemy ship. Only after silencing these were they to transfer their attention downwards with 'a fairer opportunity of clearing their decks'. The fighting tops eventually achieved complete success, both in eliminating enemy action aloft and in suppressing action on the decks below. Fanning says that Pearson appeared to direct all the tops on the *Serapis* to concentrate on the quarterdeck of the *Bonhomme Richard*; where stood Paul Jones of course, who proved luckier than Nelson.

Fanning's fighting top was well equipped in advance of action and manned, as noted previously, by a large number of sailors and marines. Their weapons included muskets, pistols and blunderbusses, which could be loaded with handfuls of pistol balls or with fire darts and other fiercely incendiary devices. These might be equipped with barbed points and hooks to latch onto sails, tarred standing rigging and the like, thus creating rapidly ascending columns of fire, which could only be approached to be doused at dire risk of being shot. Fires like this, unsurprisingly, could have very serious consequences for the effective handling of a sailing ship, especially if uncontrolled. If sufficiently far above an enemy deck, or in some exposed awkward spot, fires could prove very difficult to put out under withering small arms fire. Portable swivel guns (small cannons in effect) were also slotted in position on the fighting tops for varied use, including the launch of incendiary devices. Fanning specifically mentions 'cowhorns' in his account, by which he means 'coehorns', swivel howitzers for tossing grenades and the like at the enemy. In addition to these firearms in the fighting tops, and referring to the fighting top under his own command, Fanning – from a wide range of possibilities – refers specifically to stink pots, flasks and grenades.

Stink pots were in fact a type of crude chemical warfare; a source of choking smoke and seriously disabling fumes. Flasks were friable pots which could be filled with explosives as well as with a sticky and fiercely incendiary mix which was difficult to extinguish and was even aggravated by water. Grenades were the commonest weapon of this handy type (from the Spanish word 'grenada', pomegranate). They were hollow iron balls or sometimes thick glass balls, filled with explosive for fragmentation effect on crowded decks or amongst groups clustered around a gun perhaps, or putting out a fire. They were fused by a length of match cord which passed through a wooden plug fixed into the shell of the grenade. The match cord was treated chemically to be 'slow' burning (in other words, fizzing like a firework) on the outside of the shell, and fast burning inside to trigger an explosion. Highly effective, grenades remained basically unchanged in design for some three hundred years. Ordinarily, iron grenades weighed from two to three pounds, and at around three inches diameter fitted comfortably into the human hand. In naval actions, where they could often be dropped rather than thrown, they tended to be bigger, sometimes much bigger.

Grenade containers, looking like elongated wooden buckets with canvas shrouding fixed and drawn close around the top, were placed at their allotted stations around the ship and in the fighting tops as a vessel was cleared for action. The grenadiers carried a length of glowing match-cord in a ventilated metal match holder, often worn attached to their headgear. In close engagements, grenades could often be the decisive weapon; and alongside their well armed companions, the grenadiers were at a distinct advantage in the enlarged fighting tops of the *Bonhomme Richard*. Boarding was a prime objective during a sea battle and action aloft was very material to facilitating this, and to allowing more freedom of action by suppressing activity aboard the enemy vessel.

Seeming at the outset to be Paul Jones's greatest advantage, however, was the sheer physical presence of the *Alliance*. Like the *Serapis*, she was a new vessel built for military operations at sea; a frigate carrying twenty-eight twelve-pounders and eight nine-pounders. She certainly looked a formidable sight to Pearson as the enemy squadron steadily approached, but looks can be deceptive: Landais was in command. Pearson would have also seen that the frigate *Pallas* was no mean adversary, armed with thirty-two eight-pound guns. She was shy of action at first, but at a later stage of the battle, assisted by the *Alliance*, she would take on the sloop-of-war *Countess of Scarborough*, carrying twenty-two six-pounders. The corvette *Vengeance*, with her twelve three-pounders, had her place at the outset in the ragged battle formation shaping up to Pearson, but being relatively small and lightly armed she took little part in the developing action. She became a virtual onlooker. After the battle, Paul Jones initially blamed her captain, Ricot, for lack of effective support, especially in holding back assistance from the captured pilot boat, which had one of Jones's best lieutenants and twenty men on board. He changed his mind when persuaded after the event that he had misunderstood the situation. The Lieutenant had made the decision when he closed with the fierce action. Cottineau said in support of Ricot that in fact Jones had told ricot to stand off and, contrary to Jones's allegation, he had 'conducted himself with all possible zeal', commenting that, as far as Paul Jones was concerned 'ingratitude is one of his virtues'.

Off Flamborough Head, the situation was critical. Darkness was descending and before the moon began to rise to illuminate the scene again, Pearson made a calculated and very sensible move. Having done their duty by ensuring a good headstart for the convoy, the *Serapis* and the *Countess of Scarborough* altered course as inconspicuously as possible, in the gathering, though only temporary, shroud of darkness and mist. Hoping that their subtle move had been unobserved and would remain so for some little while, they wisely started to head themselves for the cover of the guns at Scarborough Castle. Paul Jones spotted the move using his night glasses. He could not allow the convoy or its escorting warships to get away completely unscathed if he was to avoid ridicule and, in view of events so far, look anyone in the eye again. The *Alliance* was far to windward and the *Pallas*, unable to comprehend what was going on, faltered, heading out to sea.

The moment had come either to accept an ignominious conclusion to the expedition or make a bid for glory. John Paul Jones predictably chose glory, and death for a great part of his crew: 'I was obliged to run every risk and to bring the enemy to action with the *Bonhomme Richard* alone.' The *Newcastle Courant* later confirmed his predicament: 'When Jones first attacked the *Serapis*, he was ahead of his little fleet several leagues; notwithstanding this, he engaged with all the fury of a man determined to conquer or die.' Paul Jones was without doubt out on a limb; but surely not by several leagues. The gap is suspiciously large, however; perhaps the others were hanging back to discourage Jones. They would certainly have preferred to go for the convoy, of course.

Lieutenant Richard Dale, subsequently to become one of the few lifelong friends of John Paul Jones, confided soberly after the battle:

> From the commencement to the termination of the action there was not a man on board the *Bonhomme Richard* ignorant of the superiority of the *Serapis* both in weight of metal and in the qualities of the crew.

The word 'motley' is no cliché applied to Paul Jones's crew of 322, as we have seen earlier, though they were good seamen. They faced a crew of 320 steadfast and disciplined Britons aboard the *Serapis*, augmented in Scandinavia to about 400.

At 5.30 in the afternoon Pearson, according to the time kept aboard the *Serapis*, cleared his ship for action. At six o'clock, according to the time kept aboard the *Bonhomme Richard*, with the sun sinking in an increasingly misty red glow towards the horizon, Paul Jones signalled his squadron to form line of battle, an intention which was far from realized.

John Paul took up his station on the quarterdeck of the *Bonhomme Richard*, standing on an arms chest according to one of his crew. He never left his quarterdeck throughout the desperate engagement which was to follow, receiving only one small wound that he dismissed later as 'not worth mentioning', and a musket ball through the skirt of his uniform coat.

The sea was calm and the full moon soon rose above the horizon to light up the scene for a while quite brilliantly, before the mist and clouds closed in, a scene later and memorably portrayed in his painting of the dramatic engagement by the artist James Hamilton. Flamborough Head itself was crowded with hushed spectators gazing out over the tranquil, moonlit sea.

From the *Serapis*, at about seven o'clock, the customary question was called across the water: 'What ship is that?' Fanning describes it as voiced 'in true bombastic English stile, it being hoarse and hardly intelligible'. In an effort to get closer before shots were fired John Paul replied: 'The *Princess Royal*' – he was flying a British flag. Pearson's raised gun ports revealed their awesome firepower. Within pistol shot, Paul Jones finally struck his now redundant British colours, raised the Stars and Stripes, and almost simultaneously with *Serapis*, fired a crashing broadside. Several murderous broadsides were then fired off at close range by both ships; though *Serapis* was much better positioned by Pearson to do this effectively, with some well placed raking fire bounding lethally along the vulnerable length of the *Bonhomme Richard*.

Unfortunately for Paul Jones, very early in the fight, two of his eighteen-pounders blew up, killing several men, wrecking the neighbouring guns and blowing a gaping hole in the deck above. Jones had to make an immediate decision. All of the old eighteen-pounder guns were promptly abandoned. There was more punishing cannon fire on both sides; rigging was damaged, some of it crashing down onto the decks, and lethal splinters of jagged oak tore into flesh. Pearson strove desperately to stay clear of *Bonhomme Richard*, so that his superior firepower could continue to make its telling impact. He was successful for a while. Paul Jones on the other hand strove desperately to close with the *Serapis*. He explained afterwards: 'As I had to deal with an enemy of greatly superior force, I was under the necessity of closing with him to prevent the advantage he had over me in point of manoeuvre'. He had to prevent Pearson from keeping the heavier guns of his ship in advantageous and deadly play.

Despite his best endeavours, John Paul succeeded only in getting his bows into the stern of the *Serapis* – not a very useful position. Though the boarders were crouched in their places ready to storm aboard the enemy vessel, John Paul judged the moment premature, and backed his ship away. Both captains were still trying to rake each other with gunfire from stem to stern in an effort to cause disabling damage to masts and rigging with bar and chain shot, as well as to sweep the enemy decks with lethal grapeshot, and send cannon balls ricocheting along the confined spaces between decks. Quite early in the action, whilst Jones was engaging thus with the *Serapis*, the *Countess of Scarborough*, 'raked the stern of the *Bonhomme Richard* with broadsides' (Jones) and caused serious damage and casualties.

The weight of Pearson's well placed eighteen-pounder broadsides inflicted huge damage on the *Bonhomme Richard*, smashing up and finally silencing completely her main battery of twelve-pounders. Her sides were agape with ragged holes and she was leaking ominously.

Things were not as terminal as they appeared, because of the foresight Paul Jones had shown in converting the *Duc de Duras* into a warship. He now enjoyed the advantage of the superior fighting tops mentioned earlier, an innovation that had already proven useful in combat with the *Drake*. His emphasis on small arms tactics, unusual in its intensity at the time (but soon taken up by others as noted earlier), was intended to give him an advantage at close quarters, in that he could command enemy decks and thus ensure that his own men could more easily attack his opponent's masts and rigging with disabling chain, bar and other shot from his deck guns prior to boarding, which was the ultimate aim. So successful was his overpowering small arms fire in suppressing enemy action in the open that later in the punishing engagement, the men from his fighting tops, as well as those amongst his rigging, were able to clamber over the interlocking yardarms into the masts and rigging of the *Serapis* almost with impunity, and from there intensify the hail of small arms fire and grenades upon the deck of the British man o' war.

However, in trying to bring about close action and cancel out the advantage of the *Serapis* in firepower, the *Bonhomme Richard* continued to suffer grievously from Pearson's practised manoeuvring and skilfully applied cannon fire, especially from the potentially decisive eighteen-pounders in the lower gun deck, which were tearing the very guts out of Jones's ship.

Pearson realised the grave damage he was inflicting on his adversary, and as Paul Jones had been completing the withdrawal of the bows of his shattered vessel out from the stern of the *Serapis*, the captain of the British warship, misconstruing the backing-off, unsure of the situation but hopeful, called across: 'Are you striking?'

Securing in one short exclamation his heroic place in American naval history, John Paul Jones gave the immortal reply: 'I have not yet begun to fight!' The defiant answer – if it was in fact uttered – was only too true. The fight between the *Serapis* and the already crippled *Bonhomme Richard* was to prove the longest ship-to-ship engagement in British naval history under fighting sail, a marathon approaching four hours – and it had hardly begun!

There was more manoeuvring and Paul Jones did almost manage to get himself into position to rake his enemy from stem to stern, the which advantage Pearson was engineering quite successfully for his own gunners. Paul Jones was not quite successful in this, and the badly damaged ships collided, the bowsprit of *Serapis* getting entangled in the mizzen shrouds of the *Bonhomme Richard*. The light wind pivoted the ships so that they slowly came to rest against each other, side by side for most of their length, but stem to stern. The weather had changed sides at last! Pearson dropped his anchor around this time, but the drag created failed to separate the ships as he had gambled. Paul Jones's crew leapt into action to bind the ships fast. He was elated at the turn of events: 'Well done, my brave lads,' he thundered, 'we have got her now.' They grappled to the *Serapis*, Paul Jones himself lashing firmly to his ship the stout end of a piece of rigging which, sheared through, had come snaking down from the *Serapis* onto his own deck. He now exploited the suddenly more favourable situation by concentrating on wrecking the rigging of the enemy ship as soon as possible, thus destroying her mobility. To do this with his deck guns as well as incendiary devices, he had to suppress activity on Pearson's ship by killing her crew or scattering them with musketry and grenades from aloft. He succeeded. Pearson wanted to get clear and apply his deadly guns again. His crew tried desperately to cut the grapples and break free, but in the murderous hailstorm they were unable to do so. From then on, says Fanning, several boarding attempts were made by both crews 'in quick succession, in consequence of which many were slain … on both sides'. Towards the end of the drama, with small arms ammunition running out and cannon disabled, Fanning says that fighting was done 'principally … with lances and boarding pikes; with these weapons the combatants killed each other through the ships' portholes', after disabled guns had been wrestled out of the way. But not yet.

The muzzles of the opposing death-dealing cannons were now grinding against each other. To get his starboard eighteen-pounders into play, not used so far in the battle which had been fought from the port side, Pearson had been forced to blow off his gun ports. They just could not be opened against the press of the *Bonhomme Richard*, into whose hostile port holes or shot holes his intrepid gunners had at times to poke their ramrods in order to ram home their charges and shot – an action certainly inviting a pike thrust!

Pearson was winning the heavy gun duel; the deck of the *Bonhomme Richard* was on the verge of falling into the hold, and the quarterdeck into the gunroom. Paul Jones's ship was being battered to wood pulp, but on deck and in the rigging things were different. The Americans had got the upper hand. Aloft on the *Serapis* there was eventually only one diehard left alive, popping out to snipe at them. Fanning spotted him 'peeping out once in a while' and pinpointed him for the attention of the marines the next time he appeared. 'We soon saw,' says Fanning, 'this skulking tar, or marine, fall out of the top [the foretop] upon the enemies' forecastle.'

With complete American domination aloft, the deck battery of ten-pounders aboard the *Serapis* was abandoned, and her decks were cleared of living seamen under the sheer pressure of musket and small arms fire from above, and the ripping explosions of grenades. The *Serapis* was set on fire several times by the enterprising crew of the *Bonhomme Richard*. Pearson remarked later upon '… the great quantity and variety of combustible matters which they threw in upon our decks … and in short into every part of the ship', throughout the course of the battle. 'We were on fire not less than ten or twelve times in different parts of the ship, and it was with the greatest difficulty and exertion imaginable at times that we were able to get it extinguished.' The wadding from the cannons (teased-out, tarry rope rammed down the muzzles to prevent the balls rolling out with the motion of the ship) shot in company with the iron balls, blazing across into the enemy, added significantly to the conflagrations on board both ships.

The crowds thronging Flamborough Head were viewing an awesome, and awful, spectacle. The flash of the guns lit up the clouds of drifting gunsmoke. The red glow of fires reflected on the surface of the sea and flickered in the smoke. The glare of the hellish inferno and the crashing sound of the gunfire rolling out over the calm sea were fearful to witness and shocking to the minds of the townsfolk and farm workers staring out to sea. The silvery moon still shone fitfully over the ghastly, smoke-shrouded battle scene.

When told about the fearsome sea fight which was rapidly developing, one inhabitant of nearby Scarborough remembers he '… immediately threw up the sash of the room … we had a fair view of the engagement, which appeared very severe, for the firing was frequently so quick that we could scarce count the shots.'

As the battle proceeded, the *Alliance* was generally deemed by Paul Jones and his crew to be playing a dastardly, almost traitorous part, sailing aloofly around the two ships locked together in deadly combat, and loosing off broadsides into both friend and foe, but mostly into the *Bonhomme Richard*, claimed Jones. 'Every tongue cried out that he was firing into the wrong ship but nothing availed.' He says that Landais 'passed round firing into the *Bonhomme Richard*'s Head, Stern and Broadside'. The crew repeatedly yelled across to the *Alliance* in anger and despair, quickly showing, through the drifting smoke clouds, their night recognition signal, three lanterns side by side upon the fore, main and mizzen shrouds. This, according to Fanning, '… had the desired effect, and her firing ceased'. The *Bonhomme Richard* was painted black, and *Serapis* mainly a glowing yellow-ochre in accordance with customary British naval practice. (The *Victory*, Nelson's flagship at Trafalgar, as now displayed in the Royal Dockyard at Portsmouth, is a fine example, with black and ochre bands.) As the battle had already been going on for around an hour, bathed in misty moonshine much of the time, surely Landais knew what he was doing, despite the rolling clouds of gun smoke. Fanning says that initially some of the officers and crew of the *Bonhomme Richard* believed the *Alliance* to be a British man o' war! Fanning includes a bracketed aside at this point in his account: 'The moon at this time, as though ashamed to behold this bloody scene any longer, retired behind a dark cloud.' Granted, darkness added to smoke was a pretty sure recipe for lethal confusion in an extremely fraught battle situation. But some of Landais's officers and crew told him directly and unambiguously that he was damaging the wrong ship, some even refusing to fire. However, Landais later claimed that it was his broadsides which caused *Serapis* to surrender, and Pearson could very reasonably assert in justifying his conduct later that he was defeated by two frigates, rather than by one; he claimed that *Alliance* inflicted severe damage and loss of life on his ship, and that her potent presence clinched his eventual decision to strike his colours. For what

A thoughtful contemporary painting of the battle by Sir Richard Paton. There is darkness and smoke, but the scene is not impenetrably obscured, as in Hamilton's picture. Serapis *and* Bonhomme Richard *are close alongside each other, stem to stern – their final grappled position.* Alliance *is to the right firing a broadside. Is she hitting one ship or both of them? And which ship is which? To the right and further off, the* Countess of Scarborough *and the stronger* Pallas *(under Cottineau) can be seen battling it out. The small* Vengeance *hovers behind these ships, taking no part in the action. (Courtesy the U.S Naval Academy Museum at Annapolis)*

It is worth, British newspapers concurred; the *Newcastle Courant* saying: 'Another of his squadron [the *Alliance*] immediately came up to his [Jones's] assistance, which turned the tables on the *Serapis*, and she was obliged to strike.' However, after the battle, Landais apparently told an officer, who reported the conversation to Paul Jones, that he had intended to help the *Serapis* sink the *Bonhomme Richard*, and then board the crippled British warship without too much difficulty, claiming the victory – and prize money of course – at little cost. (Jones never named this informant.) Some such intention would seem plausible in the light of his actions, which could thus be seen as logical, if not comradely!

Three midshipmen from Jones's crew – Mayrant, Coram and Linthwaite – attested to a number of clauses in a collective affidavit solicited by Paul Jones, who composed its list of twenty-five articles after the event, to present to his officers. (see Bibliography; Franklin/Olberg p625, 30.10.1779) The young midshipmen attested to numerous matters of fact, but also indicated that they 'believed' several others. One of these stated that 'Captain Landais has acknowledged since the action that he would have thought it no harm if the *Bonhomme Richard* had struck for it would have given him an opportunity to retake her and to take the *Serapis*.' However, Lieutenant Colonel Wuibert (elsewhere Wilbert, and Wiebert) attested to this statement as a matter of fact, not belief. In other words, he must have heard Landais say it. Wuibert is described below his signature as 'American Engineer and Commanding officer of the Volunteers on board *Serapis*, late of the *Bonhomme Richard*'. Like Colonel de Chamillard, Wuibert was in command of the French marines. Stack and Macarthy, both officers of Walshe's regiment and serving in the Volunteers, also attested to article 23 as a matter of fact. Cottineau attested to the article, but did not specify whether he did so as a matter of fact or belief.

What did Landais himself have to say on this matter? In his *Memorial* he says that he simply told one of his crew that if the *Bonhomme Richard* had struck at some point he would have battled to get control of both the *Richard* and the *Serapis*. He does not say that he wanted this situation to materialize, nor that he tried to help bring it about. And he does not name Wuibert. He does not see Jones's article 23 as a point of any consequence, and attempts to draw the sting from Jones's sinister interpretation of the information from his unnamed informant by saying that he repeated the statement 'several times'.

The most likely explanation of both Landais' intentions and his actions falls somewhere in the middle, between terrible perfidy and tactical sang froid. Perhaps, as he said to fellow officers, he genuinely 'thought it no harm' for the *Bonhomme Richard* to have struck, as he could have moved in to retake her and then finish off the crippled *Serapis*. Bad enough, but not aiding and abetting the enemy.

Whatever the truth of the matter, by the end of the action *Alliance* had experienced no casualties and was almost wholly undamaged by shot: one ball from the *Countess of Scarborough* had lodged in her timbers, apparently early in the proceedings, and two had bounced off. She never approached the disengaged and dangerous side of the *Serapis*. Written 'evidence' collected by John Paul Jones from officers and men after the battle – not only from his own ship – was overwhelmingly weighted against Landais; although admittedly, crews' testimonies were sometimes elicited under suspicious circumstances. But it was demonstrated to Jones's satisfaction that Landais's action off Flamborough Head was clearly underhand and beyond the pale of honour. Paul Jones considered this behaviour quite in keeping with the tenor of his previous conduct during the course of the voyage. However, he may have excessively blackened Landais's actions. Grape shot, which *Alliance* seems to have been mainly firing, was difficult to direct with reasonable accuracy onto such a restricted target, especially from the distance Jones alleged they were firing from. Whether Landais was viciously malevolent or grossly irresponsible in regulating his fire, his own crew rallied strongly to his support later. However, as we know and shall have more evidence of later, Benjamin Franklin was a sharp analyst, and his final assessment of Landais and his entire conduct was vigorously censorious. And neither Pearson nor Paul Jones seems to have had only grape shot in mind when they were referring to the serious damage to their ships inflicted by *Alliance*. Whatever damage Landais caused to either ship, and both Paul Jones and Pearson emphasise how 'effective' he was in terms of mortality and men wounded, as well as in terms of physical damage, it is certain that both ships suffered from *Alliance*'s broadsides.

According to Thomas Schaeper's careful analysis, Landais actually fired three broadsides at the close-grappled ships. The first was fired around 8.15 p.m., towards the bows of the *Bonhomme Richard* and the stern of the *Serapis*; the second just after 9.30 p.m. towards the bows of the *Serapis* and the stern of the *Bonhomme Richard*; and the third around 10.00 p.m. from almost the same position as the first broadside, again towards the bows of the *Bonhomme Richard* and the stern of the *Serapis*. By the time the first broadside was fired on 24 September night would have fallen, forcing the ships' crews to rely for visibility on moonlight and the glare of fires, hampered by a mist hanging over the scene, which, according to Paul Jones, was still there the next morning. Landais, for his part, says he was careful with his broadsides, firing the guns off not simultaneously but in series, as each gun came to bear on an aiming point aboard the *Serapis*: a light in a stern cabin. Being 'within a musket shot' as Landais puts it, 'all the guns were fired at her [*Serapis*] one by one as we went along'. As proof of commendable closeness – for accuracy – to the grappled ships (a closeness disputed by Jones), Landais cites a musket ball from the *Serapis* passing 'through a man's hat brim'. But even assuming the cannon shots were in fact expertly fired off in sequence in the first place, how effectively Landais and the *Alliance* executed their rally to the assistance of the *Bonhomme Richard* is still in doubt. One can make some kind of judgement by the practical results on board that ship. There was mayhem. Consider the three damning pieces of evidence already mentioned: the crew were yelling across that the *Alliance* was firing at the wrong ship; they put up their night recognition signals in desperation; and Fanning and his fellow crew members even thought that the *Alliance* was a British man o' war. On board the *Alliance* things were also frenetic, with crewmen complaining angrily that they were hitting the wrong ship, and some refusing to fire. Landais, in his *Memorial*, was writing in 1784, some five years after the event, having digested what everyone else had to say, so it could be argued that he had had enough time to concoct a defence. On the other hand, as Jones was writing his report in the heat of the moment, his statements within it may be rash, or driven too much by emotion and animosity.

So set in the balance against the laudable and reported damage he inflicted upon the *Serapis*, his three broadsides were something of a disaster for the *Bonhomme Richard*, an extreme case of 'collateral damage'; and culpably negligent because the dangerous tactic was used on three occasions, separated by long intervals. Peter Landais was quite sanguine about it all, considering what he did to have been the most useful thing he could, and commending crewmen who did not fire when they could not safely do so.

If Paul Jones was scornful about Landais, Pearson was in contrast wholly satisfied with the conduct of Thomas Piercy in command of the *Countess of Scarborough*, commending him for having 'given me every assistance in his power, and as much as could be expected from such a ship, in engaging the attention of the *Pallas*, a frigate of thirty two guns, during the whole action'. The *Countess of Scarborough* was no match for the more powerful *Pallas*, and after an engagement lasting, according to Piercy, about two hours, with the vastly more powerful frigate *Alliance* approaching menacingly, and with his rigging in tatters and seven guns dismounted, the *Countess of Scarborough* struck her colours. 'I saw,' says Piercy with admirable sense, 'it was in vain to contend any longer, with any prospect of success, against such superior force.' At the outset of the battle, says Piercy: 'Two minutes after you [Pearson] engaged with Jones, I received a broadside from one of the frigates [*Alliance*], which I instantly returned, and continued engaging her about twenty minutes, when she dropt astern.' As he dropped away, Landais says he instructed *Pallas* to take up the fight with the *Countess of Scarbrough*, whilst he went off to help Jones in his fight with Pearson. Piercy is then faced with the same decision as Landais:

> I then made sail up to the *Serapis* to see if I could give you any assistance, but upon coming near you, I found you and the enemy so close together, and covered with smoke, that I could not distinguish one ship from the other.

Piercy wisely held his fire, then squared up to the *Pallas*, which was approaching the hellish scene. Piercy's sensible conduct contrasts starkly with that of Landais, who did not hesitate to fire recklessly into the same smoke-confused scene against advice from all around, and with dark cloud drifting over the moon at the time.

The effects of obscuring gunsmoke upon a sea battle were well demonstrated at Trafalgar some twenty-five years later. Fortunately for the British, their approach was partly masked by smoke, though the *Victory*, leading the fleet, suffered cruelly. As that battle developed, vessels were surprised by warships suddenly looming out of the smoke at very close quarters, with some collisions, and Trafalgar was fought in broad daylight, not at night, as at Flamborough Head.

With the battle still raging around him, John Paul Jones personally took over control of the nine-pound guns on the quarterdeck, as there was no one else available to do so, and manfully served one of them by himself. He paused in exhaustion at one point, and sat down for a minute or two on a hencoop. A crewman approached and implored him: 'For God's sake, Captain, strike!' John Paul was galvanised by the despairing words and leaping quickly to his feet, replied dourly: 'No, I will sink, I will never strike,' and got back to his nine-pounder, knowing full well that his ship was in desperate trouble and indeed very close to sinking.

At around this time (close to 9.30 p.m. according to Pearson), William Hamilton, a Scottish member of Jones's crew, worked his way along a yardarm stretching out over the deck of the *Serapis*, with a basket of hand grenades and a glowing match. Paul Jones later talked about 'his extraordinary presence of mind and intrepidity' – qualities that would undoubtedly strike a chord with his commander: 'As the flames from their railings and shrouds [part of the tarred standing rigging] added to the light of the moon,' Hamilton threw grenades amongst clusters of men, and 'was even skilful enough to throw several into their hatchways.' One of these dropped into a hatch where it ended up in amongst some scattered eighteen-pounder cartridges. They caught, and there followed, says Lieutenant Richard Dale of the *Bonhomme Richard*, 'a most awful explosion', whose 'effect was tremendous', when it ripped along the gun deck and killed or badly burned about twenty men and powder monkeys, and put five eighteen-pounders out of action.

Watchers on board Paul Jones's ship could see through the gun ports hapless crewmen on the *Serapis* burnt agonisingly naked of their clothes, except for their shirt collars. Some of the crew manning the guns of the *Serapis* were obliged to jump overboard between the two ships to escape the inferno, and were lucky to get

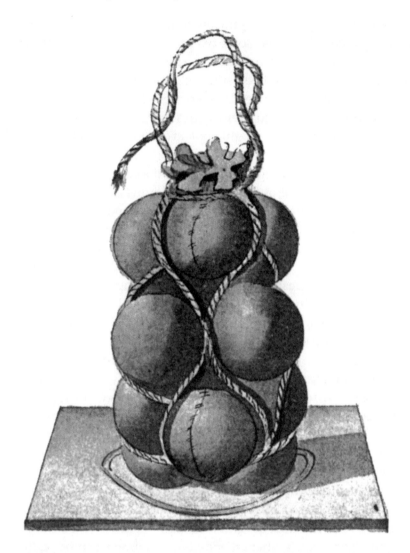

Quilted grapeshot, in use when Paul Jones successfully took on the Drake *and the* Serapis. *The drawing is by Captain A.S. Fraser RA, 1828, in the keeping of the Royal Artillery Institution Library, Woolwich. The packages of shot – standardised by then at nine balls, of varying dimensions depending on the bore of the gun, were often made up on board ship. Canvas bags were sewn, and a bottom plate of wood or iron with a central iron spindle pushed down inside. The nine balls were then stacked inside around the spindle, in three tiers. After this the bag was quilted tightly in a mesh of cord, to facilitate insertion and ramming down the barrel.*

back on board scorched, raw, and dripping with salt water. One man in the sea, Robert Ozard, got hold of a rope and clambering up it, managed to haul himself over onto the deck, only to find that he was about to be shot by a marine. As he cried out, 'O Lord,' in despair, his voice was recognised by the marine, and at the same time the watchful Pearson called out: 'It's one of our people, don't kill him.'

The scorched flesh of suffering crewmen was rubbed with hogs-lard by the surgeon's orderlies in the crowded cockpit. Nathaniel Fanning is horribly graphic on the effects of Willie Hamilton's grenade, saying that most of those injured '... lingered along for two or three days ... burnt in such a shocking manner that the flesh of several of them dropped off from their bones, and they died in great pain'.

Following the explosion the *Serapis* was now on fire again, the glow visible to the crew of the *Bonhomme Richard* through her gun ports. As Lieutenant Wright of the *Serapis* put it at the court martial, 'the starboard side was all in a blaze'. But the *Bonhomme Richard* was also burning, as well as filling steadily with water. Paul Jones talks coolly about the explosion caused by Willie Hamilton's grenade 'burning a number of people' and does not at the time he made the remark seem to have really appreciated the seriousness of the event for the *Serapis*.

In desperation, Paul Jones now concentrated the whole fire of his three remaining nine-pounders against the mainmast of the *Serapis*, himself firing double-headed shot and the others suppres-sant grape and canister shot. After the explosion tore through his ship, Pearson had been on the verge of striking, but in an extraordi-nary twist was forestalled by the actions of the chief gunner of the *Bonhomme Richard*. Not seeing the Commodore, perhaps thinking he was dead, and after agreeing with two other wounded petty officers that the ship would sink rapidly if she did not surrender, he ran to haul down the American ensign, only to find it shot away. He yelled across to Pearson for quarter. 'What damned rascals are them?' shouted John Paul angrily – very much alive. It is said that he ran across and hurled his pistol at the Chief Gunner, dropping him to the deck.

There is some variation between reports of an exchange between Pearson and Paul Jones that followed. Soon after the battle, the

Newcastle Courant in 'particulars', which, the newspaper claims, 'may be depended on as authentic', says that Pearson 'called out to him [Jones] to strike, or he must infallibly go to the bottom'. One source reports Paul Jones as replying politely; 'No, sir, I haven't as yet thought of it, but I'm determined to make you strike.' The *Courant* quotes a rather pithier version: 'Jones replied, with an oath, "I may sink but I'll be damned if I'll strike"'. Pearson in his dispatch says that in fact he called across two or three times around this point and got no reply, but forlornly sensing a chance to snatch a victory out of the appalling carnage at the last, he 'called for the boarders' and sent them across hoping to force the issue, but they were repelled 'by a superior number lying under cover' and awaiting them – including Paul Jones wielding a boarding pike.

It was now very dark and getting on for ten o'clock. An ominous five-foot depth of water was sloshing around in the hold of the *Bonhomme Richard*. The prisoners were released around this time and most turned their hands to manning the pumps with great urgency, though it was a lost cause, and the water kept on rising. According to Lieutenant Dale, on his release, one of the prisoners:

> ...a commander of a twenty gun sloop taken a few days before passed through the ports on board the *Serapis*, and informed Captain Pearson that if he would hold out only a little while longer, the ship alongside would either strike or sink.

Pearson did hold on, but Jones showed no sign of striking, and though the *Bonhomme Richard* was indeed sinking she did not actually do so for a couple of days. She was also still on fire, with her guns all but completely knocked out. Only the three nine-pounders on deck were still smashing doggedly away at the mainmast of the *Serapis*, which was tottering. The mainmast made a good target in the obscurity says Jones in his *Memoir*, because it was painted 'yellow' (yellow ochre to be more precise) and stood out. The enemy eighteen-pounders which remained were still wreaking some havoc down below, though many of the balls were by now passing clean through the gaping hull to drop harmlessly into the sea beyond, without doing any more harm.

Things could not go on much longer. When his mainmast began to totter alarmingly; with his crew unable to appear on deck without being shot; only four eighteen-pounders still in increasingly ineffective action below; the powerful *Alliance* hovering undamaged close by; and with the *Countess of Scarborough* having already surrendered to the more powerful *Pallas; and* after a long-fought and bloody battle, the beleaguered Captain Pearson decided that the time had come to strike. At the outset of the action Pearson had ordered the red ensign purposefully nailed to the staff, and he now had to rip it away with his own bare hands. The last straw, according to Pearson, was the action of the *Alliance* in 'coming across our stern and pouring her broadside into us again, without our being able to bring a gun to bear on her'. Pearson concluded that he '... found it in vain, and in short impracticable, from the situation we were in, to stand out any longer with the least prospect of success; I therefore struck'.

With the mainmast at last crashing to his deck from the single-minded, personal attention of Paul Jones, the hapless Pearson was, upon striking, directed politely aboard the *Bonhomme Richard* by Richard Dale. 'Sir', said the First Lieutenant, 'I have orders to send you on board the ship alongside'.

As custom demanded Pearson handed his sword to Paul Jones, who handed it back with a word about his bravery. He then invited Pearson into his cabin for a glass of wine – a glass or two, says Nathaniel Fanning.

In his Report Paul Jones says that 'the British colours were struck at half an hour past ten o'clock', revising this in his later Memoir by saying it was 'after 11 o'clock when the battle ended ... it had lasted more than four hours'. Lieutenant Dale described the battle as 'a most obstinate contest of three and a half hours'. Mid-shipman Fanning says that the 'memorable battle' lasted 'a few minutes more than four hours'.

Jones, again in the later Memoir, singled out Lieutenant Richard Dale by name from amongst a number of officers whom, he said, 'conducted themselves in a very admirable manner during the action'. He was more appreciative also by now of what Willie Hamilton, whom he describes as 'this brave man', had contributed to their victory with his lucky but boldly delivered grenade.

In the confusion at the end, Fanning spotlights an incident not mentioned by Paul Jones in his Report, but referred to in his later Memoir. A small party of men, whilst the surrender proceedings were underway, says Paul Jones, made off in a small ship's boat, which was at that time 'laying alongside', says Fanning. He says that these men were in fact a few escaping English prisoners, the Master-at-Arms having released all the prisoners to save them from drowning if the ship sank – and to help save the ship by manning the pumps. Fanning talks of thwarting a serious attempt to take over the ship, and Paul Jones in his Report refers to: 'My treacherous Master-at-Arms [who] let loose all my prisoners without my knowledge'. He continues, 'My prospect became gloomy indeed. I would not however give up.' He achieved his victory not long afterwards. Escaped English prisoners, giving sworn testament before the Mayor of Hull, became the source of some alarming – but uncorroborated – tales about Paul Jones, including his piratical appearance, 'dressed in a short jacket and long trousers, with about twelve charged pistols slung in a belt round his middle, and a cutlass in his hand'.

After the engagement, Jones directed Richard Dale to follow behind him with the *Serapis*. However, after cutting the lashings between the two ships, the lieutenant says, he could not get the her to move off behind the *Bonhomme Richard* as she got underway. Dale says :

> Excited by this extraordinary circumstance I jumped off the binnacle, where I had been sitting, and falling upon the deck, found to my astonishment I had the use of only one of my legs: A splinter of one of the guns had struck and badly wounded my leg without my perceiving the injury until this moment. I was replaced upon the binnacle.

The sailing master of the *Serapis* came up to him as he sat there and told him the simple reason for their failure to get underway as ordered: the *Serapis* was – as you may have remembered – firmly anchored! Dale sent someone below to cut away the cable, and was then carried on board the *Bonhomme Richard* to have his wound attended to. He was only one wounded man amongst an obscene number of other casualties.

The close fight between *Bonhomme Richard* and *Serapis* had lasted for an unprecedented length of time, the ships locked in a deadly embrace for most of that time. John Paul described his flagship as

'… mangled beyond my power of description … a person must have been an eyewitness to form a just idea of the tremendous scene of carnage, wreck and ruin which everywhere appeared'. Estimates of the casualties vary considerably, influenced perhaps by some understandable reluctance to admit the true scale of the human cost, but they were at a frightful level. The two ships between them seem to have ended the engagement with between a half and two-thirds of their combined crews killed or wounded, with the *Bonhomme Richard* suffering by far the most. Pearson estimated the American ship's casualties at just over three hundred, which looks unrealistic as it would have accounted for almost the whole crew (though maybe all *were* wounded to some extent). Paul Jones himself never actually produced a toll of his own killed and wounded. Following the engagement off Flamborough Head, he looked over the wrecks of both ships, contemplating sombrely the scenes of blood and death before him. Reflecting on it later he said: 'Humanity cannot but recoil from the prospect of such finished horror, and lament that war should be capable of producing such fatal consequences', words which somehow seem curiously detached from the hideous human reality of the event which he himself had brought about. In his defence, though Paul Jones clearly enjoyed adventure and its risks, he indicated on several occasions that he did not relish war as such. And perhaps his words seem more bloodless to a modern audience than they would to his contemporaries. However relentless and single-minded in a battle situation, he was a considerate and compassionate man in his general attitude and in individual cases. An example of this was alluded to earlier; in his treatment of one of the pilots captured off Flamborough Head, John Jackson, who lost an arm during the course of his involuntary involvement in the subsequent fight with the *Serapis*. Paul Jones returned him to his home port in his own pilot boat, with the then considerable sum of £250 in his pocket. He also wrote to the Corporation of Hull, saying that Jackson had been taken at gunpoint, and that if the Corporation would certify in writing every two years that he was still alive the American government would grant Jackson half pay for life. It was not Paul Jones's fault that this arrangement, although seemingly approved by Franklin, was not honoured by Congress. The story gained currency in Britain and was another nugget of information helping to burnish John Paul's image.

The danger was still acute even after the battle was over. Fanning recounts that fire on board the *Richard* was 'within the thickness of a pine board' from the powder magazine. The powder was ordered out of the magazine. As they emptied the powder room, crewmen and assisting English officers were alike 'much frightened ... the fire was at that moment in and about the powder room, and we expected every moment to be blown into the air'. Unsurprisingly, the job was done 'in a few minutes'. After eventually putting out other serious fires with difficulty, they could concentrate on manning the pumps and preventing the ship from sinking! Their sustained pumping was, however, to no avail. On the second morning after the engagement, and despite their unremitting efforts to save her, the *Bonhomme Richard* took in more water and, with the American flag still flying, finally sank bows first into the North Sea, having many dead still on board.

Landais claims that Paul Jones deliberately sank the *Bonhomme Richard* because, 'had she been brought in, it would have been a palpable witness against him', further alleging – without support – that Jones 'had unplug'd the shot holes to make her sink'. There is no end to the unremitting allegations of fault and wrongdoing poisonously lacing Landais's account in his *Memorial*; he was a very aggrieved man; one might say driven mad by his sense of injustice.

In 1975 a search for the *Bonhomme Richard* was started with modern equipment, and within about twelve months a wreck was discovered which had the right length and breadth. Moreover, it was found at a place where a fisherman had previously dredged up from the bottom a cannon dated 1775 – about the right time to be from Paul Jones's ship. However, she was one shattered vessel amongst many wrecks lying on the bottom of the North Sea thereabouts. Nothing sensational seems to have transpired since (at the time of writing), though a wreck in that vicinity, perhaps the same one, has been registered with the Receiver of Wreck. (The Receiver of Wreck is a British government official whose main task is to process reports of wreck so that owners can attempt to retrieve their property, or ensure that lawful finders of wreck receive an appropriate reward.) In 2006 a new attempt using US Navy divers was undertaken, with a resumption of efforts scheduled for 2007. There are problems, in that the *Bonhomme Richard* drifted some distance from the battle scene before she sank, and may now be overlain by a more recent iron wreck. Any productive activity on such a famous sunken vessel, leading to her identification and excavation, would not fail to attract media attention, especially in the US.

Contrary to Captain Pearson's later statement, all the wounded seem to have been got out before the ship sank, but it is recorded that the vessel was not cleared of goods before she went down. In fact, she took down with her many of the valuable personal belongings of Paul Jones himself, including, he says, 50,000 livres, and a number of 'invaluable papers' – these surely lost forever in watery dissolution.

Before she eventually sank, Nathaniel Fanning had looked her over, taking 'a full view of the mangled carcasses of the slain on board of our ship; especially between decks, where the bloody scene was enough to appall the stoutest heart. To see the dead lying in heaps – to hear the groans of the wounded and dying – the entrails of the dead scattered promiscuously around … was enough to move pity from the most hardened and callous breast'.

According to Paul Jones, in the morning after the battle the weather was cloudy and foggy, and when it cleared around 11 o'clock all of the enemy convoy had taken refuge under the fortress of Scarborough, with not a single sail to be seen along the coast. However, the fascinated observer at the sash window of his house in Scarborough maintained his vigil. He noted that six ships, one of which had lost her main mast, kept their station all the following day, but were gone the following morning. Still on the look-out the following morning, he observed that before the arrival of any second Baltic fleet, a powerful force of eight British warships hove into sight, but were soon seen to sail off 'in search of this rascal Jones', as the Scarborough man put it.

The American squadron had sailed off – or limped off in the case of Paul Jones – to the Texel as originally planned, and as luck would have it, were never intercepted by any of the British warships sent searching for them. On board the *Serapis* now, he was in company with the rest of the squadron for some while, until, as he says, 'they left me'. On boarding the captured *Serapis* he had transferred his flag to her after his own ship sank, and with jury-rigged masts (temporary rigging), he was '… tossed about in the North Sea by contrary winds for ten days before reaching the Texel'.

Paul Jones wanted the task force to head for Dunkirk, a friendly French port, whilst the rest insisted on making for the Texel, a neutral, and to Jones a problematical, Dutch port. But the Texel was the concluding destination set down in the orders regulating their cruise, and for better or for worse, Jones went along with them. However, the Dutch were reluctant to allow the squadron into the roadstead initially, and with pursuing British warships by now, says Fanning, 'but a little more than a cannon shot' away from the crippled squadron, Jones threatened to barge his way in. Fortunately, the threat impressed the prevaricating Dutch admiral involved, and the regrouped squadron entered the roadstead of the Texel together, in triumphal style, on at 6 am on 3 October 1779; just two days past the date prescribed in their orders (and only one according to Jones, who gives the date of the 2nd).

Looking rather like an anarchist's cartoon bomb, this design remained fundamentally unchanged for 300 years. The fuse passed though the friable iron casing via a bored wooden plug into the interior, which was filled with 'powder ground most subtily.' It was a grenade like this that Hamilton threw down the open hatch of the Serapis *with such terrible consequences. (Courtesy the Royal Armouries Museum, Leeds)*

9

Trophies –
The Conquering Hero

John Paul Jones led his task force into the Texel on the quarterdeck of the *Serapis*, with an American flag flying triumphantly from the British mast-head. The occasion was one of exultation, and having triumphed in the face of serious adversity Paul Jones must have experienced a sense of fully justified pride. To his disgust, however, when they eventually left the Texel all the ships in the squadron, including the captured British warships (except the *Alliance*, which was an American ship), were flying French colours. Paul Jones just had to put up with it.

Fanning thinks that after their arrival in Holland, success went to Paul Jones's head. In Amsterdam he was, says Fanning, 'caressed' and 'treated like a conqueror', though the Dutch were not at war with Britain. 'This so elated him with pride', Fanning censures, 'he had the vanity to go into the state house' and show himself off to the general public from a 'balcony or piazza'. Fanning's judgement seems harsh, in view of all the trials Paul Jones had endured to achieve his success, and now to have it recognized in spite of some eager detractors.

The highly colourful voyage of the *Bonhomme Richard* squadron with its spectacular climax was acclaimed ecstatically in France; it was in such welcome contrast to the miserable Combined Fleet disaster off the south coast of England. With the French fleet limping back into Brest just two days before his victory, John Paul was idolised in Paris. His exploits and persona sparked off a new rage in female fashion – hats 'à la Paul Jones'. One of these creations somehow featured the unlikely combination of a grenade symbolised by a pomegranate encircled by a victory crown of laurel. Only thirty-two years old and debonair, with the weather-beaten good looks of a seafarer, he was persuaded to wear a laurel wreath in a box at the Paris Opera, to adulatory applause. He received an engraved gold-hilted sword from the King of France, and was personally decorated by the King, basking in the title of chevalier.

In America too the intrepid actions of Paul Jones were acclaimed, making an especially welcome impact in a year when things were not going well for the Americans in their war with Britain. He received the formal thanks of a grateful Congress, and though it was to be eight long years after the event and marred by a certain amount of political quibbling in the early stages, the rare distinction of a Congressional Gold Medal. Congress resolved unanimously:

> ... that a medal of gold be struck and presented to the Chevalier John Paul Jones in commemoration of the valour and brilliant services of that officer in command of a squadron of American and French ships under the flag and commission of the United States.

No other naval officer was awarded a Gold Medal by Congress during the American War of Independence, and only five army officers (with George Washington himself amongst the select few) were singled out for the same recognition. On the obverse of his unique gold medal was a portrait bust of John Paul, and on the reverse a fine depiction of the battle between *Bonhomme Richard* and *Serapis*. The eminent French artist Moreau made a suitably impressive portrait engraving of Jones in celebration of his spectacular triumph over the British man o' war.

Since his first arrival in France John Paul had been in close contact with fellow Freemasons and, after his remarkable naval victory, was received in Paris with an altogether extravagant eulogy into the prestigious Lodge of the Nine Sisters. The Nine Sisters were the nine classical Muses, and apart from being a heroic figure in the classic mould Paul Jones had certain literary pretensions to recommend him to the lodge; as an enthusiastic versifier. Some of his compositions were love poems, and he sometimes adapted the same verses to suit different women. The Lodge commissioned a fine portrait bust of Paul Jones from one of its members, the talented sculptor Houdon, who also executed busts of Washington, Franklin and Voltaire, all Masons, the last two being members of the Nine Sisters Lodge itself. Freemasonry, which embraced female Lodges of Adoption, became the focal point of John Paul's social life in Paris. It was through the Masonic connection that he came to know his 'Delia', the young Comtesse de Nicolson.

Puzzlingly for an American naval captain with a regard for regulations and etiquette, Paul Jones is reported to have appeared in public around this time wearing an American uniform, but jauntily sporting 'a Scotch bonnet edged with gold' upon his head. Paul Jones was born in the once notoriously lawless region straddling the boundary between England and Scotland, so perhaps here was an example of the independent spirit of the border people showing through, the, by then, more refined, but formerly wild, hard men, the border reivers, 'that will be Scottish when they will and English at their pleasure' – or American in the case of Paul Jones!

His high-profile adventures in British home waters were to be the pinnacle of John Paul's career. His place in the hall of fame was secure. It had all hung on his decision at the critical moment to go for the *Serapis* on his own, rather than lose the Baltic convoy without even a shot being fired. If Paul Jones had not spotted and correctly interpreted Pearson's stealthy change of course in the gathering darkness off Flamborough Head at the start of the action and before the moon came up, he would have been thwarted in everything he so desperately sought, except his share of the prize money. There would have been no honour and no everlasting glory. Pearson performed his escort duty admirably, in that Paul Jones did not get to a single ship of the convoy. But he had taken plenty of other prizes of course, and there had been a very valuable total haul for the squadron – and the 'concerned'. Towards the end of his report to Benjamin Franklin on the expedition, Jones says: 'As the great majority of the actors in it have appeared bent on the pursuit of interest only; I am exceedingly sorry that they and I have at all been concerned.'

Sadly, the eventual end of the *Serapis* was ignominious. Soon after arrival at the Texel, the vessel was reported to be in a filthy and shameful condition, with rotting human body parts lying about. Once this was brought to his attention, Paul Jones, who must have had plenty of experience of filth aboard slave ships in his earlier days, had the ship thoroughly cleaned. In the exhausted aftermath of the gruesome battle off Flamborough Head, things would have been lax without the disciplinary presence of John Paul on board; he was busy being adored elsewhere by the general populace!

Some time later, whilst *Serapis* was stationed by the French in the Indian Ocean, an open signal lamp was being used one night to cast a light on the broaching of a keg of high-proof brandy, to water it down into grog. The liquid contents of the keg were set alight, resulting in an uncontrollable fire that completely burnt out the ship. Less dramatically, the captured *Countess of Scarborough* became a merchant vessel, which was what she had been before being adapted as a warship by the British navy.

The British Government claimed, unsuccessfully, that the *Serapis* and the *Countess of Scrarborough* were not legal prizes, because they were taken by rebels under the command of a subject of the King, a subject who was nothing more than a traitorous renegade.

Pearson and Piercy, the respective captains of those ships off Flamborough Head, came out of a court martial with honour, having 'done infinite credit to themselves by a very obstinate defense against a superior force', the court reasonably declared. They had, in facing up to and finally engaging with the American squadron, steadfastly and successfully carried out their primary duty of ensuring the safety of the convoy of merchant ships, something that Pearson was justifiably proud to put to the Admiralty. As he saw it, his ship had 'not been given away'. The Admiralty agreed and in due course Pearson received a knighthood. Both Pearson and Piercy were given the freedom of several towns, including Scarborough and Pearson's home-town of Appleby. Pearson was also presented with handsome pieces of silver plate by grateful mercantile interests: the Russia Company, and the Royal Exchange Assurance Company.

Paul Jones had two warships as prestigious prizes out of the engagement – and an impressive collection of prisoners with which he hoped to twist the arm of the British government over the treatment and release of American captives. It was extremely galling to Paul Jones that the French Government exchanged them for French prisoners, not Americans. In the longer term, however, the objective of prisoner-of-war status was secured.

Considering that he had been defeated, Pearson could perhaps be seen by some, including his recent adversary, as fortunate in being awarded a knighthood. When he heard of it, Paul Jones quipped:

'Should I have the good fortune to fall in with him again, I'll make a Lord of him'.

Not long after the squadron's arrival in the Texel, Landais was called to Paris as a result of Paul Jones's allegations against him; 'cowardice and bad conduct', according to Fanning's pithy summary. Before he went to see Franklin, Landais quarrelled with Cottineau, who had testified in favour of Paul Jones and who declined to support evidence which Landais had prepared. According to Fanning, Landais challenged Cottineau to a sword duel, a challenge which Cottineau accepted. Landais had the better of it and Cottineau was, says Fanning, very dangerously wounded. Landais then challenged Paul Jones to a duel, as might have been expected in view of threats made during the expedition around the British Isles, and Paul Jones's angry rise to the challenge. However, as Fanning relates, Paul Jones, 'perhaps not thinking it prudent to expose himself with a single combatant who was a complete master of the small sword, declined'. Instead, the practically minded Jones, ignoring his earlier rash acceptance of the Frenchman's challenge, ordered Landais' immediate arrest! Landais eluded capture and decamped for Paris, and his inevitable interrogation by Benjamin Franklin. He did not consider Paul Jones a man of honour, and said so.

Eventually, Landais went back to America where, following involvement in further alarming transgressions unrelated to Paul Jones and the *Bonhomme Richard* cruise, and having been relieved of command amidst allegations of insanity, he ended up in irredeemable disgrace. However, he lived defiantly on in New York for forty years: 'He subsisted in the utmost independence on his scanty income, refusing all presents', said a contemporary, writing in *The Talisman*. He succeeded in outliving virtually all his detractors, finally giving up the ghost at the age of eighty-seven. In his latter days he cut a wizened and rather bizarre figure, wearing pitifully threadbare clothes and invariably sporting the American cockade. Each year, on the Fourth of July, Independence Day, he wore his old and increasingly badly fitting American naval uniform, the large, antiquated brass buttons tarnished by age. The uniform 'wrapped his shrunken person like a cloak', the coat tails flapping against his heels as he walked. The writer states at the end of his vignette of Landais in the *Talisman*, 'The natural violence of his temper was not softened by age … He affirmed to the last that he, and not

Jones, was the conqueror of the *Serapis*.' According to cathedral records, Landais's epitaph, which described him as not 'dying' but rather as 'disappearing', seems to have been destroyed in a catastrophic fire that gutted old St. Patrick's cathedral not very long after Landais died. Before asserting that it was he who conquered the *Serapis*, Landais had certainly read the long letter Pearson had written to the Admiralty giving his own account of the action off Flamborough Head, a letter published in full in the newspapers in Britain, and which Landais referred to in his *Memorial*. The tenor of Pearson's letter would have bolstered him in his bold assertion of conquest, however dubious it might have seemed to others.

Pearson states, as noted earlier, that the *Alliance* caused serious damage to *Serapis* at the end of the action, her undamaged presence being also the immediate cause of him striking his colours. He says, furthermore, that 'the largest of the two frigates [*Alliance*] kept sailing around us the whole action, and raking us fore and aft, by which means she killed or wounded almost every man on the quarter main decks'. Paul Jones gives the credit for the casualties to his swarms of sharpshooters aloft. Tellingly, *Alliance*, with damning evidence of causing serious – Jones says treacherous – damage to the *Bonhomme Richard*, emerged from the cataclysmic action almost completely unscathed; which perhaps says much about her real effectiveness at Flamborough Head, including her distance from the action. However, Piercy cites the overpowering arrival of the *Alliance* on the scene as the immediate and justifiable reason for his striking after a two-hour fight with *Pallas*.

Having obtained his commission in dubious circumstances, as Benjamin Franklin discovered on looking closely into the matter after the termination of the *Bonhomme Richard* cruise, Landais was first sent to France from Boston as Captain of the *Alliance* in 1778. He had to quell a mutiny on board while crossing the Atlantic. He was instructed by the American Navy Board to inform Franklin of his arrival; 'whose orders you are then to obey'. The Navy Board notified Franklin to this effect. Landais was to 'follow such orders as he may receive from Your Excellency, which he is strictly to obey'. Which is why Landais had to explain himself at some length to Franklin after the expedition had ended. In particular, Landais vehemently denied – as he naturally would do of course – that he deliberately fired on the *Bonhomme Richard* in the heat of battle. Paul

Jones insinuates this, Landais alleges, because he was trying to avoid opprobrium for the huge loss of life aboard the *Bonhomme Richard*; as Landais says: 'to extricate himself, he wanted to charge me with their blood'. He says that Franklin, 'who had listened attentively, all the while', expressed the thought that 'I might by mistake have fired upon the *Bonhomme Richard*. Supposing I had, it would not be a guilt in me, but only a mistake, which might have happened in the night'. However, he is very concerned that his action might be considered deliberate, and asserts that the 'refined treachery, and blackness of mind' necessary 'to destroy Captain Jones, as hinted by him' is unimaginable in relation to Pierre Landais. As he did not himself fire a cannon, he says, the alleged deed could only have been done either by ordering his officers to fire, or by persuading or bribing them to do so. Such an order would have seen him clapped in irons, and even supposing that suborning the officers was feasible, would the gunners and all the crew have obeyed them in firing upon their American brothers? 'Franklin agreed', says Landais, 'that it was not likely', and that this was indeed Franklin's view is confirmed in his own later written comments on the subject. But there were documented protests from the crew of the *Bonhomme Richard*, and also from amongst those on board the *Alliance*, about the damage the *Alliance* was doing to the flagship from a distance and in the darkness. The difficult situation was basically the same as that which had caused a more cautious Piercy to reluctantly withhold the assistance of his firepower from Pearson, who fully appreciated his dilemma and acknowledged his openly expressed reason for desisting, and made no adverse comment. Landais evidently had no such qualms, and rounded off his conversation with Franklin on this particular point of culpability by saying:

> Since Captain Jones is capable of devising such a charge against me, to justify himself and appear mighty and glorious, after having been released by the *Alliance* from the sad fate he was so nigh falling into, it may be imagined what he is capable of.

Landais was fighting for his own reputation, but history had made its judgement on both men's reputation by the time John Paul Jones's body was belatedly brought back to America in 1905. President Theodore Roosevelt, expressed an altogether different view of the

man who wanted to 'appear mighty and glorious' in an address to
the United States Naval Academy at Annapolis, saying that he was
not only a proper subject for admiration and respect, but an object
lesson for naval officers, who should have:

> ... an eager desire to emulate the energy, the professional capac-
> ity, the indomitable determination and the dauntless scorn of
> death which marked John Paul Jones above all his fellows.

In contrast, Benjamin Franklin, in a strictly private missive to
Landais (for his eyes only he assured him), has this to say of Paul
Jones's inimical Captain:

> I think you are then so imprudent, so litigious, and quarrel-
> some a man even with your best friends, that peace and good
> order, and consequently the quiet and regular subordination
> so necessary to success, are, where you preside, impossible;
> these are within my observation and apprehension; your mili-
> tary operations I leave to more capable judges.

He finishes by saying that if he had twenty ships at his disposal,
Peter Landais would not get one of them.

In honouring Paul Jones in the immediate aftermath of events
with the *Ordre du Mérite Militaire* with its associated title of chevalier, and his personal gift of the gold hilted sword, the King of
France was clearly as impressed by John Paul Jones as was Theodore
Roosevelt in his assessment over 125 years later.

The British government saw things rather differently, but its psy-
ops and propaganda were poor, partly because it was not in possession of the facts. Much of the cruise of the *Ranger* and of the *Bonhomme
Richard* expedition – especially at Whitehaven and Edinburgh – could
have been presented as a catalogue of failure and fiasco. The British
alleged that the easy prize-ship pickings were mere piracy. Had they
known more about the extraordinary background and personal dra-
mas that characterised Paul Jones's tours, the renegade could have
been turned into a mockery, and even his victories over Royal Navy
warships cast in a less glorious light.

Public attention in Britain focussed on the inept failure of the
government in searching out and catching the rascal. The situation

was summed up very well in a letter from the First Sea Lord of the British Admiralty, urging a Captain Reynolds instantly to sea in search of the *Bonhomme Richard* squadron: 'If you can take Paul Jones, you will be as high in the estimation of the public as if you had beat the Combined Fleets.' British squadrons were, in fact, out frantically looking for him in overwhelming force, but the wily will o' the wisp outfoxed them all on both voyages. British newspapers had been pretty matter of fact in reporting events at Whitehaven, but after the battle off Flamborough Head a more urgent, even hysterical note can be heard. The *Morning Post and Daily Advertiser* on 14 October 1779:

> Paul Jones in his action with the *Serapis* conducted himself like the pirate, and not the hero. He meanly sued for quarter, when his intentions were murder; thus taking advantage of our Englishman's humanity to make American treachery triumphant; on land the rebels fight from lurking holes, and seek the blood of their enemies like cowardly villains. At sea they cry for mercy, to mask the malice of premeditated assassination.

The editor and his crew were clearly rattled!

Paul Jones stayed on in France for a while, basking in his glory and enjoying his celebrity, whilst at the same time attending to certain matters arising out of his exploits, such as the conduct of Landais and question of prize money. Despite his spectacular triumph over the naval might of the British he was conscious that in inshore waters and with safe haven nearby, the Baltic Fleet had got away unscathed. But given the effective interposition of Pearson in the *Serapis* and Piercy in the *Countess of Scarborough*, there had not been much he could do about it. He returned after a while to America, but without accomplishing anything spectacular in the interim. He did however, at the start of the crossing to America, gain the grateful admiration and heartfelt thanks of crew and passengers alike, when, by an extraordinary and prolonged feat of matchless seamanship, he saved his ship *Ariel* from going down with all hands in a fearsome storm off the coast of Brittany, with the sea running 'mountains high', says Fanning. Soldiers set to manning the pumps broke off from pumping to start praying, and had to be kept at the 'cranks' (pump handles) with 'naked hangers (swords) over their heads', with a threat of 'instant death if they quit their duty'. The ship ended up totally dismasted and badly damaged - but still afloat, by the time the tempest blew itself out.

After the ship had been repaired, and just before setting out again to cross the Atlantic, Paul Jones arranged a social event on board the *Ariel*, which included an elaborate dinner in the afternoon and a sham sea fight in the evening, recalling the battle with the *Serapis*, especially in the use of the fighting tops, where Fanning was in command again! Fanning says that when festivities started around 3 o'clock the quarterdeck 'had the appearance of a lady of quality's drawing room', carpeted, and with an elegant awning and elaborate hangings, as well as pictures, 'many of which were quite indecent especially to meet the eyes of a virtuous woman'. He complains about the food: 'For nearly twenty hours preceding the serving up of dinner, we were almost suffocated with garlick and onions, besides a great many other stinking vegetables.' The sham fight took place in the evening a little after sunset, involving about an hour and a quarter of deafening explosions, smoke and stink. 'Some of the ladies were much frightened', and the fight would have lasted much longer had not some of them 'intreated Captain Jones to command the firing to cease'. At about midnight the festivities came to an end and the midshipmen helped a few drunks back to their homes. Fanning concluded censoriously: 'I believe it must have cost himself, as well as the United States, a vast sum of money.'

Crossing the Atlantic soon after this talk-of-the town event in Lorient, there was a brief encounter with the *Triumph*, a twenty-gun British privateer, which proved to be a case of the trickster tricked. As usual Paul Jones got close by unsportingly flying the British flag, opened fire at close range and soon caused *Triumph* to strike her colours. The cheers aboard *Ariel* were short-lived however, because at an opportune moment the captain of the vanquished privateer successfully crammed on sail and, equally unsportingly, bolted.

Paul Jones made one or two fleeting visits to England in the aftermath of his cruises around the British Isles, and later he was even bold enough to spend a little time in London. He did not exactly advertise his presence in England, but on one occasion a naval acquaintance bumped into him in Cranborne Alley, off Leicester Square in London. They walked together for a while and went into a shop, where Paul Jones bought a pair of boots and had them sent to his hotel. On another occasion he was recognised in Harwich and besieged at an inn by a raucous mob, before making good his escape.

During the periods when he was back in America, and when not, then through correspondence, Paul Jones expended a lot of effort on the question of improving naval efficiency, always an interest of his, especially through training. He seems to have been the prime mover in the setting up of the Naval College at Annapolis. All the time though, he was seeking promotion to flag rank as a rear admiral, which he felt to be no more than his due, judged on his performance and seniority. Eventually he returned to Europe, bitter that this promotion had not come, to act as prize agent for the American government. Once there, and mainly on the advice of Thomas Jefferson, by then the American ambassador in Paris, he quite soon accepted an offer from Catherine the Great to enter the Russian navy as a rear admiral.

At last he had attained the flag rank that he was forever aggrieved at being denied in America, with a promise of supreme command in fighting the Turks in the Black Sea. The Ambassador in Paris wrote to George Washington: 'The Empress has engaged Commodore Paul Jones in her service. He is to have the rank of Rear Admiral, with a separate command, and it is understood he is in no case to be commanded.'

10

A Russian Bearhug –
Success, Scandal, and the Secret Police

Paul Jones was keen to take up his challenging appointment, and being anxious to get to Russia after reaching Sweden in winter, he felt compelled to brave the crushing ice floes of the freezing Baltic by hiring two small open boats. It was a dangerous and toilsome voyage, with the vessels having to be hauled over sea ice in numerous places. The smaller vessel, though not its crew, was lost. The crew of the second vessel had to be forced at pistol point to complete a trip they had not bargained for. Though well rewarded for their gruelling efforts, they were frostbitten by the end of their ordeal and no doubt glad to see the back of their alarming passenger. Thus it was, with inimitable panache, that John Paul heralded his entry into the Russian capital of St Petersburg. His stay in Russia proved short and bizarre; and the obscure circumstances surrounding it warrant speculation, especially as he never fully recovered from the traumatic experience.

The sprawling, autocratic Russian Empire and the fledgling liberal democratic republic which was the United States of America were a world apart politically as well as geographically. Russia did not recognise the United States diplomatically. At his first encounter with his new and unlikely employer, Paul Jones, the bold fighter for freedom and glory, chose to proudly present to Catherine the Great, the sixty-year-old imperialist despot, a copy of the American Constitution. Despite what might have been seen as a somewhat tactless gesture, the two of them made a favourable personal impression upon each other.

Whereas Paul Jones was a colourful and controversial figure with a burgeoning reputation, the key players on the Russian stage were larger than life in a much more lurid sense, including Catherine and

John Paul's future Commander, Prince Potemkin, her greatest passion and ever-enduring confidant; and on the available evidence, very likely to have been her secret second husband.

By the time Paul Jones arrived in St. Petersburg, Catherine had already become Empress, and sole ruler of Russia, as a result of having engineered the deposition of her inconsequential and apparently semi-imbecilic spouse Tsar Peter III; in the nick of time, as he himself was just about to get rid of her. Peter was locked away and soon killed off with Catherine's connivance. Whilst married to the sterile and impossible Peter, Catherine had already experienced two miscarriages by one of a chain of lovers, Sergei Saltykov, a young man of twenty-six. 'He was as beautiful as the dawn', she later wrote in her memoirs. Apparently unknown to her husband, she gave birth to a son by Saltykov, eventually to become Tsar Paul I. Still married to the living Peter she had subsequently had another son, fathered this time by a dashing young soldier named Gregory Orlov. After being successfully carried and born clandestinely, this child was secretly fostered as Alexis Bobrinsky, later to become Count Bobrinsky and progenitor of a celebrated Russian family. Much earlier there had also been a daughter, Anna, by Stanislaus Poniatowski, a Polish aristocrat, but the child had died in infancy. 'God knows where she gets her pregnancies from,' Tsar Peter had once exclaimed aloud in company. His mother, the Tsarina Elizabeth, was not so baffled. She had for reasons of state connived in the quasi-official liaison with Saltykov. The hapless Tsar Peter, who had a long standing mistress (ugly by common consent), whom he much preferred to Catherine, had added to his exasperated remark the resigned comment: 'I suppose I shall have to accept the child as my own.' Though Catherine was hardly an icon of moral rectitude, she understood the importance of an outward show of such.

Paul Jones also made an initially favourable impression on Prince Potemkin, who was blind in one eye as the result of a brawl over Catherine, and with a severe squint in the other. He was personally daring in battle, and exposed himself recklessly – heroically some said – on several occasions. Once she had become powerfully attracted to him physically, Catherine had raised Potemkin from obscurity, conferring position and title on him and eventually putting him in overall charge of Russian forces. She came to rely on him to run the imperial machine, and he did not let her down. On the contrary, his performance in administering the Russian colossus was extraordinary, and generally acknowledged. Potemkin had animal qualities which greatly appealed to Catherine. Many people, though, saw him rather as vain and of a cruel disposition. He certainly enjoyed a sumptuous lifestyle and a happily chaotic love life, which supposedly included the seduction of five young nieces – he is said to have referred to them collectively as his chicken run. He reproached Catherine for having had fifteen lovers before him, but arranged many more young men for her pleasure when the fires of passion died down between the two of them. She described Potemkin as 'one of the greatest, oddest and most amusing originalities of this stern age'. At home it was his habit to wear nothing but a large negligently drawn dressing gown to cover his otherwise naked body, and swathed thus would receive all comers, from ambassadors to ladies of the court, as well as Catherine herself. The French ambassador penned an interesting sketch of Potemkin, contrasting the 'liveliness of his mind' with the 'flabbiness of his body', noting his fortitude in the face of danger and difficulties, as well as his sad disaffection with his own successes: 'Everything had to be complicated with him: business, pleasure, moods, surroundings'. He described Potemkin as rude to people who showed deference, and friendly to those who were familiar in their approach; he said Potemkin made promises easily but rarely fulfilled them, and never forgot anything he had seen or heard; he read little but was nevertheless well informed. 'Because of his unstable temperament his general behaviour and way of life were indescribably eccentric', commented the ambassador dispassionately.

The pugnacious Paul Jones was eager to show his mettle in this new, exotic milieu. Catherine had territorial ambitions against Turkish possessions in the Black Sea, Greece and the Balkans. Once on active service with the Russian fleet in the Black Sea, he soon became known as Pavel Ivanovitch Jones (sometimes rendered Dzones) which he no doubt found reassuring as well as amusing.

The tough and prickly little Scotsman became quickly disillusioned with the way in which things were organised. As can be appreciated from his past conduct, he found it particularly hard to stomach the fact that victories in battles which in his view he had won were credited to others. He had been promised an independent, untrammelled command, but this did not materialise. He found that he was only one of four rear admirals and his situation was not a happy one. His relations with Prince Potemkin, and with other commanders involved in the Black Sea operations, especially the Prince de Nassau with whom he soon became at daggers drawn – as he had been with Landais – deteriorated rapidly. Jones attracted some resentment, and one Englishman engaged in the naval operations asserted forcefully: 'Nothing but the presence of the enemy could induce us to serve with him, and no consideration whatever could bring us to serve under him.' Despite his undoubted abilities, Potemkin demonstrated to a man like Paul Jones a great deal of incompetence in operations in the Black Sea. The imperial favourite's relative, Nassau, early on told Paul Jones, now his colleague, that any advantage or victory gained over the Turks should be exaggerated to the utmost. He replied, with a note of derision, that he had never 'adopted that method of making myself of consequence'. In fact, his contribution to operations in the Black Sea was significant, though largely disparaged by Potemkin and Nassau. Paul Jones says, for example, that it was his idea prior to an important action to arrange for the placing in advance of a powerful shore battery on Kinburn Point (a commanding spit of land) in anticipation of the withdrawal of the Turkish fleet to that very area. As predicted, this withdrawal did indeed take place, and the shore battery had a decisive effect on the subsequent outcome of the naval engagement; but someone else got the credit.

The plans put forward by Paul Jones for reforming the Black Sea fleet, though sidelined at the time, were later implemented but without acknowledgement to him. He soon saw himself as being used 'to draw the chestnuts from the fire for them'. Potemkin eventually felt it necessary simply to suppress John Paul's professional account of operations against the Turks. De Segur, a diplomat friend of Nassau writing far away in St Petersburg, describes Paul Jones's account of events in the Black Sea as 'blinded by jealousy', but an English diplomat and historian named Eton, an eyewitness to the Black Sea operations, who also read Paul Jones's suppressed account at the admiralty office in Kherson, was convinced that the official record of the campaign was 'nearly a romance'. The mendacity of official logs in the Black Sea is confirmed in the affair of the frigate *Alexander*, which Paul Jones saw lost with his own eyes, but which nevertheless remained on the list of active Russian vessels.

Nassau in his turn also fell foul of Potemkin, as did the American Lewis Littlepage, in command of a gun-boat division in the Black Sea and very well disposed towards Paul Jones. The web of intrigue that was Russia did not suit the direct and forthright nature of Paul Jones, and he and Potemkin were opposites temperamentally; though he seems to have earned the respect of his subordinate Russian officers and to have got along well with them. He also made a favourable impression on the local Cossack crewmen – at least in them he had found a group at last who seemed to appreciate his distinctive leadership qualities.

Even though Paul Jones was now of flag rank, the old spark of derring-do had not deserted him. For example, before an imminent sea battle, he made a personal survey of the Turkish fleet during the night, rowed around quietly through the densely packed ships by a Cossack sailor named Ivak, using muffled oars whose blades Jones had tied round with rags himself. Beforehand, as fondly recounted by a very old Ivak many years after the event, they had a meal from a shared cooking pot with other Cossacks. Paul Jones, now showing some grey hair, contributed a generous quantity of brandy to the proceedings, but ended up shedding a tear with the rest of the party over the mournful songs that they were soon singing. Eventually shaking off the melancholic mood, he leapt up and announced purposefully; 'It's time to go.'

Accompanied by Ivak he headed for the Turkish fleet in the small rowing boat, which Ivak said responded to his handling of the oars and John Paul's handling of the rudder, 'like a tricky little fish'. They encountered some Turkish Cossacks crewing one of the Turkish vessels, threw over a bottle of vodka, and got the password for the night by pretending they were delivering salt to the fleet. They worked their way through the forest of ships, surviving a number of challenges, until they came to one of the biggest vessels. Ivak held the boat steady whilst Jones wrote in large heavy letters with a lump of chalk 'TO BE BURNED', and signed it 'PAUL JONES'. Telling his story in old age, during a chance encounter which luckily captured the tale before he died, Ivak concluded: 'It seems that some men are born to command.' Maybe Paul Jones would have had a happier time in British waters with Cossack crews! The bold chalk message was left untouched by the presumably uncomprehending Turks, only to be seen by the flotilla of Russian ships as they moved into action the next day (though presumably most of them could not read it either). This very ship was in fact singled out and burned by the *Vladimir* during the successful engagement, with Rear Admiral Pavel Ivanovitch on board, directing operations.

Maybe the well attested night survey was foolhardy and irresponsible for an officer of flag rank, but it certainly impressed the fleet with the personal qualities of this particular leader and invited comparison with the contrasting conduct of some of his colleagues. Sir Samuel Bentham, a naval engineer engaged by Potemkin, provides an example. Samuel was the capable brother of the British philosopher Jeremy Bentham, whose clothed and hatted skeleton now sits eerily in a chair within a large glass case at University College, London, (at his own behest). Not long before Paul Jones was engaged in the Black Sea campaign, Jeremy Bentham was working for Catherine and Potemkin, though in a prestigious civil capacity rather than a military one like his brother.

Samuel, who was especially well thought of by Potemkin, was put in highly successful command of a flotilla of very powerful, innovatory gun-boats, which Samuel himself had conceptualised and prepared for action against the Turks in the Black Sea. The Russian forces secured such a victory over the Turks that Potemkin could not help but consider himself 'the spoilt child of God'. However, as an experienced observer, Sam commented tellingly on that part of the attack organized by Nassau, in which he himself took a creditable and decisive part: 'We had about as much discipline as the London mob.'

Paul Jones would not have overseen such chaos. An Irishman serving with the Russians included a comment on Paul Jones in a letter written to his father back at home in Dublin, in full knowledge of his past depredations: 'Be his crimes what they may, he is a most excellent and intrepid marine officer, whose valour on this and the subsequent attack has obtained him vast honour'.

This assessment was in a similar vein to Ivak's fond and respectful opinion of Paul Jones and his leadership qualities. During the course of his narrative, Ivak – who was close to a hundred years old when his story was recorded – produced for examination a dagger that Paul Jones had given to him during the Black Sea campaign. It was engraved with the words: 'From Pavel Jones to his friend Ivak the Cossack'.

The episode involving Ivak was not the only manifestation of derring-do to cause a stir, but Paul Jones soon became resigned to unsatisfactory relations at higher levels in Russia, writing sadly: 'Since I am found too frank and too sincere to make my way at the court of Russia without creating powerful enemies, I have philosophy enough to withdraw into the peaceful bosom of friendship.'

He was torn from this peaceful bosom however, and just when he needed friends, when, out of the blue, he was accused of raping a ten-year-old girl named Katerina from the German colony in St. Petersburg. It did not really help much when her age was revised upwards to twelve or more. She said that she went to sell butter to Paul Jones, and had never seen him before. Locking the door, she said, he grabbed her round the waist and struck her a punch in the face, bloodily cutting her lip on her teeth. She said he pressed a white handkerchief to her mouth, took her into another room and sexually assaulted her; she losing consciousness in the process because of the pressure of the handkerchief, and thus being unable to shout out. Afterwards he told her not to tell her mother, and threatened to stab her if she talked to anyone. She said he spoke very bad Russian.

This whole violent episode sounds quite out of character. There are conflicting accounts as to what really happened. It emerged that the girl was not so innocent as her age would seem to suggest, her mother eventually admitting that she was sexually experienced; and old enough for marriage. It later emerged that she had seen John Paul Jones not once, but on a number of occasions, having first met him some while before when he was staying at the London Tavern, as she told the police later when she revised her story. Paul Jones did at an early point (within a day or two of the original allegation), admit in a letter to the chief of police that there had been some 'badinage' with Katerina, a 'lost girl' (*fille perdue*) whom he says he thought several years older than was alleged. 'Badinage' is probably sexual activity of some kind, since he also stated that 'she amiably agreed to do all that a man would want of her', adding that she had come to his house a number of times, and that he always gave her money, perhaps more than the butter bill. He was adamant in denying criminality, asserting that there was no question of violence, rape or loss of virginity. One of his servants, the German Johann Bahl, whom Jones complained indignantly was kept in police custody for two days and terrified into a statement by the threat of the knout (a brutal Russian whip), alleged that after the 'happening' Katerina's eyes were red with tears, her face swollen and her lips covered with blood. In contradiction, Paul Jones penned a letter, supported by three respectable eyewitness affidavits, to the effect that Katerina spoke in a casual manner when the eyewitnesses saw her after she returned from seeing Paul Jones to collect her gloves and a jug. She had been calm and composed when she left, and was in no way distraught, with no bruising or evidence of injury such as swelling or blood, and with no evidence of tears. These eyewitnesse were Jones's official interpreter and secretary, Dmitriovski, his allocated orderly, a Cossack seaman named Yakovlev from the Black Sea; and his coachman Vasiliyev, also on duty with him. Other people employed in the house contradicted the allegations against Paul Jones, Bahl being the exception.

However, after word of the allegations had rapidly and mysteriously got around St. Petersburg, and Paul Jones had been socially outcast by acquaintances in the Russian capital, pressure was put on the police to drop the case. Paul Jones thought initially that the motive for the whole thing was money, and that Katerina's mother was at the root of it; but the mother's detected liaison with a mysterious establishment figure wearing 'decorations', and the inexplicable dropping of the case after he had been discredited by rumour, compelled him to change his mind. He felt that there had been someone behind the mother, angling for just that outcome: the ruin of his reputation. He had witnesses to put forward evidence, and further investigation of the facts might well have exonerated him, defeating the malicious objective. Jones discovered that the aristocratic city governor had told lawyers in St. Petersburg not to 'meddle with [his] case', explicitly forbidding them to help him. He found, to his dismay, that his own written statement was put aside or rejected, purportedly because he had penned it in French. He quickly realised that he was being denied the opportunity to defend himself. Not surprisingly, Paul Jones wrote indignantly to his powerful commander, Prince Potemkin:

The charge against me is a dastardly fraud. I love women, I admit, and the pleasures that one enjoys only with that sex; but to get such things by force is repellent to me. I cannot even contemplate gratifying my passions without willing consent.

I give you my word as a soldier and as an honest man that if the girl in question has had relations with no one else, she is still a virgin.

Although he was John Paul's commander, Potemkin was not going to spring to his defence. For reasons of state and perhaps through personal animosity, he may have been involved in contriving the distortion of this liaison into the violent rape and deflowering of a child, an allegation which resulted, on the face of it, in the departure of Paul Jones from Russia.

The Comte de Segur, then the French Ambassador and an intimate of Potemkin, stood by Paul Jones in his predicament. He had known Paul Jones in America as a fellow member of the Society of the Cincinnati (see page 232) and despite his disparaging comments on Jones's version of the Black Sea campaign, was well disposed towards him. He did some fruitful detective work on his behalf and made favourable representations to the lukewarm Potemkin. He was scathing about Katerina's mother, whose husband, he says, 'certifies that she is a pimp and whose daughter solicits the inns'. Segur's intervention was not enough, though he later wrote an article in a French publication explaining things favourably for Paul Jones after his dogged enquiries. As regards any conversation with Katerina in 'bad Russian', Paul Jones says in a letter directly appealing to the Empress, 'It is impossible that anyone has heard me speak two words in this language, inasmuch as I do not know it at all'.

Paul Jones had confronted Potemkin forthrightly on more than one occasion, and the autocratic prince did not enjoy the experience, stamping his feet with rage at a man who did not act at all like a Russian serf, or even a courtier for that matter. He did not react favourably either when John Paul stood up to him to champion the rights of Russian seamen, though he seems later to have paid some material regard to the sentiments expressed. Potemkin appears pretty early in their relationship to have had very little time for Paul Jones, a feeling that he communicated directly to Catherine. For example, the gist of a letter regarding Paul Jones from Potemkin to the Empress was noted in the diary of her secretary: 'He is bold only for profit. He used to be a pirate. He never had command of many ships. He is afraid of the Turks. Nobody wants to serve under him and he wants to serve under nobody.'

Though some of the sentiments would have been warmly echoed by the British, who were well represented in Russia, the overall view so glibly presented seems unsupportable. Paul Jones was demonstrably not afraid of the Turks, nor was he ever a pirate. Although viewed as such by the British, throughout the American War of Independence he was a commissioned officer of the American Government, confirmed by his Captain's commission so reverently preserved in the shrine at Annapolis. The ragtag crews he took into British territorial waters would have collapsed in rueful laughter at the allegation that he was bold only for profit; the crew of the *Ranger* in particular wished fervently that he had been more the pirate and less the seeker after glory; and the crew of the *Bonhomme Richard* certainly knew the dire human cost of his thirst for glory. He had been in successful command of quite a number of ships, had never lost one to the enemy, and had been successful in playing, for the first time, his part as a fleet commander in the Black Sea. His personal relationships were in some ways a problem, but it should be remembered that he had been promised an independent command in the Black Sea, which he did not get. In one acrimonious exchange with him, Paul Jones actually asserted that Potemkin had treated him very unfairly, and Potemkin, remarkably, agreed, but said it was too late to do anything about the matter. However, he and Catherine thought enough of Paul Jones to delay his departure from Russia for a short while – for fear he would transfer to the service of Sweden with whom the Russians were at war – and to pay him a retainer with the same object.

Prince Potemkin, a fascinating character who on campaign was accompanied by a bizarre retinue, eventually died of apoplexy (a stroke in other words), in the midst of the steppe. He was lifted from his coach and laid on the grass near the roadside, as he requested, under a hastily erected tent of skins thrown over a frame of Cossack lances. He expired in the loving arms of his niece Sashenka Branicka, not long after deliberately gluttonising in a high fever – perhaps with a death wish it is said – on an incredible amount of rich food and drink: ham, salted goose and several chickens washed down with generous amounts of varied wines and spirits. However, by the time a thoughtful Cossack had driven his lance into the exact spot where Potemkin gave up the ghost, soon marked by a still-extant stone monument on the grassy steppe, Paul Jones had been long gone from St. Petersburg, and would soon depart rather more quietly from this world. Fortunately, his indignant letter to Potemkin regarding Katerina, written two weeks after the event, survives; as does his letter to the Chief of Police in St. Petersburg, written only two days after the allegation, but which did not see the public light of day until just after the Second World War.

In 1926, not so long after the Bolshevik revolution in Russia, a woman turned up at the American consulate in the Baltic city of Riga in Latvia, trying to obtain an American passport. She styled herself Baroness Weissereich and claimed to be descended from a son of John Paul Jones and Princess Anna Kourakina, a maid of honour at the Russian court of Catherine the Great. She possessed a ring engraved 'J.P.J.', together with extracts from what was deemed on examination to be only a 'suppositional diary' – in other words, a fake. The story that she told was looked into and deemed to be bogus. A passport was refused and the claimant disappeared into oblivion. There is, it is true, no written evidence of Paul Jones having an affair with such a person at the Russian Imperial Court, but he did apparently have a short affair with a Princess Naryshkyn, of whom more will be said later. Amours in Russia were to be expected, since – as 'Delia' found – he was not without charm, and had enjoyed any number of affairs, including one with the illegitimate daughter of Louis XV in Paris. There could be descendants at more than one port of call, including the Russian Imperial Court. The affair with the Russian princess Anna Kourakina, if indeed it did occur, was alleged to have met with the disapproval of the Empress, and to have been therefore connected in some way with the spurious charge of rape.

Although the mysterious applicant for the passport at Riga may have had her request rejected, she had, in mentioning Anna Kourakina, unwittingly introduced a most intriguing and virtually unremarked aspect of John Paul's truncated stay in Russia; terminated by the appalling allegation of criminality centred on Katerina. Quite unknowingly, in mentioning a female member of the princely Kourakin clan, the 'Baroness' had suggested a possible connection, albeit tenuous, between Paul Jones and an important family with at least one very prominent member at the highest level of Russian Freemasonry (see Appendix IV). John Paul was, as we have seen, very much involved in the Masonic movement. It was a connection which, starting in Kirkcudbright at a time of crisis in his career over the flogging and subsequent death of Mungo Maxwell, continued through his life in New England and early service in the American Navy, and publicly reached a highpoint during his sojourn in Paris, when he was accepted into the prestigious Lodge of the Nine Sisters. With such a consistent Masonic record, there is little doubt that Paul Jones would have sought contact with Freemasons in Russia. The movement had been burgeoning rapidly there since the first lodges were tentatively established before the middle of the eighteenth century. A good many years before Paul Jones arrived in St. Petersburg, a substantial proportion of the highest military and civil service officials had become Masons, inspired by the ideas of congregation and self-improvement, allied to rationalism, deism – and self-interest. By the 1750s a lodge comprising mainly officers and theatre people had been founded in St. Petersburg, an already well-established social milieu that might very well have attracted Paul Jones. However, by the time he stepped ashore from his fraught Baltic crossing in 1788, any attempt to become involved with Russian Freemasonry could well have been, as far as Catherine the Great was concerned, an inexcusable mistake.

Catherine, now a dauntingly autocratic woman of more than sixty, had been brought to Russia from Germany as a young girl of sixteen in order to marry the future Russian Tsar, as she did. She was tender hearted and liberal in outlook in her earlier years in Russia, with a great deal of sympathy for the lot of the serfs, as well as for Masonry, which she saw then as conducive to implementing her own enlightened social policies. Her attitude changed with age. She was especially disaffected by a dangerous and terrible insurrection of serfs led by a brutal Cossack deserter named Pugachev, who claimed to be Catherine's husband, the dead Tsar Peter. The imposture animated the serfs, poor as it was. As the Cossacks crudely put it: 'Does it matter whether he is the Tsar or not? We could make a prince out of shit'. The dire impact of Pugachev on Catherine's thinking as well as upon Russia, can be deduced from her assessment: 'Nobody since Tamerlaine has caused such destruction', putting Pugachev in the same league as the 'Scourge of God'. In due course the insurrection, characterised by wanton and imaginative cruelty towards the landowning classes, was ruthlessly, though not easily, crushed. Pugachev was eventually carted off to Moscow in a cage and publicly decapitated. Catherine breathed a sigh of relief. She was a born survivor, and as her long reign continued, she became increasingly seen, in her own eyes as well as by her subjects, as the very embodiment of the Russian soul, the 'little mother' of her people. At the same time she became ever more the tyrant, eventually giving away thousands of state serfs without a qualm, some as valuable gifts to her many lovers.

By the time John Paul Jones arrived in Russia she had developed a deep antipathy towards the growing Masonic movement. By then she considered it a dangerous hotbed of subversion and revolution, a sentiment fuelled by time and events, reinforced by the sometimes alarmist revelations of the Russian secret police. In the literary Lodge of the Nine Sisters in France, Paul Jones had been associating with fellow Masons of some distinction and of liberal thought and inclination, including notables such as Benjamin Franklin and Voltaire. Franklin had been responsible for introducing Freemasonry to America. Thomas Jefferson and George Washington were both Freemasons. However, more germane to Catherine's hostile attitude was the situation in Europe. In France, now on the eve of the Revolution, both Danton and Robespierre – soon to become architects and then quickly victims of the Terror – were also Freemasons, but cast in a different mould. The Russian secret police monitored developments in Russia with increasing concern, until in 1792, more than two years after John Paul had left Russia under a cloud to take up residence in France again, the leading Freemasons were arrested and all Masonic lodges in Russia – 'secret and absurd gatherings' Catherine called them – were closed down on her direct order.

Even her former friends were not exempted from the proscription. Catherine felt that to expose a people used to abject and grinding slavery to the blinding light of freedom was courting disaster on a grand scale, and she greatly feared the 'fermentation of the scum'. According to her later opinion, freemasonry was '... one of the greatest aberrations to which the human mind had succumbed'; she thought it was a 'mixture of religion and childish games', but at the same time dangerous in its secretiveness, its male exclusivity, manifest foreign contacts, access to substantial funds of money, and insidious penetration of the higher echelons of Russian society and the military. Three years before Paul Jones came to Russia, Catherine had poured ridicule on the Freemasons in a trio of satirical comedies that she penned herself, whose titles reveal the gist: *The Deceiver*, *The Deluded* and *The Siberian Shaman*.

The pragmatic Tsarina considered that the personality of her son, Grand Duke Paul, was so flawed that he was unfit to wield supreme power in Russia, and made alternative arrangements in favour of her grandson Alexander. In the event Paul did succeed his mother, but reigned for only a few years before he was assassinated. In view of her opinion of him, as well as for reasons of state, Catherine had been particularly shocked and disturbed to discover that Paul had been clandestinely approached to be Grand Master of the Order of Freemasons in Russia. He had in fact become involved with the Freemasons at least six years before Paul Jones arrived in Russia in 1788. Prince Alexander Kourakin, a close friend of the Tsarina's son Paul since their childhood, was a prominent Freemason and instrumental with others in drawing him into the movement. Portraits showing Paul wearing Masonic emblems started to circulate, but although he was well disposed towards Freemasons when he became Tsar, later in his life Paul abandoned Masonry and derided it in much the same vein as Catherine had done. Among the Masonic associates of Prince Alexander Kourakin was the prosperous Russian nobleman Nikolai Novikov. He was a prominent publisher, an important focus of Freemasonry, and also a man of an increasingly mystical turn of mind that was drawn inevitably to this aspect of the Brotherhood's philosophy. In her earlier, more liberal days Catherine had been a patron and friend of Novikov, and had even written anonymous pieces for inclusion in his magazine *The Painter*. She turned against him as he became more deeply involved with Freemasonry, and came in the end to regard him as 'a very great rogue'. One Masonic group, dubbed the 'Martinists', with which Novikov was involved, were alleged by the secret police to have drawn lots to determine which one of them would assassinate the Empress.

Eventually, in 1792, Novikov was arrested and without a public trial – a course that Catherine judged most prudent – sentenced to fifteen years incarceration in the Schlusselburg fortress, the state prison in which her husband Tsar Peter had come to his untimely end. Although Novikov was not arrested until 1792, police inquiries into the Masonic movement were very well advanced and generating great and increasing alarm when Catherine recalled John Paul Jones from the Black Sea to St. Petersburg in 1789. It is worth noting that the *modus operandi* of the secret police was as you would expect; dirty tricks were not the worst of their faults. It is said that the chief inquisitor Sheshkovsky was not averse to knocking out a few teeth with his walking stick when opening the interrogation of a freethinker, Masonic or not. Alexander Radishchev, regarded as the first Russian radical but only a half-hearted freemason (he was too much of a rationalist), quoted with approval the words inscribed beneath Houdon's bust of Benjamin Franklin: 'He wrested lightning from the heavens and the sceptre from the hand of kings.' Radishchev was exiled to Siberia in 1790. It will be remembered that the sculptor Houdon, a member of the Masonic Lodge of the Nine Sisters in Paris, executed the bust of his fellow-mason John Paul Jones hard upon the spectacular vanquishing of the *Serapis* in 1779. The secret police would not have been ignorant of such disquieting connections. It is said that Potemkin was one of the few of Catherine's court intimates who did *not* become a Mason in the days before the Empress turned irrevocably against the movement.

Prince Alexander Kourakin's involvement with Freemasonry had been quite overt, and to the great displeasure of Catherine. He had ended up exiled to his estates in the country; until recalled to St. Petersburg and official prominence for a short while when Paul succeeded his mother. Alexander Kourakin's younger brother, Alexis, despite a personal taste for oriental luxury, debauchery and the arbitrary seizure of other people's property, was a liberal statesman and the proponent and active practitioner of a scheme which led eventually to the emancipation of the serfs. His beliefs and actions characterised eighteenth-century Freemasonry in Russia, as the all-devouring guillotine, it seemed to some, did the Brotherhood in revolutionary France.

Other members of the eminent Kourakin clan participated intimately in the life of the Russian court, but in less politically controversial ways. By way of example, Princess Helena Stepanovna Kourakina was considered a notable society beauty. She was the daughter of Field Marshal Apraxin, a former political intimate of Catherine, and had married into the Kourakin clan. In due course she became the acknowledged mistress of Count Peter Shuvalov, Catherine's Grand Master of Ordnance. Before too long, whilst still Shuvalov's mistress, she had an affair with a dashing young guardsman named Gregory Orlov, the best looking of five popular brothers, all well placed in the army and instrumental in gaining sole power for Catherine by removing her incompetent husband the Tsar. Gregory Orlov, generally reputed to be a sexual athlete, soon attracted the attention of Catherine, whereupon he dropped Princess Helena Stepanovna to become the lover of the Tsarina, who soon found herself pregnant by him. Helena Stepanovna had already had a relationship with Catherine's husband Tsar Peter III before his untimely death. She had been brought secretly to him at night by Naryshkyn, one of the Tsar's cronies, and a member of the same clan as the Princess Naryshkyn with whom Paul Jones apparently had the short affair mentioned earlier. It was said of Princess Helena Kourakina that 'her brazenness was such that after the night was over … wishing to show everyone that she had spent the night with the monarch', she insisted on dashing open the discreetly closed blinds of the carriage in which she was being escorted home. The same observer noted: 'The whole Court had reached such a state that almost everyone kept a mistress openly; and women sought lovers for themselves without hiding the fact from their husbands or kinsmen.' Helena Kourakina's life is well documented. One cannot help wondering what relationship she had with the mysterious Anna, cited by the 'Baroness'!

It is not positively known whether John Paul Jones was involved with the Freemasons whilst in Russia, but on balance it is almost certain that he was, and in view of his known Masonic associations in the past, probably in quite exalted circles. Was it more than coincidence that the desperate woman who turned up in Riga claimed descent from John Paul Jones through Princess Anna Kourakina, a maid of honour at Catherine's court and a relative of Prince Alexander Kourakin, one of the leading lights of Russian Freemasonry? She does not herself appear to have been aware of any Masonic connection, which makes her story even more intriguing, and worth considering. Masonic connections in Russia, and involvement with Freemasonry in the fermenting French capital, as well as in America – where revolution had been successfully accomplished – would have alarmed Catherine the Great. Such a revelation could well have been instrumental in engineering the disgrace and departure of Paul Jones from Russia, under a convenient cloud of sexual scandal. It was a subtle move: expulsion on underlying political grounds but without giving any offence to the new United States of America or to the French, who idolised the American naval hero, apparently a valid course of action on moral grounds, despite the effectiveness of John Paul against the Turks in the Black Sea. His efforts there, though recognised by some, had been disparaged to Paul Jones's uncomprehending indignation, and probably with more malice and calculation than he ever realised. It would be ironic if the felicitous connection with Freemasonry made at a critical moment in his early life in Scotland, proved eventually to have been at the root of his undoing in Russia.

By the time Paul Jones arrived unsuspectingly in St. Petersburg in 1788 to take up his naval post, which had arisen through the gratefully acknowledged assistance of Thomas Jefferson, a fellow Mason, the whole Masonic question in Russia was coming to a head. An American of Paul Jones's reputation could not simply be cast off or incarcerated on patently trumped-up charges like so many native Russians were to be in the very near future. In January 1789, having been recalled to St. Petersburg by Catherine, he wrote to Jefferson with no inkling of imperial disfavour: 'I have only at present to inform you that I returned here from the Black Sea a short time ago, by the special desire of her Imperial Majesty; but I know not yet my future destination'. His expectation was that he would be engaged in the Baltic to fight in the war against the Swedes. This was based on an explanation given by Potemkin for his going north, and an assurance of greater things in the offing from Bessborodko, Catherine's Foreign Minister. However, when he arrived in St. Petersburg he was left stewing in idleness, and any expectations came to nought.

Jefferson replied to Paul Jones in a letter delivered by courier and dated 23 March 1789, which stated that John Paul's recent communication was the first they had heard of him since he left Copenhagen in 1788. All his correspondence had been seized by the Russian secret police. In the same month came the rape charge. Defence documents which he submitted were disregarded and legal assistance for his defence was forbidden, as noted earlier. The French Revolution erupted in May, and the Bastille fell in July.

Though Paul Jones had made a very favourable impression on Catherine when he first came to Russia in 1788, she had radically changed her view of him by the time he died in Paris in 1792. At the time of his death she wrote a letter in French which included an assessment of his character: 'This Jones was a wrongheaded fellow, well worthy of being lionised by such a loathsome rabble', meaning the citizens of Revolutionary Paris, some of whom – rather than the Americans – had arranged for a volley of shots to be fired by a detachment of grenadiers over his lead coffin as it lay in its lonely grave.

Paul Jones was a lover of liberty after the American style, not afraid of expressing his thoughts; for example, when he championed the rights of Russian seamen. He had no sympathy for the developing excesses of the French Revolution, though Catherine may well have thought otherwise. Written in French rather than in her native German or in Russian, Catherine's brief epitaph is distinctly political rather than moral in tone, reinforcing the surmise that in relation to the rape allegation Paul Jones may have been a victim of sexual entrapment for political reasons. Catherine uses the phrase 'mal tête' to describe Paul Jones. This is a phrase with no modern French equivalent, and may well be simply Catherine's own idiosyncratic turn of speech, invented to give expression to an idea of him that she had in mind; 'wrongheaded' seems a fair English equivalent, and like 'mal tête' is without sexual overtones.

Catherine's aggressive contempt may have been prompted by the funeral oration which she very soon came to know about. There was a reference to 'the pestilential air of despotism' that hung over the Russian Empire, and a personal reference to her as the 'Semiramis of the North' – Semiramis being a powerful queen of ancient Assyria, notorious in legend (as was Catherine in real life) for an unassuagable sexual appetite.

In the relatively short span of life left to him after his return to France, Paul Jones tried to keep up a correspondence with Catherine, perhaps if only to justify his retainer. He suggested actions after the fashion of Whitehaven and Leith, but the proposals came to nought, as did a scheme for furthering Russian interests by getting the better of the Turks through an expedition round the Cape of Good Hope.

Eventually Catherine was sharply dismissive of him, reminding him enigmatically that he was well aware why she had dispensed with his active service in Russia. 'I have nothing more to say to Paul Jones,' she finally let him know through an intermediary, 'Tell him to go and mind his own business in America.' To Catherine, the United States was probably not so much the Land of the Free as the Land of the Freemasons – in view of the fact that most of the Founding Fathers, the signatories of the Declaration of Independence and the authors of the American Constitution, were determined Freemasons as well as fervent republicans.

John Paul handled his first battle fleet command in the Black Sea with credit, vouched for by numerous affidavits from subordinate officers who had witnessed his performance. It is very likely that his disastrous encounter with the young Katerina in St. Petersburg was foolish (and perhaps engineered by others), rather than felonious as alleged. Taking into account these professional and personal circumstances, it seems reasonable to search for some deeper explanation for Paul Jones being bundled out of Russia so peremptorily. In the prevailing political atmosphere, a longstanding connection with Freemasonry, though the threads are admittedly still elusive in Russia, could well have been the underlying factor that precipitated his fall from imperial grace. John Paul's very brief entanglement with the Russian Bear was definitely not a happy experience for him. In fact, it proved to be his last throw of the dice.

Conclusion –
'The Sweets of a Private Life'

John Paul eventually found his way back to France. When younger
he had contemplated making his fortune and going back to live in
Kirkcudbright. He had also contemplated a farm in New England.
But Paris seems to have drawn him as much as any place. It must
indeed have seemed like home in many ways: he was most benevo-
lently regarded there, and had a pleasant social life in cosmopolitan
company. In his later years, as the Protestant clergyman said in his
funeral oration: 'He preferred the sweets of a private life in France.'
This was before the horrors of the French Revolution. John Paul
did not live long enough to witness the execution of the King and
Queen and the tumbrils rolling to the guillotine during the Reign of
Terror. He corresponded with his family, and very much wanted to
visit his sister who was living in Dumfries; but it was not to be.

Many, including his contemporaries, have expressed their views
about the personality of Paul Jones and his relationships with other
people. In interesting contrast to the more usual tenor of these is
the view of an artist acquaintance in Paris, who frequently attended
relaxed supper parties arranged by two sisters, at which Paul Jones
was also a guest: 'I have never met so modest a man. It was impossible to get him to talk about his famous exploits, but on all other
subjects he willingly talked with a great amount of sense and wit'.
This is another facet – the salon face one might say – of an officer
and gentleman of complexity.

Such apparent self-effacement must be contrasted with his decision in 1777 (as mentioned earlier), with the cruise of the *Ranger*
in prospect, to provide himself with an elaborate Achievement
of Arms: a coat of arms of his own design emblazoned upon an
ornate shield. The Achievement of Arms as a whole constituted an

important personal statement, and the fact that he modified it more than once as his life progressed clearly demonstrates that it was significant to him. Paul Jones on occasion revealed a wry sense of humour, and it is possible that the design of the fraudulent shield might have been tongue in cheek. That he had no misgivings about the whole thing is demonstrated by the fact that he modified it boldly and without qualms at the height of his career, to take into account his new honorific status as Chevalier, conferred upon him after his spectacular encounter with the *Serapis*. After this much vaunted event, and with the agreement of the American government, he was invested by King Louis XVI of France with the Order of Military Merit. Appropriately, as he saw it, the helmet above the shield in his 1777 composition was now replaced by a coronet, with a screaming eagle topping it – perhaps a reference to the Society of the Cincinnati which had as its emblem a gold eagle suspended from a pale blue ribbon edged in white. John Paul Jones was one of the one thousand originating members of the Cincinnati, which was open initially to United States Army or Navy officers who had served in the War of Independence. Controversially, it was – and remains – a hereditary organisation with a strong component of mutual assistance. George Washington was elected the first President-General of the Society, and Thomas Jefferson was an early critic! Cincinnatus was a hero of early Rome, who left his plough to serve Rome as dictator on two triumphant occasions, after each of which he returned humbly home to his farm. Whatever the inspiration behind the screaming eagle, the eight-pointed gold star of John Paul's French 'Ordre du Mérite Militaire' is shown suspended by a ribbon below the shield in his revised Achievement of Arms, which is supported by an infant Neptune wielding his trident. Owing to his humble beginnings, his character, his often fortuitous career shifts and powerful social contacts, Paul Jones was an eager recipient of the honorific trappings of his times.

The contrasts between his professional and social life are reflected in his writing: on the one hand, the concise and direct reports admired by Admiral Morison, and on the other the overly ornate, fashionable, quasi-literary style. His Masonic connection meant as much to him as anything, and he seems to have valued and enjoyed the social life which it generated until his death. But one cannot help feeling that his essentially bogus coat of arms exemplifies the assessment in the *Dictionary of National Biography* in 1892: 'Unfortunately, Jones's statements, when not otherwise corroborated, cannot be trusted.' Any aspersions against him are, however, counterbalanced by such assessments as that of the Irishman writing home to his father in Dublin from the Black Sea theatre of operations; who recognized Paul Jones as 'a most excellent and intrepid marine officer' whose valour in action 'obtained him vast honour' amongst fellow combatants.

The most estimable distinction granted to him, and one that he greatly prized, was surely the unique Congressional Gold Medal, voted to him in 1787 by a Congress appreciative of his outstanding exploits in British waters. As noted earlier, his medal, awarded for 'valour and brilliant services', placed John Paul Jones in the exalted company of only a handful of other officers – including George Washington – who were formally singled out for full Congressional appreciation throughout the entire War of Independence. And he was the only naval officer in the war to be awarded a Congressional Gold Medal.

What did Chevalier John Paul Jones think of himself? In a letter to Catherine the Great he suggested: 'So far from being harsh and cruel, nature has given me the mildest disposition. I was formed for love and friendship, and not to be a seaman or a soldier; as it is, I have sacrificed my natural inclination.' Perhaps in the interlude between parting company with the slave ship *The Two Friends* in Jamaica and securing his passage home to Kirkcudbright in fortuitous command of the *John* (with the playbill bearing his name as the single scrap of sure documentary evidence for a whole year's gap in his life) Paul Jones tour in the West Indies as an actor with a troupe of travelling players was true to his nature. In view of his literary interests and his ability to quote Shakespeare and other poets with facility, this is feasible. His letters reveal an articulate and sensitive, though self-centred, personality. He enjoyed versifying, and used it to good effect with women. When young, in the early days of the American War of Independence, he tried to make contact with Phyllis Wheatley, a slave girl kidnapped and brought over to America to be sold in Boston at the age of eight, who was acclaimed by some in England and America for her poetry. There may be in these earlier events in his life a hint as to what John Paul meant by the 'sacrifice of my inclination'. The theme of love and friendship in that letter recurs in his reply to another letter received from two Frenchwomen of his acquaintance, who thought that he preferred love to friendship. In a style that would have been looked at askance by many of his more rough and ready fellow officers, he wrote to them:

> You may be right, for love frequently communicates divine qualities, and in that light may be considered as the cordial that Providence has bestowed on mortals to help them to digest the nauseous draught of life. Friendship, they say, has more solid qualities than love. This is a question I shall not attempt to resolve; but sad experience generally shows that where we expect to find a friend we have only been treacherously deluded by false appearances, and that the goddess herself [Venus, the goddess of love] very seldom confers her charms on any of the human race.

This statement would have surely puzzled his shipboard colleagues, had they seen it; but the two French ladies probably thought it an elegant reply to their question, full of the sensibility appropriate to the Chevalier. Unfortunately, despite his genuine yearning for love and friendship, Paul Jones died starved of both.

On 1 June 1792, John Paul Jones, all unknowing, was appointed by President George Washington, with whom he corresponded, to be the American consul for Algeria; with a commensurate salary. The object was to negotiate a ransom with the Dey of Algiers for the captain and crew of an American ship captured seven years previously and virtually forgotten – they were on the verge of converting to Islam in despair of ever being rescued. He was also tasked to reconnoitre the coast, with a view to future punitive expeditions. Paul Jones would have been pleased at this recognition of his talents and of his usefulness to the United States. He died at the age of forty-five, just before the documents reached him.

He was found lying face down across his bed; a victim of kidney disease, jaundice and pneumonia (the immediate cause of his death), as the autopsy in 1905 revealed. Two compassionate friends had kept him company to the end: Samuel Blagden, an American Colonel of Dragoons, and a retired French army officer named Beaupoil. His effects were auctioned off under the auspices of Gouverneur Morris, the American Envoy in Paris, including his Congressional Gold Medal, which promptly disappeared. Fortunately, the gold-hilted sword presented to him by the King of France was preserved for his family, to be handed on in due course to Richard Dale, who served so loyally on the *Bonhomme Richard*. It remained in Dale's family until 1938, when it was presented to the Naval Academy at Annapolis, where it now rests close by John Paul's sarcophagus, together with his service sword from *Serapis* days.

Unfortunately, only the die of the Gold Medal survives, but a copy struck from it is displayed in the crypt. Although possible, it is unlikely now that the original medal handled by Paul Jones will ever turn up. What a find that would be. The contrasting fates of the gold-hilted sword and the gold medal reflect the contrasting contemporary attitudes to Paul Jones in France and America at the time of his death. His mortal remains, remarkably and recognisably preserved as it turned out, survived to grace the great patriotic ceremony at Annapolis, and the belated valediction: 'In life he honoured the flag, in death the flag shall honour him.' Had things gone differently, he would have died an honoured figure in America, not a neglected one in France; dependent for his meagre burial rites on French sentiment rather than on American gratitude.

In a Christmas Day letter to 'Delia' in Paris, from Portsmouth in New England, some ten years before his death, John Paul had some exciting news: On the 26th [of June] I was unanimously elected by Congress to command the *America* of seventy four guns.' The *America* was hugely significant to John Paul. At that time under construction, the *America* was in fact the first Ship of the Line, or capital ship, to be built in the United States. Paul Jones was understandably gratified to be selected to be her captain, and by vote of Congress. There had been a decision to promote him to Rear Admiral, but Congress did not feel able at that time to provide a command appropriate to the rank; the Americans having lost almost all their warships to the British, so it was not acted upon. In contrast to his colleagues, John Paul Jones had never lost a single ship under his command to the enemy, so when he was informed that the *America* was to be presented as a gift to France, his bitter disappointment can be appreciated. Yet with a good grace he stood on board when she was completed and personally supervised the perfect launch of the *America*, in decidedly tricky circumstances of current and underwater topography, before her departure from the Land of the Free.

After the war was over and won, the navy which John Paul Jones had known since its inception was virtually dismantled, and he was bound for Russia, to further his naval career there. This was the man whom Benjamin Franklin had once considered to be the chief weapon of burgeoning American might in Europe, and whom Thomas Jefferson once saw as the principal hope, as he put it, of America's future efforts on the ocean.

One woman with whom he had an affair called him 'my adorable Jones' another, as previously quoted, said she felt like wrapping him in cotton wool and putting him in her pocket. In contrast, many of the male establishment figures whom he encountered did not see him as in any way charming, nor did his officers and men, some of whom plotted to throw him overboard, and on another occasion conspired to leave him stranded ashore to fall into the hands of the enemy. However, in Russia he got along very well with Cossack mariners, whose background no doubt instilled in them a different attitude to authority and a different notion of leadership. This multifarious character, who sailed under several colours, some of them false, does not seem at first sight a promising prospect for heroic status, his once forgotten mortal remains recovered with difficulty and entombed in a hallowed and magnificent black marble sarcophagus.

There might well have been no heroics. The enshrinement of John Paul Jones in the hall of fame of American military history owes everything to the boldness, novelty and spectacular impact of his two warring cruises into British home waters between the spring of 1778 and the autumn of 1779, and especially to his epic fight with the *Serapis*, an event which emblazoned glory across an otherwise sombre background of failure, setback and despair, for the French and their Armada as well as for the Americans in New England. As far as the British were concerned, Paul Jones took the edge off their joy at the abject failure of the diabolical Franco-Spanish invasion attempt.

Magnifying the effect of the publicity attendant on all these events was the fact that the rude intrusion of Paul Jones into their territorial waters was unprecedented in the living memory of the

British people, and had in fact been a rare event in the whole of British history. True, William of Orange had landed with an army at Brixham a century earlier, but he had more or less been welcomed with open arms. The rarity of Jones's incursion and his outrageous actions (together, perhaps, with a kind of 'race-memory' of terrible, alien seaborne invasions by the Vikings?) provoked a furious reaction in Britain. The government was apoplectic. The importance of this in American propaganda at home and in Europe cannot be overstressed. At Flamborough Head, Paul Jones was too embroiled in a desperate and unpredictable struggle to anticipate the impact that victory would have on the newspaper headlines. Although he had a keen awareness of the importance of publicity and an eye on his reputation, in his planning Paul Jones was primarily intent on transforming the mode of action of the new United States Navy from mere commerce raiding into international warfare, bringing the war in America home with a salutary shock to the British Isles, through both damage to shipping and coastal attack.

Whatever motivations were at work, and despite spirited and deadly intent, the cruise of the *Ranger* and after that the cruise of the *Bonhomme Richard* squadron manifestly teetered on the brink of failure. The propaganda effect clouded the dour realities, and the cruises were only redeemed and glory plucked from fiasco by the way in which Jones sought out and victoriously took on the British. Considering the usual ignominious fate of American warships at the hands of the Royal Navy, these triumphs were extraordinary. Some of his actions could be considered foolhardy, but the personal bravery of John Paul Jones was incontrovertibly outstanding. The desperate fight of *Bonhomme Richard* with *Serapis* was and remains, as described earlier, the longest ship-to-ship duel in British naval history, and it was in the thick of this extraordinary engagement that Paul Jones, when asked if he was about to surrender, pugnaciously uttered the words which won him undying fame: 'I have not yet begun to fight'.

These stirring words, yelled across at Pearson by Paul Jones amidst the din, blood and confusion of the battle off Flamborough Head, are the reason why his body lies in the crypt of the American Naval College. They represent the right attitude of mind for a warrior, and John Paul Jones is a warrior hero, before all else. The bronze inscription inlaid in the marble floor before the sarcophagus,

4

quoted at the beginning of this book, sums up what is ultimately important about John Paul Jones for the Americans:

HE GAVE OUR NAVY ITS EARLIEST TRADITIONS OF HEROISM AND VICTORY

Though born a Scotsman, he is a true American hero, and one in the American Grain.

Did he really holler those famous words over the din of battle? They do not appear in letters of bronze on his splendid shrine. Surely he *ought* to have said them! He certainly did say something like them, probably quite early on in the harrowing engagement when the *Bonhomme Richard*, having taken a cruel battering from Pearson's eighteen-pounders, appeared to be backing off in defeat. It would have been an appropriately uncertain moment for Pearson to put the question, and for Jones to make his defiant and adamant reply, as, instead of striking his colours, he prepared to grapple his ship inseparably to the *Serapis* and use his calculated superiority aloft to turn the tables on the British; though at an obscene cost in lives and men hideously wounded. Had he uttered the words, as suggested by some, towards the end of the punishing three-and-a-half hour battle, with mangled dead and groaning wounded crowded everywhere, they would have amounted to no more than the rantings of a lunatic, rather than the bravely defiant words of a hero. John Paul Jones was no madman, and was in truly heroic control of himself throughout the engagement. In the heat of battle he even found time to take a crewman to task for using foul language: 'Mr. Stacey, it's no time to be swearing now – you may by the next moment be in eternity; but let us do our duty'.

Richard Dale, the stalwart first lieutenant on the *Bonhomme Richard* is the authority for the words 'I have not yet begun to fight', as well as for their utterance at the earlier moment, though his recollections were only recounted – or rather, recorded – more than forty years after the event; by Colonel Sherbourne, an early biographer of John Paul Jones. Dale was an experienced seaman, present on board throughout the engagement, and in as good a position as anyone to know what went on during the course of the raging and smoke-shrouded night battle, though he must have spent much of his time on the main and lower decks. John Paul's own statements as to what he actually said come only at second hand, and in one case from an account penned seventeen years after a small dinner party, where Paul Jones told the story of the action off Flamborough Head to fellow guests!

President Theodore Roosevelt was instrumental in every way possible in resurrecting John Paul Jones from the dead. The transformation took place in the franctic years of the naval arms race leading up to the First World War, at a time when Roosevelt was intent on increasing American naval strength beyond recognition. Paul Jones thought along similar lines and would undoubtedly have approved of Roosevelt's approach. Plucked from obscurity, he gave Roosevelt psychological assistance in achieving his aim! Roosevelt himself once referred to Paul Jones as no more than a 'daring corsair', but was persuaded – and pleased – to see him in a different light in 1905, when he authorised the search for the lost grave and the transportaton of the body to America.

Without denying his importance to America as the key figure in transforming commerce raiding into naval war, or his demonstrably intrepid conduct and his great personal bravery, the undeniably farcical side to the exploits of Paul Jones in British waters has to be admitted. This does not detract from the man's reputation, because the farcical element to events invariably arose out of the actions of others: mutinous and unenthusiastic officers and crew, the injunctions of the concordat from his task force's financial backers – and the weather!

Since the body of Paul Jones was brought to Annapolis with such ceremony, there seems to have been in America a tendency to transmute the image of him as the man of heroic action, the fighter for freedom and glory, into the embodiment of wisdom and nobility; Father of the United States Navy. To accompany the 1905 State Funeral at Annapolis, Congress ordered the production of a commemorative publication, part of which read: 'There is no event in our history attended with such pomp and circumstances of glory, magnificence, and patriotic fervour.' Words that pretend to as much as the enormous sarcophagus in which rests the small, wiry body of the dynamic Captain.

The story of John Paul Jones is treated on the whole very respectfully by American writers; though they acknowledge the warts, particularly his knack of antagonising people. But on the whole they do not really recognise any farcical side to his activities, even though the lost-boat shenanigans off the west coast of Ireland and the antics of the crew at Whitehaven, for example, undeniably have a ridiculous element to them, as even John Paul Jones would have ruefully recognised after the event.

In England, the fact that Paul Jones's activities were a propaganda triumph rather than a strategic military strike helped his quite swift transition from pirate to raffish folk-hero. Within three weeks of the sea fight off Flamborough Head, the *Morning Post and Daily Advertiser* for 15 October printed the opinion: 'His gallant behaviour would have been extolled to the skies, if his bravery had been exerted in our service, but as he fought against us, we cannot find it in our hearts to allow him any merit at all.' The actions against the *Drake* and the *Serapis* and the attempts on Whitehaven and Leith had made him into a bogeyman in the papers. Paradoxically, the magnanimous comment in the *Morning Post* quoted above was printed just the day after the almost hysterically vilifying piece quoted earlier appeared in the same newspaper, describing Paul Jones as conducting himself 'like the pirate, and not the hero', referring specifically to his action with the *Serapis*.

John Paul Jones certainly did not have the Nelson touch where his officers and crews were concerned, nor did he have the chance to emulate Nelson's unrivalled catalogue of exploits. Comparison with Drake, though perhaps fairer, is not to his advantage either, though his temperament and exploits, as well as his attitude of mind, were similar. Like Drake he took many prizes, but he failed at Whitehaven and Leith, whereas Drake succeeded, for example, in 'singeing the King of Spain's beard', as he put it, with thrilling and deadly panache when he attacked the gathering Spanish Armada inside the harbour at Cadiz; and successfully attacked and sacked towns in Spanish America.

Paul Jones of course had much less time in which to really show his mettle than Drake had, and in the fledgling United States Navy John Paul was forging naval tradition where there was none, and had to contend with very awkward human material: officers of doubtful status, New England free thinkers volunteering just for the easy money, a mongrel crew of Americans, Frenchmen and Britons at loggerheads with each other. It cannot be denied that no one has ever equalled John Paul Jones in the memorably heroic quality of his victory over the *Serapis*, including Drake.

If Americans see no comedy in John Paul Jones now, the British saw no humour in him in the eighteenth century for quite different reasons. The fact of his presence in British waters was not funny. But he was a renegade who developed an unexpected image, eventually with something of Robin Hood about him. The image softened further with the passing years and became totally divorced from reality in the late nineteenth century operetta *Paul Jones*, composed by Robert Planquette, a prolific creator of such works, with words by H.B. Farnie. This operetta is a lighthearted and frothy affair, bearing no relation to reality in either setting or incidents, as is freely acknowledged in the fairytale introduction; the authors admit the piece is 'a purely fanciful episode in [Paul Jones's] adventurous career'. A totally unrecognisable Paul Jones sings sea shanties. On the opening night at the Prince of Wales Theatre in London, the part of Paul Jones was played by a Miss Agnes Huntington, with a chorus including the Lassies of St. Malo as Man o' Warsmen. It was probably never staged again. Curiously enough, Pierre Landais was born at St. Malo, which is proposed in the introductory text of the operetta as the possible birthplace of Paul Jones. Jones would have been appalled at the thought of such a horrendous confusion of identity, and might well have turned in disgust in his lead coffin! The operetta is expanded upon a little more in Appendix V.

The United States, in the person of Gouverneur Morris, was quite happy to see John Paul Jones laid to rest in a cheap and obscure grave, not much more than a decade after his vaunted exploits had taken place; and was very late in formally acknowledging his status, before going overboard on it in 1905. In view of this profound lack of recognition for over a hundred years it is perhaps lucky for the posthumous reputation of John Paul that the likes of Gilbert and Sullivan rather than the unmemorable Farnie and Planquette did not latch onto him first; though the centrepiece of the battle off Flamborough Head would have been a heavy obstacle indeed to humour or mockery of any kind, even for them.

The curtailed service of Paul Jones in Russia remains obscure. In the short time afforded him after his enthusiastic reception there by Catherine and Potemkin, he aquitted himself quite well professionally. Personally, he seems to have provoked a mixed reaction, as might have been expected in view of his known character, and to have been his usual amorous self. It would be interesting to have access to the files containing correspondence intercepted and kept by the Russian secret police, specifically that addressed to Thomas Jefferson in Paris; the prominent Freemason and the congressman who penned the stirring preamble to the American Declaration of Independence, following consultations in a committee that included Benjamin Franklin. Perhaps this correspondence still languishes somewhere in a forgotten Russian dossier. It would be fascinating to know what it was about Paul Jones that was deemed sufficiently threatening to single him out for quite such intensive secret surveillance, apart from his ranking in the naval hierarchy. It is not that his letters to Jefferson, for example, were simply intercepted and then quietly posted on; none of them were ever delivered, and the dismayed John Paul had to make special courier arrangements to eventually contact Jefferson in Paris. The files would explain a lot.

John Paul Jones was idolised in France, and is still considered a rather romantic figure there. When his funeral cortege wound its way through Paris the streets were modestly lined with applauding citizens. However, events in France (in part inspired by the example of the American Revolution across the Atlantic) would make Jones's death a quickly forgotten sideshow. The Bastille had been stormed in 1789, and three weeks after his funeral the Protestant graveyard in which the body of Paul Jones was interred was swamped by the hurriedly buried bodies of the Swiss Guard who fell almost to a man as they tried in vain to stop an enraged mob from taking over and sacking the royal palace of the Tuileries on August 10, 1792, an act very soon followed by the imprisonment and then guillotining of the King and Queen. At his graveside, the Protestant minister officiating struck an appropriate and very prescient note in his valediction: 'We have just returned to the earth the remains of an illustrious stranger, one of the first champions of the liberty of America', he announced at his commencement. He concluded with the rousing words:

> Link yourselves with the glory of Paul Jones by imitating his contempt for danger, his devotion to his country, and his noble heroism, which, after astonishing the present age, will continue to be an imperishable object of veneration for future generations.

In comparison, a more specific and therefore more poignant valediction was made by Colonel Sherburne in 1821, in the introduction to his biography:

> The venal British press and British antipathies have been the source of his defamation. The present work, written from authentic documents, will redeem his name from the odium hitherto cast upon it. The labors of John Paul Jones for the furtherance of the American cause were incessant. Whether in port or at sea he was indefatigable. He had a genius prone to adventure, and of all the naval commanders of that day, he planned and executed, both in America and in Europe, the most annoying expeditions against the enemy.

Fittingly enough, a party of Masonic brethren from the Lodge of the Nine Sisters was amongst those in the funeral procession marking the exit of John Paul Jones from this world, and they were in solemn attendance at his interment.

The last vestiges of the harbour works at Carsethorne, the playground of the child John Paul Jones and the cradle of seafaring dreams.

Appendix I:
The Little Cottage In Kirkbean

As I pointed out in the introduction, for many years now I have lived with my family in Cumbria, the English county of Whitehaven, the place of John Paul's apprenticeship to the sea and whose once-crowded commercial harbour was the target of the night attack by the *Ranger*, and Appleby, the old market town in the Vale of Eden, close to which Richard Pearson, captain of the *Serapis*, was born at Langton. Pearson, the eldest child in a very large family of brothers and sisters, went to the local grammar school at Appleby until, like Paul Jones, he joined the navy at the tender age of about fourteen.

In the summer of 1997 I set out from Kendal, a town in Cumbria not far from Appleby, and made again the leisurely journey from England into Scotland, to the Scottish side of the Solway Firth to revisit the sturdy, whitewashed stone cottage in Kirkbean parish where John Paul was born, on 6 July 1747.

John Paul had an older brother, the family's eldest child – who went eventually to live in America – two older sisters, and a younger sister. Two other children died in infancy. The family of seven shared a small living room with an open fireplace for warmth and cooking. There was a bedroom for the parents, screened off from the living room by a simple wood partition, with an open stairway from it giving access to the loft where, in the usual fashion, the children would have slept. Their father was the Head Gardener on the Arbigland estate, within which the tied cottage stood.

Looking outwards from the back of the cottage, the view is over broad farmlands sloping gently away towards the Solway Firth, where sweeping tidal flows give rise to alternating expanses of shining sea and vast brown sand flats. The English shoreline and the mountains of Cumbria are visible in the distance.

The seas between England and Scotland are pretty empty of ships now, but in the childhood days of John Paul there would have been numerous vessels plying their trade on the waters of the Firth. The nearby haven of Carsethorne would have been irresistible to an inquisitive local youngster of normal boyish interests. Carsethorne today consists of not much more than a strip of houses along the seafront. There is no harbour now, the only vestiges a few weather-beaten timbers and posts standing starkly along the foreshore. Across the wide estuary of the River Nith, where it meets the tidal waters of the Solway Firth, lies Caerlaverock Castle. In a not too distant past, vividly alive in folk memory when John Paul Jones was a boy, this fortress, now a picturesque ruin, was the power base of the Maxwells, one of the worst of the ruthless reiving clans, or 'names' as they were known, who long plagued the borders. Maybe the lurid tales arising out of the callous deeds of such notoriously wicked, but bold men, influenced John Paul's young imagination. Fanning asserts in a footnote to a page of his memoirs that: 'Jones had a wonderful notion of his name being handed down to posterity'. The incredibly rich store of border ballads, which would have been familiar to him, showed how both fame and notoriety could indeed live forever, once recorded by a balladeer.

In the usual Scottish way, John Paul's basic education was well provided for at the village school in nearby Kirkbean. He proved to be intelligent and imaginative, and had a flair for language. Between the cottage where he lived and the village school lie the grounds of Arbigland House, extensively planted with trees, some no doubt put there by his father.

The whitewashed cottage is now a heritage site. A neighbouring cottage has been converted into an informative visitor facility and there is a large landscaped car park. A short way off, just inside the garden hedge, are two flagpoles side by side, flying the American Stars and Stripes – the present day version – and the Scottish Saltaire, the flag of St Andrew. Between them there is a short pillar of squared stone with an iron plaque, subscribed by the firm in New England that built the modern warship USS *John Paul Jones*.

The site of John Paul's birth was not always so trim. When Lieutenant Alexander Pinkham, who caught the essence of the matter when he judged that Paul Jones 'created the spirit of my country's infant Navy with his fight against the *Serapis*', visited the cottage in 1831, he found it in a distressingly ruined condition. When he left he trustingly left behind twenty-five gold sovereigns for its restoration. Fortunately, it was restored, and in 1993, nearly a hundred and seventy years later, both cottage and grounds were opened to the public.

In 1953 the Daughters of the Revolution were instrumental in the addition of a commemorative plaque on the front wall of John Paul's cottage birthplace, hailing him as an 'illustrious hero of the American Revolution'. The Daughters appear to be a formidable band, who would not countenance any belittling of an established national hero – the patron saint of the Naval Academy, as an article in the *Washington Post* once described him. They would not, and in all conscience could not, see the less heroic side to his exploits, nor the importance of his luck in spotting Pearson's shrewd and subtle change of course in the gathering darkness off Flamborough Head: an observation which with little doubt made the difference between imperishable glory and oblivion.

Ten years earlier, there had been another example of female cooperation in commemorating Jones, in the wartime spirit of 'hands across the ocean'. On 30 April 1943, a replica of the flag that went to the bottom of the North Sea with the *Bonhomme Richard* in 1779 was presented in London to Admiral Stack of the USN. Like the orginal Stars and Stripes reputedly made by the collective efforts of the women of Portsmouth, New England, this replica was made by half a dozen Lady Mayoresses (of York, Sheffield, Leeds, Hull, Bradford and Bridlington) plus female members of the the British armed services and the wives of Yorkshire farmers and fishermen. It was presented to Admiral Stack, the commander of the USN in Europe at the time, by Mrs Evelyn Cardwell MBE, who lived close to Flamborough and whom the King had decorated for her disarming and capture of a German airman in the dark days following the evacuation from Dunkirk. Admiral Stack promised that the flag would be flown to Annapolis and displayed in the US Naval Academy Museum, where generations of midshipmen would see it as a symbol of the common aspirations of the British and American peoples. The promise was kept, but unfortunately, the attentions of generations of children and deterioration of the fabric have apparently all-but destroyed it.

At the cottage, listening to a homely Scottish voice playing the part of John Paul's mother, Jeanie, recapturing for visitors the everyday life of the family of seven, one gets the feeling that his real-life mother would have had a much less grandiose view of her extraordinary son and his war record than the Daughters of the Revolution. The National Library of Scotland characterizes Paul Jones as a 'Scottish Adventurer' in its manuscripts index, and John Paul's mother might well have seen him in this way too. She would have frowned on his politic change of name, and would have been nonplussed and probably amused by his odd Coat of Arms. She would, in the way of mothers, no doubt have seen the less heroic side of him quite clearly, and even the amusing aspects of her son's highly unconventional behaviour – though she died not knowing the half of it! She would have felt his 'badinage' with Katerina as something of a body blow to family honour. The contived situation would have been grounds for a blood feud in only quite recent Border history. No matter what Jean Paul might have thought privately of her younger son's behaviour, if anyone had attempted to belittle his achievements in British waters she would surely, in true motherly fashion, have rallied to his defence. The Daughters of the Revolution would do the same, and in so doing they would only be reflecting the feelings of all right-thinking Americans, and in the author's opinion, the truth.

His father passed away knowing even less of his son's doings than his mother, as he died when John Paul was only about twenty. The stone slab in the churchyard at Kirkbean capping the monument to John Paul's father reads: 'In memory of John Paul Senior who died at Arbigland the 24th October 1767, Universally Esteemed.' There is a gap for the eventual insertion of other names, though the tomb was never used again, and across the foot of the stone, 'Erected by John Paul Junior'.

The modest memorial tomb, erected by Paul Jones in the churchyard at Kirkbean as a last resting place for his father, with a gap in the superscription to allow for inclusion of the names of other family members in due course; though none was ever buried there.

John Paul always kept in touch with his sisters, and took a special interest in the children of his favourite younger sister Janet, who lived in Dumfries. It is slightly uncomfortable to sit in the sparse little cottage and, whilst listening to the quiet motherly voice, contemplate the implausible claims that John Paul Jones was the illegitimate child of his father's brother, or of the Earl of Selkirk, or – even less likely – the Duke of Queensberry, who had a connection with the Selkirk family. Coping with her household of more than seven at one point, one wonders how Jean Paul would have found the time for dalliance, even if she had the inclination.

Musing idly in front of the now cold and cheerless fireplace in the cottage, one wonders what Jean Paul would have made of a very strange fact noted by Lincoln Lorenz in his biography of Paul Jones. At seven o'clock in the evening, on the day and at the very time at which her son's body was leaving his home in Paris for interment in a pauper's grave, Gouverneur Morris, responsible for this sorry state of affairs and unable to attend the funeral because of his dinner engagement, was almost struck dead by a bolt of lightning as he strolled through the streets of the French capital. Recalling Paul Jones's wry sense of humour, one cannot help interpreting this sudden bolt from the blue as his supernatural equivalent of an eighteen-pounder – John Paul's parting shot.

Appendix II:
No More Than A Privateer?

On 7 August 1780, almost a year after the dramatic conclusion to the marauding expedition around the British Isles by his task force, Paul Jones wrote a letter to Benjamin Franklin, mostly concerning prize money and the wages of his crew. At the end, however, he raised a matter referred to earlier in this narrative:

> Mr. Gillon of South Carolina has taken much pains to promulgate that you wrote him a letter with an assurance that the *Bonhomme Richard* was a privateer. This has already done me much harm; and as it is not true, I beg your Excellency to contradict it.

On 12 August 1780, not long before the *Bonhomme Richard* squadron set sail, Franklin responded in a letter expressing best wishes for the voyage and covering several official matters. It also included the following passage:

> Depend upon it I never wrote to Mr. Gillon that the *Bonhomme Richard* was a privateer. I could not write so, for I never had such a thought. I will next post send you a copy of my letter to him; by which you will see, that he has only forced that construction from a vague expression I used merely to conceal from him (in answering his idle demand that I would order your squadron, then on the point of sailing, to go with him to Carolina) that the expedition was at the expense and under the direction of the King, which is not proper or necessary for him to know. The expression I used was that the *Concerned* had destined the squadron for another service. These words, the *Concerned*, he and the counselor, have interpreted to mean the owners of a privateer.

Looking at the words, they could very easily have done so. By 'the counselor' Franklin no doubt meant Arthur Lee, his strange fellow commissioner whose sanity he had been worried about for quite some time. Lee hated both Franklin and Paul Jones, and very soon conspired with Landais to regain command of the *Alliance* for the latter, who promptly took off in her for America, to the dismay of both Franklin and Paul Jones.

In signing his letter to Franklin dated 29 June 1779, Alexander Gillon described himself as 'Commodore of the Navy of the State of South Carolina'. His letter was asking for assistance in relieving the 'bleeding inhabitants of South Carolina and Georgia'. He asked in particular if 'you will please to consider whether the fleet I lately saw at L'Orient might not immediately proceed to the relief of them [sic]

States'. He says he knows 'the exact force of the fleet' and is 'convinced it is equal to the purpose required'.

In his reply, dated 5 July 1779, Franklin turned down Gillon's request in the following terms:

> The zeal you show for the relief of Carolina is very laudable: and I wish it was in my power to second it by complying with your proposition. But the little squadron which you suppose to be in my disposition, is not as you seem to imagine fitted out at the expense of the United States; nor have I any authority to direct its operations. It was from the beginning destined by the concerned for a particular purpose. I have only, upon a request that I could not refuse [from Sartine] lent the *Alliance* to it hoping the enterprise may prove more advantageous to the Common Cause than her cruise could be alone. I suppose too, that they are sailed before this time.

It was a copy of this particular letter that Franklin said he would send to Paul Jones for reassurance. Gillon, incidentally, supported Landais's claim to the *Alliance*, which was snatched from Paul Jones and borne off to America as noted above, with, Paul Jones indignantly asserts, the heroic crew of the *Bonhomme Richard* in irons down below, because of their loyalty to him.

Peter Landais looked upon matters concerning the so recent expedition in his own way. He saw a copy of a letter from Sartine to Franklin and picked up on a seemingly insignificant point; 'in speaking of the *Alliance* he [the French Minister of Marine] calls her an American Frigate'. He says that, as far as the French were concerned, this:

> ...implies a King or Republic ship from 20 to 60 guns: but speaking of the *Bonhomme Richard*, he don't say she was a French or American Frigate, or a French one in the American Service, which he could not have omitted had she been either of the three.

Read in conjunction with the terms of Franklin's letter of polite rejection to Gillon, this was taken by Landais to 'prove' that the *Bonhomme Richard* 'was a privateer belonging to the concerned, as expressed in his Excellency's letter'. One cannot help feeling that Landais was clutching at straws, and he was not aware of Franklin's statement to Paul Jones, that 'the expedition was at the expense and under the direction of the King'. However, Landais gives 'another proof' of his contention: 'Captain Cottineau told me he was concerned in the *Pallas* for the sum of eighty thousand livres, and the *Vengeance* was Mr. Le Ray de Chaumont's property.' Moreover, he says, the preparation of the *Bonhomme Richard* for their cruise around the British Isles was not arranged for 'as the King's ships are', and that Chaumont was involved in financing it. For good measure, Landais queried the validity of Paul Jones's French Commission.

More than his vehement words on the matter, Jones's actions demonstrate that his operations in British waters did not fit the 'privateer' label. The 'concerned', whoever they were collectively, tried to hamstring him with the concordat, but in the end they failed; but not without profit, notably due to Landais, who knew perfectly well that he was acting the privateer and did what was expected of him! As far as Landais was concerned, the defining moment of Paul Jones's 'privateering' was when the British discovered the planned joint assault on Liverpool by sea and land forces under the command of Paul Jones and Lafayette respectively. In the words of Landais, the subsequent splash of publicity across the newspapers 'made the execution of it impracticable'. The *Bonhomme Richard* suddenly lost her fitness for purpose, with the roundhouse now something of a liability on deck rather than a convenience. 'The former plan being put aside', says Landais, 'there was no immediate employment for those vessels, and if they had been disarmed, part of the expenses for fitting them for sea, must have been totally lost.' Landais then speculates: 'Somebody of power and influence being well acquainted with the case, I suppose, associated together, and obtained them for a cruise, answering for them, and accordingly became concerned in that little squadron.'

So did a planned amphibious assault on Liverpool turn into a privately financed privateering expedition? If it did, it was not obvious to Paul Jones, the man in charge of the squadron, who did not acknowledge it and was at pains to deny it, and certainly acted as though there was more to the expedition than mere profit.

In trying to define Paul Jones's authority and 'official' position, it is instructive to look into his correspondence with the American Commissioners in France, who were his immediate employers of course. On 15 September 1777, before the cruise of the *Ranger* had taken place, Paul Jones wrote to the Commissioners in Paris: Benjamin Franklin, Silas Deane and Arthur Lee. The last paragraph reveals his thoughts on the successful prosecution of naval warfare by the United States:

> I have always since we have had Ships of War been persuaded that small squadrons could be employed to far better advantage on private expeditions and would distress the Enemy infinitely more than the same force could do by cruising either jointly or separately. Were strict secrecy observed on our part, the enemy have many important places in such a defenceless situation that they might be effectually surprised and attacked with no very considerable force. We cannot yet fight their navy as their numbers and force is so far superior to ours: therefore it seems to be our most natural province to surprise their defenceless places and thereby divide their attention and draw it off from our coasts.

His operations in British waters were rooted in this brief but telling statement. In his very short initial account of the *Ranger* expedition to the Commissioners he says: 'On the morning of the 23rd I landed at Whitehaven and burned shipping; if we could have arrived earlier we should have destroyed the town, but we did show the enemy that what they have done in America can happen to them.'

After his exploits with the *Ranger* had been concluded, and in anticipation of the expedition of the *Bonhomme Richard* squadron, Paul Jones wrote another letter, this time for the French Minister of Marine as well as for the American team in Paris. Its contents show the same thinking:

> Three fast frigates with tenders might burn Whitehaven and its fleet, rendering it nearly impossible to supply Ireland with coal next winter.
>
> The same force could take the bank of Ayr, in Scotland, destroy the town and perhaps the shipping at Clyde, along with Greenock and Port Glasgow. The fishery at Campbeltown and some Irish ports are also worthy targets.

It might be equally expedient to alarm Britain's east side by destroying the coal shipping of Newcastle. Many important towns on the east and north coasts of England and Scotland could be burnt or captured.

The success of these enterprises will depend on surprise and dispatch; it is therefore necessary that the ships sail fast, and carry sufficient forces to repel the enemy. If successful, any one of these projects would occasion almost inconceivable panic in England. It would convince the world of her vulnerability, and hurt her public credit.

Other projects might be to intercept Britain's West India or Baltic fleets, her Hudson Bay ships, or destroy her Greenland fishery.

Such a strategy is not that of a privateer.

Benjamin Franklin entered into the spirit of things with gusto. He opened a letter to Lafayette, dated 22 March 1779, with the words: 'I admire much the Activity of your Genius, and the strong Desire you have of being continually employ'd against our Common Enemy'. He goes on:

It is certain that the coasts of England and Scotland are extremely open and defenceless. There are also many rich towns near the sea, which 4 or 5000 men, landing unexpectedly, might easily surprise and destroy, or exact from them a heavy contribution, taking a part in ready money and hostages for the rest. I should suppose, for example, that two millions Sterling, or 48 millions of Livres might be demanded of the town of Bristol for the Town and Shipping; twelve millions of Livres for Bath; forty-eight millions from Liverpool; six millions from Lancaster, and twelve millions from Whitehaven. On the East side there are the towns of Newcastle, Scarborough, Lynn and Yarmouth; from which very considerable sums might be exacted: and if among the troops there were a few horsemen to make sudden incursions at some little distance from the coast, it would spread terror to much greater distances and the whole would occasion movements and marches of troops that must put the enemy to a prodigious expense, and harass them exceedingly. Their Militia will probably soon be drawn from the different Counties to one or two places of encampment; so that little or no opposition can be made to such a force, as is above mentioned, in the places where they may land.

If there's a slightly unhinged pirate around here, it's Franklin!

He goes on to say that the practicalities of all this are beyond his scope to reasonably comment upon, but expresses the opinion: 'In war, attempts thought to be impossible, do often for that very reason become possible and practicable; because nobody expects them, and no precautions are taken to guard against them.' This is really no more than an expansion upon what Paul Jones had so succinctly broached to the Commissioners, in the letter heralding his arrival in France.

Franklin was a remarkable man, acknowledged as such by his admiring contemporaries, and a marvellous ambassador for the fledgling United States. Apart from his official duties on behalf of America, he found time to experiment with lightning, invent bifocal spectacle lenses, write *Poor Richard's Almanac*, and be involved in profitable commercial activity. He must have been pretty exasperated in carrying out his official duties at times, if a passage in a letter to the Revd. Samuel Cooper, dated 2 December 1780, is anything to go by:

> Dr. Lee's accusation of Captain Landais for insanity was probably well-founded; as in my opinion would have been the same accusation, if it had been brought by Landais against Lee: For tho' neither of them are permanently mad, they are both so at times; and the insanity of the latter is of the two the most mischievous.

In another very exasperated letter, directly to Arthur Lee, Franklin expresses, 'my Pity for your Sick Mind' and warns Lee, that 'if you do not cure yourself' all will end in 'Insanity'. He refers to 'jealousies, suspicions and fancies that others mean you ill'. He ends: 'God preserve you from so terrible an Evil'.

Paul Jones, with plenty of potential to be exasperating himself, might have differed with Franklin on his relative assessment of Lee and Landais, though he would have recognized in Landais much of what Franklin saw in Lee!

Appendix III:
Pearson and Piercy and the Battle off Flamborough Head

Following the successful encounter of his task force with the *Serapis* and the *Countess of Scarborough*, Paul Jones arrived triumphantly at the Texel, and dropped anchor in the roadstead there on 3 October 1779. By that time he had completed his comprehensive report of the whole expedition, including a detailed account of the dramatic action off Flamborough Head. It was in the form of a very long letter addressed to Benjamin Franklin. This letter, which constitutes the 'official' account, was in fact dated the very day they anchored in the Texel. It could hardly have been more promptly dispatched for the attention of America's Minister Plenipotentiary in France, and in due course for the attention of the President and Congress in the United States.

At the Texel, Pearson and Piercy were both technically prisoners, incarcerated on board the *Pallas*. Soon after arrival, however, Pearson completed his own account, also in the form of a letter, of the prolonged action off Flamborough Head; and on 6 October dispatched it to the British Admiralty in London, where it was received on 11 October. It was published in the *London Gazette* the following day, and subsequently in the *London Evening Post* on 17 October. Piercy had already penned a short account of his action in command of the *Countess of Scarborough*, addressed formally to Pearson his superior officer and then fellow prisoner and dated 4 October, the day after their unlooked-for arrival in Holland.

These two letters formed an important element in the proceedings of the court martial held aboard HMS *Daphne* in Sheerness Harbour more than five months later, on 10 March 1780. There were nine members of the Court: eight fleet captains and the president, Robert Roddam, Vice Admiral of the Blue Squadron, with a judge advocate in attendance. The letters were read at the commencement of the court martial proceedings, but would have been already well known to the members of the court from their newspaper publication, and would have been the subject of trenchant discussion – whether public or private, informed and otherwise – for several months before the Court assembled aboard the *Daphne*. Both letters were vouched for as a true record of events during the course of the proceedings, and were readily accepted as such by the court. Pearson himself refers to his letter as 'my publick letter', and the Court also refers to it in these terms. So there had been ample opportunity for comment, whether favourable or adverse.

The record of events written by Paul Jones has formed the basis of most accounts of the Battle off Flamborough Head, with Landais's version virtually dismissed as worthless, the product of a deranged mind even, though it is supported in a number of respects by Cottineau and others.

The task force accounts are coloured by the personalities of their authors. The letters of both Pearson and Piercy, produced with the certainty of intense professional scrutiny in the offing, are dispassionate in tone and in view of their eventual acceptance by the court martial, both can be taken as reliable. Paul Jones said that Pearson needed to make the most of the intervention of *Alliance* to justify his striking – as Pearson says, in the face of a substantially superior force. Paul Jones disparaged the part played by the *Alliance*, and had to undermine Pearson's account to give plausibility to his damning denigration of Landais. However, Cottineau claimed that the *Alliance* did in fact play a significant part in events, much along the lines set down by Pearson in his letter to the Admiralty, and as confirmed by Piercy as far as Landais's influence on the striking of the *Countess of Scarborough* was concerned.

A Royal Navy court martial, always a serious affair, was particularly tough in the latter half of the eighteenth century. Some twenty years earlier, Admiral John Byng, the son of an aristocrat, had been tried by court martial in Portsmouth. He was found guilty of not doing his utmost against the enemy in connection with the loss of Minorca during what has been described as 'an unofficial war of outposts between the British and the French' at various locations around the world, in the years which immediately preceded the Seven Years War. Byng was condemned to death, and publicly shot on the quarterdeck of a warship at Spithead on 10 March 1757. There was a lot of sympathy for the unfortunate Admiral, not least in Parliament; though not from the King. Unfortunately for Byng, the Articles of War had by then been revised to allow no punishment but death for an officer of whatever rank who did not do his utmost in action against the enemy, whether in battle or in pursuit. Voltaire, coining a phrase that has survived to the present day, commented wryly that the execution of Byng was carried out *'pour encourager les autres'*.

Pearson, assisted by Piercy, had prevented any attack on the Baltic fleet – their prime duty as escort – but they had lost two Royal Navy warships to (as far as the British were concerned) a Scotch renegade and a pack of French privateers flying the flag of the rebellious colonials, at a time when Britain had been under dire threat of Franco-Spanish invasion. This could have proved a daunting defeat to explain, were it not redeemed by the truly heroic nature of the engagement off Flamborough Head. As they were careful to point out, neither Pearson nor Piercy had given their ships away, and, badly damaged though these ships were, with grievous loss of human life, they only yielded them in the end to the greatly superior force represented by the potent and virtually undamaged *Alliance*. Both British captains knew that they would have to face the close scrutiny of a court martial, and would need evidence that would stand up to public exposure in the newspapers; no stone was likely to remain unturned in judging their case.

In the terms of the Articles of War, it was duly found that Pearson and Piercy had done all that they could in the action off Flamborough Head, and both were exonerated – and without the necessity for intense examination during the actual court proceedings. However, aspersions had been cast on the conduct of a Lieutenant Stanhope, First Lieutenant on board the *Serapis*. This matter was examined in some detail to establish the facts in his case. The Lieutenant had gone overboard in the huge explosion set off by the grenade dropped fortuitously through the hatch to end up amongst spilled powder and cartridges on the gun deck of the *Serapis*. On struggling back on board, he went down to the cockpit 'dripping wet' and 'much scorched on his hands and face'; as the purser stated in evidence. After his burns were dressed with hogs-lard 'he came into my cabin', the purser went on, 'and refreshed himself'. The purser lent him a pair of shoes as he had none at that juncture, and helped him to wring out his clothes. Stanhope then went back to his guns. He went below again some time later, 'appearing to me to be in much pain' said the purser. He 'asked for a little wine and water'. They exchanged a few words about the action and Stanhope then went dutifully back to his guns again. Stanhope's conduct was looked into at some length through the questioning of several eyewitnesses, with a favourable outcome for the unfortunate Lieutenant, as he was found not to have culpably lingered away from his station. On the contrary, more than one witness commended his conduct, and Pearson himself expressed faith in him from the outset of the proceedings.

The fact that Pearson and Piercy were not closely examined on their conduct during the court martial in itself says a lot for the reliability and veracity of their accounts of the action off Flamborough Head. No-one challenged them effectively at any stage; neither friend nor foe, nor the newspapers. In relation to Pearson's crucial emphasis on the part played by the broadsides of the *Alliance* in damaging *Serapis* and influencing his decision to strike, John Paul alleges that Pearson was simply trying to 'stretch a point and save his own credit'. In jarring contradiction to Jones's own damning account of the conduct of Landais, who, he says, directed his guns at the *Bonhomme Richard* malevolently, Pearson was in agreement with Landais that there was no treacherous assault on Jones's ship. Paul Jones hints, somewhat half-heartedly, at a conspiracy against him, but the concord between Pearson and Landais regarding the actions of *Alliance* was supported by Cottineau's written account. He specifically says *Alliance*, towards the end of the battle, 'raked the *Serapis* two times', and attributed any accidental damage inflicted on Jones's ship to 'the clumsiness of its cannoneers'.

Cottineau's account was presented to Chaumont in the form of a letter and an accompanying memoir, hostile to Paul Jones, which John Paul knew nothing about, though Chaumont passed copies to Franklin. These documents were not publicised by either Chaumont or Franklin.

Though Paul Jones was utterly damning of Landais in his prompt report to Benjamin Franklin from the Texel, he had adopted a less condemnatory view by the time he wrote a long, racy and colourful account of the action off Flamborough Head for presentation to the King of France in 1785, very much in the hope of gaining fresh employment with the French navy. He allowed, at two points during his narrative, that Landais fired his broadsides at the combined bow and stern target presented by the *Serapis* and the *Bonhomme Richard* as they fought locked together. In effect he was by that time saying, six years after the event, that he considered the actions of Landais to have been reckless rather than malevolent. On this new tack there was no longer a need to cast doubt on Pearson's view. Nevertheless, towards the end of his account to King Louis, Paul Jones attributed the eventual sinking of the *Bonhomme Richard* principally to the 'blows she had received in the bow from the *Alliance*, causing holes that could not be closed'.

In a rancorous sea of conflicting opinion and contested fact, Pearson and Piercy seem to stand forth stolidly as reasonable and reliable eyewitnesses – as far as the events directly affecting them are concerned at any rate. And there is a reassuring immediacy about their accounts. Paul Jones reported to Franklin on 3 October, Piercy to Pearson on the 4th, and Pearson to the British Admiralty on the 6th, only three days after their arrival at the Texel. Pearson's letter is a very long and detailed account of the whole engagement. Piercy's is much shorter but throws valuable light on the actions of the *Alliance* in decisively threatening the crippled *Countess*; as well as on the dark, smoke-obscured scene which dissuaded him from firing his guns in assistance because, as he says, 'I could not distinguish one ship from the other'. Pearson approved of his decision. Confronted with the same scenario Landais, as we have seen, had no such qualms; and he reaped the whirlwind of his clumsy, perhaps callous, intervention.

All in all, one could well understand why the court martial, whose professional seagoing members would have been aware of the dissent amongst the cruise participants in France, was favourably impressed by the evidence of Pearson and Piercy. Here are the findings of that court martial, held on board the *Daphne* at Sheerness:

> Having examined the evidence in support of the [indecipherable] matter as well as what everyone had to offer and [indecipherable] considered the same The Court is of opinion that the Captains Pearson and Piercy assisted by their officers and men have not only acquitted themselves of their duty to their Country but have in the execution of such duty done infinite credit to themselves by a very obstinate defence against a superior force.

As far as the aspersions against Stanhope were concerned, the court 'proceeded to examine into the cause of it and from the evidence given is of opinion that such aspersion is malicious'.

As a result of their deliberations: 'The Court do therefore unanimously acquit the said Captains Pearson and Piercy their Officers and Men for the loss of their respective Ships in the most honourable manner and they are hereby most honourably acquitted accordingly'.

Sources for the various accounts of the action off Flamborough Head are indicated in the bibliography.

Appendix IV:
The Strange Case Of The Russian Princess

When the personable young woman introducing herself as Baroness Helmy Weissereich turned up at the American consulate at Riga, the capital of Latvia, in 1926, she must have caused something of a stir. She wanted to live in the United States she said, and requested that she be granted an American passport. She had no money and knew no one to receive her in America; but, she said, her great-great-grandfather was John Paul Jones, a man illustrious in the annals of American history. She offered proofs of her claim in the form of a gold ring engraved with the initials J.P.J., a family heirloom, she said. She claimed it was given originally by Paul Jones to her Russian ancestor Princess Anna Mihailovna Kourakina, a Maid of Honour at the court of Catherine the Great, and a secretary and confidante to the Empress, being privy to her personal and other secrets. She also produced documents in support of her claim: letters, and what she claimed was Anna's diary, but although the pages appeared venerably yellow, its age was soon called into question. It was a diary in which John Paul and her thoughts about him naturally feature very prominently. Some extracts from what was reputed to be the diary of Catherine the Great also came to figure in the controversy. Its authenticity was soon questioned.

The Anna Kourakina story was first publicly recounted by Valentine Thomson in 1934. She said that it had been 'just brought to light after the death of her [Anna's] last known descendant' – Helmy. The diary kept by the Russian princess had descended to Helmy through her family. Miss Thomson's enthusiastic account of the whole thing amounted to close on 7,000 words, and opened with a haunting photograph of Helmy Weissereich in the pages of the *New York Times Magazine* on Sunday 23 September 1934. The story was given the front page, and completed the following Sunday. Miss Thomson says that Helmy's request for a passport was turned down because: 'The technicalities of the immigration system barred the way,' and Helmy 'was fated never to see America.' However, restless in spirit like John Paul, according to Valentine Thomson, 'she wandered to Casablanca, Morocco, and fell in love with a young American'; such a perfect destination for the mysterious woman, as a hotbed of espionage. Before anything more came of the affair, however, she returned to Russia for some reason and died not very long afterwards.

Valentine Thomson says that she first heard of Helmy when the young woman was working under communist rule in one of the galleries at the Imperial Palace in St. Petersburg – Petrograd, not yet Leningrad. Miss Thomson says she was

'... actually classifying a collection of pictures which Anna, under Catherine's imperious direction, had bought in Paris in 1787'.

In the bibliography of his book *John Paul Jones: A Sailor's Biography*, (1959), Admiral Samuel Eliot Morison refers readers to Valentine Thomson's 1934 *New York Times* two-part article: 'for the Anna Kourakina story', which he reduces to a dismissive seven-line footnote. Rather than being scuppered by the 'technicalities of the immigration system', as Valentine Thomson claimed, Admiral Morison says that Helmy was turned down because her story 'was investigated and found to be false', the story being, moreover, 'supported by phony extracts from a non-existent diary of Catherine II'. He does not say who investigated Helmy's story, why it was deemed false, nor how thorough the investigation was, and the matter of the investigation does not seem to be documented at all. Of course, it would not have been the first time nor the last that a would-be migrant cooked up a plausible story to swing the decision of a harrassed administration. Morison says curtly that there is no evidence for the story told by 'the applicant', and that there is 'no likelihood that Jones ever had an affair with a lady at the Russian court'.

Writing earlier in 1943, Lincoln Lorenz, the other major biographer of John Paul Jones, notes in the preface to his book *John Paul Jones: Fighter For Freedom and Glory* that in the interval between an earlier biography in French entitled *Le Corsaire chez l'imperatrice*, published in Paris but undated, and her American biography *Knight of the Seas*, published in New York in 1939, Valentine Thomson has changed her view of Baroness Helmy Weissereich's story. In the earlier biographical work, writes Lorenz:

> She fully certifies to the truth of an elaborately told romance between Jones and the Russian princess Anna Kourakina, while in the other she retracts her previous assurances of the veracity of the narrative and sets it apart in an appendix as a plausible but unauthenticated legend.

Lorenz refers briefly to certain specific quite unbelievable aspects of the story, and says that 'not one authenticated document supports the tale', which is, in his opinion: 'Amorphous as fiction and baseless as history'. In *Knight of the Seas* Valentine Thomson says that the Anna Kourakina story fits in with 'certain old, persistent legends', but that 'convincing as its evidence may seem, cannot be verified from contemporary testimony and so must in the interests of historical accuracy be regarded as a beguiling and plausible legend, reposing very possibly in fact'.

However, in view of what she unwittingly said at the consulate, Helmy's story may have had at least some basis in truth. Valentine Thomson's story in the *New York Times* is rich in detail, authentic or not. What exercises this author is not the truth or lies told by Helmy, but the Masonic connection it points to as underlying Paul Jones's effective expulsion from Russia.

Neither Valentine Thomson nor Lincoln Lorenz, nor Admiral Morison, seem aware of the significance that a connection between Paul Jones and the Kourakins might have. Helmy herself is unaware of the Masonic connection or its significance; and she would certainly have used any such knowledge she may have had to bolster her case in Riga. If her story was a complete fabrication, how is it that Helmy came to choose the Princess Anna Kourakina as the lynchpin of her case at the Consulate? Before she is dismissed out of hand, the way in which she establishes the connection between Princess Anna and Commodore Paul Jones merits consideration.

Anna says that they first encountered each other – falling in love at first sight of course – not in Russia but in Paris, and before Paul Jones entered into the service of Catherine the Great. According to Anna's diary, produced by Helmy in Riga, they met each other one winter evening at the Russian Embassy in the French capital. Both were attending a dinner given by the Russian Ambassador, Baron Simolin, in honour of America's representatives in France. Valentine Thomson says that their encounter marked the beginning 'of one of the great loves of history', as Jones surrendered to an 'overpowering and fatal passion'. Paul Jones never mentions Anna. However, according to her own story, Anna already knew about Paul Jones before they met, having been present at a meeting in Russia between Baron Simolin and Catherine late in 1787, at which Paul Jones was discussed and a portrait of him produced by the Ambassador for the Empress to study.

When Catherine eventually retired, Anna says that she and Simolin conversed about life in Paris and he gave her the portrait, saying significantly, 'You will like him.' She was evidently destined to return to Paris with Simolin; presumably (if the matter is factual) to buy the pictures for Catherine mentioned above. The Ambassador's duties involved a variety of activities, from buying the latest fashions for Potemkin to dispense to his women, to conducting the inevitable espionage work associated with the Embassy.

Anna may have been sent to Paris to buy pictures, but in the context of the varied work undertaken by the Embassy, she may have had another task to perform. It would have been a willing task, judging by the reaction noted in her 'diary', when she saw John Paul's portrait in Russia: 'Strange to confess he has cast an uncanny spell on my heart. He may be a desperado or a renegade. I do not care. His personality thrills me.' Once in Paris she is clearly amused at his low opinion of her worldly capabilities in relation to a secret assignment involving the French queen, saying: 'my admiration and love for him have grown stronger' and that, at the prospect of his going to Russia, 'my heart throbs with excitement'. It certainly looks as though the indomitable Jones had made yet another conquest, though possibly with some aid from the Russians.

The Russians, and Catherine in particular, were very impressed by Paul Jones's recent exploits; and Catherine keenly wanted him to enter into her service in Russia; to fight against the Turks in the Black Sea. Thomas Jefferson, Franklin's successor in Paris by that time, and well disposed towards Paul Jones, was in discussions with Simolin about the matter. Jones was tempted, but reluctant to accede to the Russian requests, which were persistent and flattering in both professional and personal terms, because he would have much preferred advancement in the United States. He had also dallied with the French, producing his long biographical account for the French King, and was negotiating with the Danes. What might tip the scales in Russia's favour?

Perhaps it was the classic spook 'honey trap' that swung the mind of Paul Jones towards service in the Black Sea. Anna thinks that Paul Jones followed her personally to St Petersburg when she returned there, and that she was in effect the reason why he entered into Catherine's employ. Jones himself, and everyone else for that matter, says that he went to Russia for the position offered to him, plus further prospects of honour and glory of course. Valentine Thomson says that 'the little princess, back again in Catherine's palace, knew better'. After their first encounter at the Russian Embassy dinner – if there was indeed such an encounter – there would have been plenty of opportunity to meet whilst the pictures were assessed and bought. It was here that the secret matter involving Queen Marie Antoinette, which Jones apparently could not bring himself to believe a young woman like Anna was capable of handling, was dealt with. No doubt the princess entered eagerly into Parisian social life, perhaps, like Paul Jones, networking congenially in Masonic circles; after all, her family was very prominent at the highest levels of Freemasonry in Russia. Paul Jones would without any doubt have sought immediate contact with fellow Masons on arrival there, through the usual introductions and the several Masons he knew who were serving there already. However, through Princess Anna Mihaelovna's Kourakin clan he would have had an enviable introduction indeed to the Masonic scene.

In her 'diary', Anna's thoughts were turning on libertarian issues. She mused on peasants '... living in wretched homes lost in the vast country, breathing only love and obedience, while at court they believe only in reckless force, money, honour and sensuous pleasure'. As she confided to her diary, the gallant Marquis de Lafayette, a Freemason like Paul Jones, said to her: 'Revolutions are miracles of history which take place when life becomes too congested with hardships.' He told her that he thought the recent revolution in America, in which he played a significant part, might be repeated in France. De Segur, the French Ambassador in Russia, who befriended Paul Jones in extreme adversity there, was a Freemason and no doubt known to Anna. Ambassador Simolin, clearly well known to Anna, was, if not a Freemason, of liberal outlook in the Masonic vein. Simolin almost fell foul of the mob later, trying to help the escape of the French king from the Tuileries. Freemasons from Russia mingled easily with those in France, as Catherine well knew. The cultured Masonic social scene would certainly have facilitated a relationship between Paul Jones and Princess Anna Mihaelovna.

The enigmatic Baroness Helmy Weissereich and her tale about Princess Anna Kourakina are not essential to adjudge the Masonic connection as fundamental to Paul Jones's experience in Russia. Other lines of enquiry, though complicated, can lead to the same conclusion.

Past biographers of Paul Jones, as well as Paul Jones himself and his friend De Segur, have been unanimous in smelling a conspiracy to discredit him through the grossly distorted circumstances of the juvenile rape allegation; but their attempts to find a culprit, or culprits, have been unconvincing. Personal animosity, professional jealousy, punctured pride and other motivating forces have all been put forward as causes; but they lack adequate strength in trying to explain what took place, and cannot really account for the overall methodical organisation and exercise of veiled power that was in evidence.

The rape episode bears all the hallmarks of the secret police. A powerful Masonic connection, through Anna Kourakina or otherwise, would in the political context of Russia and Europe in the late eighteenth century, have furnished a more than adequate reason for ousting Paul Jones. Catherine the Great, perhaps in consultation with the dreaded Sheshkovsky, who headed the secret police throughout her long reign, and who she was always ready to see, would have been the logical instigator of the action; the details of the scheme being worked up by others. Drastic action against the whole Masonic movement was in the offing. Catherine was chillingly ruthless even with her friends on the Masonic issue.

In her (supposed) diary Anna registered a change in Catherine's attitude towards her, noting: 'She has become so strange and cold towards me'. She was somewhat puzzled, but thought – perhaps not entirely correctly – that this was because the Empress simply disapproved of her passionate relationship with Paul Jones. According to one of Admiral Morison's 'phony extracts' from the 'non-existent diary' of Catherine the Great, Anna soon died in childbirth. She was said to be bearing the legitimate son of Paul Jones, at the Convent of Novo Devichy, where she had been sent by the Empress.

Five years after her *New York Times* Magazine story, Valentine Thomson, on reflection, sets Helmy's narrative apart in the final chapter of her biography of Paul Jones Knight of the Seas as, in the words of Lincoln Lorenz, which echo her own words, 'a plausible but unauthenticated legend' – a turn of phrase which, of course, leaves open the possibility of some basis in fact. Helmy's story, however seriously flawed it might seem, should not be totally ignored; if only because she centred it on Princess Anna Mihaelovna Kourakina, and the 'diary' provides such interesting and plausible detail.

Authentication of this diary, if it is still in existence somewhere, would be quite an exciting application of modern forensics: The USN would surely have an interest in the verdict of science, one way or the other; as no doubt would American Freemasons; not to mention the immigration service! As Valentine Thomson says in that final chapter: 'Time has not diminished the fascination of that suppositional diary.' She enigmatically describes it, within parentheses and inverted commas as: '(now "lost")'. There is no further explanation.

Catherine let slip a revealing remark to her German confidant and old crony Baron Grimm, in a letter which she penned to him at the beginning of September 1791, with Paul Jones by then back in Paris. 'I have emptied my bag', she said, in relation to her dealings with Jones She meant not her handbag, but her bag of tricks! This turn of phrase has resonance in the world of espionage. How far would she go in plotting against the Masons? The key players in the child rape scandal were all Russo-Germans, as was the unreliable Katerina herself. Was she cynically and very effectively planted on Jones from the outset; as some kind of 'jail-bait'? Perhaps Catherine would not have gone so far, but Sheshkovsky, her brutal secret police chief, would. Certainly Princess Anna Mihaelovna would have been traumatically disillusioned by events. Valentine Thompson says that Baron Grimm was also, at some stage at least, a Freemason.

Helmy's fascinating intrusion into the life story of John Paul Jones is not only colourful, but perhaps significant in a way she did not at all realize; if, that is, there is some nugget of verifiable truth in the tale of her ancestry. Her case should at least be looked into again. It is too late for the passport, but a closer look at Catherine the Great's 'bag of tricks' might yield more of the truth! And a final observation: if the Helmy story is a complete fabrication, then in the author's opinion, she was not the sole fabricator. There is simply too much detail. By the time Helmy makes her claim in Latvia, Stalin is in complete control, and his instrument of terror, the OGPU, forerunner of the KGB, has been recently formalised. The famous Zinoviev forgery had been released two years before. Just as the secret police had in all probability been responsible for Jones's fall from grace, is it not credible that 'Helmy' was a failed Soviet plant, an attempt to place a sleeper in a potentially revealing social milieu in the United States? A delicious irony.

Appendix V:
Two Shipboard Romances

As we have seen, the exploits of Paul Jones were the subject of popular ballad makers and a popular dance reflected his amorous exploits. He even influenced women's fashion in the aftermath of the battle off Flamborough Head. As memory dimmed, things went wildly awry for John Paul when Farnie and Planquette decided to make him the subject of one of their musical endeavours; published in 1889 and according to the title page, based on an earlier work by Chivot and Duru. Though they speculate about Paul Jones's nationality (could he have been French?) in the opening paragraph of their plot synopsis, their opera comique is, they say, 'a purely fanciful episode in his adventurous career'. They were the authors of numerous comic operas besides *Paul Jones,* such as *Rip Van Winkle* and *Nell Gwynne.*

Presumably Miss Agnes Huntington, who played the part of Paul Jones in the three-act composition on its opening night at the Prince of Wales theatre in London, did so in the Principal Boy style of traditional pantomime, with requisite thigh-slapping. The stalwart crew of the *Bonhomme Richard* feature in the opera of course. The love interest (the main point of the opera) is supplied through a star-crossed romance between Yvonne, the 'pretty niece' of Paul Jones's apprentice master Bicoquet, an ageing St Malo ships-chandler, and not Mr. Younger of Whitehaven. Bouillabaisse, a curmudgeonly old smuggler who becomes bosun of Paul Jones's ship, has a young wife named Chopinette. She is hostess of the Harbour Inn, and her domestic tiffs and flirtations with Haricot, employed by Bicoquet, form the opera's sub-plot. The whole opera becomes more and more fantastical in both settings (including the Spanish Main and an island off the Mosquito Coast), and plot (involving seagoing canoes and Indian disguise). There is a happy ending of course for the gallant Paul and his lovely Yvonne, brought about by the opportune arrival of the crew of the *Bonhomme Richard*, to rescue their Captain from his Spanish captors.

One of the more attractive lyrics, which epitomizes the tone of the whole composition, is a Barcarolle, entitled 'Trio of the Winch', rendered by Miss Huntington in the part of the dashing Paul Jones:

> *Paul*: Upon a May day morning
> To dance along the sea,
> A weatherly craft
> The wind blowing aft,

That's the height of delight for me;
There's sea-bloom on our faces,
A perfume of the foam,
And merry our song
As we're darting along
O'er the harbour to our home

Ensemble: Yo ho, yo ho, heave lads, yo ho,
Outside the breezes merrily blow,
Yo ho, yo ho, heave lads, yo ho,
Our lasses are waiting I know

Paul: White is the feath'ry billow,
And blue the deep below,
But her hand is as white,
And her blue eye as bright,
That is waiting for me, I know!
And on this fair May morning,
I'll hand nor net or line
For under the tree
She'll whisper to me
Of the love that makes her mine!

The lyric might well have appealed to the poet (or poetaster) in Paul Jones – as no doubt would Miss Agnes Huntington.

Whilst working on this book at the reference library in Carlisle, I came across a truly outrageous version of the raid on Whitehaven, which the author vowed at the outset to be authentic. It was a very slim bound volume of only twenty-one pages. The main heading was Tales for the Tea Table. The sub-heading was 'No VIII: Paul Jones or Whitehaven in 1778'. The contents of the little book, which was undated, were brown with age. Someone subsequent to binding had glued inside the front cover an article from the Carlisle Journal of 18 April 1905, reporting that Horace Porter, the American Ambassador in Paris, 'after a search of six years, has just discovered the remains of Admiral Paul Jones, the Father of the American Navy'. It goes on to say: 'The body was well preserved, having been immersed in alcohol and packed round with hay and straw. The persons present at the disinterment were struck by the resemblance of the head to the bust of the Admiral and to his portraits as shown on existing medals.' The body had long, tied-back hair, said elsewhere to be sandy in colour.

The article is headed: 'The Apotheosis of Paul Jones: The Famous Pirate's Remains Found'. Setting aside the pirate reference, the article itself is succinct, accurate and informative. Glued to the back cover is a later article from the same newspaper, reporting the ceremony surrounding the reception of John Paul's remains in Annapolis. The book was put together before 1905; but just how long before that date is hard to say. It was bequeathed to the library in Carlisle many years ago as part of a very large collection, the Bibliotheca Jacksoniana, which was subsequently catalogued and the catalogue published by the Carlisle Public Library Committee in 1909. The book was catalogued as 45K, with the comment: 'Tale, taken from some publication'. 'K' was the classification for fiction! The author knows something about the topography of Whitehaven, but is breathtakingly ill-informed about the activities of Paul Jones. He says that his source is a 'gentleman', one 'whose name, had the writer permission to publish it, would alone be sufficient to stamp this narrative with the character of authenticity'. The writing is colourful and quite spirited, and it is true that the year of the attack is correct; but just a few comments and extracts will show how 'authentic' is this supposedly true-life tale of swashbuckling and romance, which casts John Paul as a hero very much in the style of Errol Flynn.

The ship in which Paul Jones stages the attack on Whitehaven is not the *Ranger*, but the *Serapis*. At one point, the crew appear as one man in answer to a sharp whistle from John Paul: 'They were fine looking fellows – Englishmen every one of them, who had previously served in the British navy', from which they were driven by bad treatment; which the author expands upon feelingly. At a tricky moment for Paul Jones in the narrative 'his sword gleamed round his head' and he roused the crew by 'uttering his well known war cry' which, in a nod to the American emblem, was 'Eagles to your prey!'

The villain in the crew is not Freeman, but some unfortunate fellow named Gibbon. Freeman is portrayed as a staunch member of the ship's company.

In view of the facts so far, it may come as no surprise to learn that Paul Jones has a wife, named Ellen, who figures prominently in the narrative, and whom he 'rescues' from Whitehaven, though only after she has learned that an English officer, whom Paul Jones spares whilst duelling with him, turns out to be her long-lost brother Henry. Upon discovering his identity, 'the lady gave a faint scream, and sank fainting upon the sofa'. She is lovingly depicted at one point 'seated at a table and pensively leaning her cheek upon her small white hand' with no-one noticing 'the tear that glistened in her bright hazel eye – for her rich auburn ringlets were now unbound, and falling over her forehead, in a great measure concealed her features from their view.' Unfortunately for the distraught Ellen, no sooner had she been reunited with her brother than she was perforce whisked away from Whitehaven, crying to him forlornly: 'Farewell – and forever'.

It is perhaps not surprising that the bride should eventually swoon: 'She almost sank from his embrace as she spoke, when Paul seizing her fainting form as he would that of a child and giving orders to his men for an instant retreat to the boats bore away his beautiful bride almost in a state of insensibility'.

They all made hurriedly for the harbour, where: 'As Paul, still bearing his almost unconscious bride, was rapidly passing the few houses near the Fort, one of which at that time bore the jolly likeness of a sailor, his eye was caught by a glance of the figure of a man skulking in a corner …' It was the traitorous Gibbon, of course. John Paul orders the crew to seize him, and after the writer has lingered long over his predicament, he was in due course strung up from the yardarm, pleading for his life and struggling. But there was no mercy: 'The lip of Paul Jones curled with very scorn as the affrighted wretch thus poured out his agonized supplications.'

. Discounting the harrowing fate of the hapless Gibbon, however, all turned out pretty well in the end. Paul Jones in company with his lovely Ellen sailed triumphantly away from Whitehaven; on board the *Serapis*. The wrong ship, once underway, 'gracefully bent to the breeze' and soon disappeared from view; 'nor was the coast of Cumberland ever afterwards visited by Paul Jones or his beautiful bride'.

This literary offering is anonymous, and in comparison one can only say thank goodness for Farnie and Planquette, who were at least open about writing fiction, not fact. But then, John Paul Jones has always been a controversial figure about whom fact and fiction are sometimes difficult to distinguish.

Before we leave this odd work, there are a few intriguing snippets given, which, in spite of the rest, look authentic. The description of 'the few houses near the Fort, one of which at that time bore the jolly likeness of a sailor' reflects pretty well the topography near the fort, as shown on contemporary plans. One of the houses was evidently an alehouse, quite possibly Nick Allison's, especially if David Bradbury's location of his pub is correct. If so, we might now know that its signboard depicted a 'jolly sailor', even though the pub's actual name eludes us. Was it indeed The Jolly Sailor? There is a reference to the 'traitorous Gibbon ... ascending the brow by way of Rosemary Lane and Mount Pleasant in order that he might await the issue of the expected conflict without himself being exposed to danger.' This way of ascent to the heights, rising behind the Old Quay, is still possible, though the cramped houses have been swept away. This is where the inhabitants would have gathered to to watch the attack. It is also still possible to descend to the quayside by way of 'the long flight of steps' mentioned in this connection by the anonymous author. There is also an interesting remark about the *Thompson*, which was the focus of Paul Jones's fire raising. She is described as 'a coal loaden brig which had just hauled from under the hurries [coal chutes]'. In other words, though she was no longer tied up at the coal staithes, she was close by, near the Old Quay. So here is the second note of authenticity.

Maybe Freeman, at a ripe old age, was the 'impeccable' though anonymous source vouched for by the author to bolster his frivolous tale of romance and derring-do, without stirring things up for Freeman in Whitehaven, if he was still alive; and if he was, he was clearly no longer in full possession of his faculties! For what it is worth, the mystery author says he has used fictitious names to conceal identities.

Bibliography

I have taken the opportunity to offer some comment on individual publications, where this seemed appropriate.

Manuscript Sources

The following manuscript sources cover matters not readily accessible in published sources or on the internet.

Court martial documents relating to the loss of the "Serapis" and the "Countess of Scarborough" ref. ADM 1/5315 and to the loss of the "Drake" ref. ADM 1/3972.

Correspondence between Captain Richard Pearson and the Admiralty, including Pearson's report following the battle off Flamborough Head. Ref. ADM 1/2305. Consulted at National Archives (Kew): London.

Official Report Package to the Government from Whitehaven, following raid by JPJ in April 1778, including affidavit of David Freeman (deserter from "Ranger"). Ref. SP37/12: Docs. I35, 136, 136(1), 136(2). Also available on microfilm of Complete Hanoverian State Papers Domestic, Lancaster University Library, Lancaster.

Publications

Alden, John R. *A History of the American Revolution.* Da Capo Press, New York, 1969. A standard one-volume history of the American War of Independence, with excellent reviews.

Alexander, John T. *Catherine the Great: Life and Legend.* Oxford University Press, Oxford. 1989.

The American Historical Review. Vol, XV P.567-571. A letter from the Marquess of Rockingham to the Secretary of State regarding Paul Jones, the Baltic Fleets and the defences etc. at Hull, on the eve of the sea fight off Flamborough Head.

Bradbury, David. *Captain Jones's Irish Sea Cruize.* Past Presented, PO Box 80, Whitehaven, Cumbria, CA28 6YB. A short (64 pages) but well-researched publication, with interesting new and re-assessed information; and plotting for the first time the course of the *Ranger*'s 1778 cruise from the ship's log, supplemented by sightings.

Bradford, James C. *Guide to the Microfilm Edition of the Papers of John Paul Jones: 1747-1792.* Chadwick-Healey Incorporated, Alexandria, VA, USA, 1986.

Bradford, James C. *The Reincarnation of John Paul Jones.* Naval Historical Foundation. Washington DC, 1986. This quite short (33 pages) publication is sub-titled: *The navy discovers its professional roots,* which says it all.

Caruana, David. *The History of English Sea Ordnance 1523-1875. (2 vols.)* Jean Boudriot, Rotherfield, 1997. I was particularly interested in grape-shot and other projectiles (Volume 1) and grenades (Volume 2). But the coverage is wide and detailed.

Dale, Lt. Richard. *Particulars of the Engagement between the* Bonhomme Richard *and the* Serapis: This is a discrete passage in a book by Dale's friend John Henry Sherburne; being the result of an interview which Sherburne conducted with Dale, as taken down by Sherburne. See Sherburne, J.H. (below).

Dewar, James. *The Unlocked Secret.* Corgi Books, London, 1990. Revised edition of a book first published in Britain in 1966, by William Kimber and Co. The book arose originally out of investigations by the journalist-author for a BBC television documentary on Freemasonry. The book attracted favourable reviews for its informed factual content and balanced approach. From a reading one can appreciate Benjamin Franklin's benign involvement in Freemasonry as well as Catherine the Great's malign antipathy towards it.

Donald, Thomas. *Historic Map of Cumberland. 1774.* By Cumberland and Westmorland Antiquarian and Archaeological Society, Kendal, 2002. From an original in the care of Tullie House Museum, Carlisle, Cumbria. Incorporates a good inset plan of Whitehaven, drawn almost contemporaneously with the attack on the seaport.

Fanning, Nathaniel. *Fanning's Narrative – The Memoirs of Nathaniel Fanning, an Officer of the American Navy, 1778-1783.* Arno, New York, 1967. A modern reprint of the original written around 1801, just over twenty years after the cruise of the *Bonhomme Richard*; the lively eyewitness account of a midshipman aboard that ship and in charge of one of the key fighting tops during the battle off Flamborough Head.

Farnie H.B. and Planquette R. *Paul Jones. Opera Comique in Three Acts.* Hopwood and Crew, London, 1889. Words and music. The original cover indicates their work is after an earlier work by Chivot and Duru. British Library reference Stock No. 11779.888.25.4.

Franklin, Benjamin *The Papers of Benjamin Franklin.* Ed. Barbara B Oberg. Yale University Press, New Haven and London, 1992. A very valuable source for correspondence relating to JPJ and others around 1778–79. Paul Jones's long letter to Benjamin Franklin giving his account of the *Bonhomme Richard* expedition is dated the 3rd of October 1779, and runs from page 443 to page 462 in the volume relating to that year.

Gilkerson, William. *Boarders Away,* Volume 2. Andrew Mowbray Inc., Lincoln, USA, 1993. Detailed study of small arms and combustibles used at sea between 1625 and 1826, with particular reference to the period of the American War of Independence. Volume 1 covers other weapons used by boarders such as cutlasses, boarding axes, boarding pikes etc.

Gilkerson, William. *The Ships of John Paul Jones.* Naval Institute Press, Annapolis, 1987. Absorbing and attractively illustrated with drawings and paintings.

Hay, Daniel. *Whitehaven: An Illustrated History.* Michael Moon, Whitehaven. 1979. A substantial book, good general background to the raid on Whitehaven.

Hosking, Geoffrey. *Russia, People and Empire 1552-1917*. Harper-Collins, U.K, 1997.

Jones wrote an autobiographical account of his services during the American Revolution for formal presentation to the French King, Louis XVI. Unfortunately this original has been lost, but it is still extant in a translation into French by Benoit Andre, published in Paris in 1798 under the title *Memoires de Paul Jones*. This has been re-translated into English, for example in an edition by Gerald W. Geralt; *John Paul Jones' Memoir of the American Revolution, Presented to King Louis the XV1 of France*; Washington DC, Library of Congress, 1979. It can conveniently be consulted via the internet. An extract covering the battle off Flamborough Head, under the heading "A Filey Story", can be accessed at http://www.lealman.fsnet.co.uk/filey8a.html. Paul Jones's document in fuller form can also be accessed at http://www.americanrevolution.org/jpj.html (Scholars Showcase).

Landais, Peter. *Memorial, to justify Peter Landais' conduct during the late war.* Peter Edes, Boston, 1784. Micro-film, British Library. An essential reference for any balanced view of the exploits of Paul Jones.

Lang, David Marshall. *The First Russian Radical: Alexander Radishchev 1749-1802*. Allen and Unwin, London, 1977. Includes enlightening coverage of Freemasonry in the Russia of Catherine the Great.

Lorenz, Lincoln. *John Paul Jones: Fighter for Freedom and Glory.* U.S. Naval Institute, Annapolis, 1943. A landmark and well-documented biography, with an extensive bibliography.

Lorenz, Lincoln. *The Admiral and the Empress.* New York, 1954. Uses transcripts from Russian archives to add to his 1943 biography.

Mackay, James. *I Have Not Yet Begun to Fight: A Life of Paul Jones.* Mainstream, Edinburgh, 1998.

Montefiore, Simon Sebag. *Prince of Princes: The Life of Potemkin.* Phoenix Press, London, 2000. A magnificent biography that deals splendidly with Potemkin in all his aspects. There are interesting references to Paul Jones, as well as coverage of naval and military events in the Black Sea.

Morison, Samuel Eliot. *John Paul Jones: A Sailor's Biography.* Little, Brown and Co., Boston, 1959. A perceptive biography by a fellow sailor. The author was a Rear Admiral in the US Navy – the rank to which Paul Jones aspired – and a prominent naval historian. Includes a plot of the cruise of the *Bonhomme Richard* from the ship's log book and illustrations of the positions of the ships during the battle off Flamborough Head.

Morison, Samuel Eliot. *The Arms and Seals of John Paul Jones.* In 'American Neptune', October, 1958, pages 301 to 305.

Prebble G. H. (Editor) *The Diary of Ezra Green MD Surgeon on Board the Continental Ship of War* Ranger. Boston, 1875. This work has been Reprinted in the U.S.A. for the New England Historical and Genealogical Register. See www.history.navy.mil/library/guides/rg45-m.htm. See also the Naval Historical Appendix at www.americanrevolution.org/navapp.html for related references.

Reynolds, Edward. *Stand the Storm: A History of the Atlantic Slave Trade.* Allison and Busby, London, 1985. A graphic and informative account of the trade and its background.

Richardson and Schofield. *Whitehaven and the Eighteenth Century British Slave Trade.* Transactions of the Cumberland and Westmorland Antiquarian and

Archaeological Society. 1992, Article XV, pages 183 to 204. Provides insight into Paul Jones's initial involvement in the slave trade.

Schaeper, Thomas J. *John Paul Jones and the Battle off Flamborough Head: A Reconsideration.* Peter Lang, New York, 1989. A close study of the battle that includes Cottineau's letter and his memoir to Chaumont, copied to Benjamin Franklin.

Scott-Hindson, Brian. *Whitehaven Harbour: A History of the Harbour.* Philimore, Chichester, 1994.

Seitz, Don C. *Paul Jones: His Exploits in English Seas During 1778-1780.* Dutton, New York, 1917. Extensive compilation of contemporary accounts collected from English newspapers etc. Includes newspaper publication of Pearson's letter to the British Admiralty in full, and Piercy's letter to Pearson.

Sherburne J.H. *Life and Character of the Chevalier John Paul Jones,* Wilder and Campbell, Washington, 1825. A second edition was published under the title *"The Life and Character of John Paul Jones, A Captain in the United States Navy, during the Revolutionary War,* by Adriance, Sherman and Co., New York, 1851. Includes the Minister's diatribe on the seashore at Kirkaldy, and Richard Dale's account of the battle off Flamborough Head, as narrated to his friend John Henry Sherburne. Contains also Jones's Reports to the American Commissioners in France on the cruises of the *Ranger* and the *Bonhomme Richard,* and correspondence with the Selkirks.

Thomson, Valentine. *New York Times* Magazine, 23rd and 30th of Sept. 1934. The Anna Kourakina story (see Appendix IV) Available at British Library's Newspaper Library, London, and archives of the *New York Times.*

Thomson, Valentine. *Knight of the Seas: The Adventurous Life of John Paul Jones.* Liveright Publishing Corporation, New York, 1939. The publisher's dust jacket is a confounding of chocolate-box romance and swashbuckling derring-do. The material relating to Anna Kourakina appears, not in an appendix, but as the last chapter, 'The "Secret Romance" of John Paul Jones and Princess Anna Mikailovna Kourakina'.

Troyat, Henri. *Catherine the Great.* Aidan Ellis, Henley-on-Thames, England, 1978 A fascinating biography by a master of the genre, translated from the French. The author was born in Russia as Lev Trassov, but was educated in France, and became a member of the Academie Francaise.

Waliszewski, K. *Paul the First of Russia, the son of Catherine the Great.* Archon Books, Hamden, Conn., U.S.A, 1969. Useful for the political background to John Paul's brief sojourn in Russia.

Walsh, John Evangelist. *Night on Fire: the first complete account of John Paul Jones's greatest battle.* McGraw Hill, New York, 1978. Like Morison, Walsh provides good illustrations of the relative positions of the *Serapis* and the *Bonhomme Richard* during the course of the battle off Flamborough Head; and also compares eyewitness and historians' accounts.

Warner, Jessica. *John the Painter: The First Modern Terrorist.* Thunder's Mouth Press, U.S.A., 2004. A fascinating examination of a bizarre and deadly character from the eighteenth-century underclass.

Watson, Stephen J. *The Reign of George III: 1760-1815*: Vol. 12, Oxford History of England, Oxford University Press, 1960.

Wilson, Timothy. *Flags at Sea. A guide to the flags flown at sea by British and some foreign ships, from the 16th century to the present day, illustrated from the collections of the National Maritime Museum.* Her Majesty's Stationery Office, London, 1986.

Index